Lewis Yablonsky was born and grew up in Newark, New Jersey. He was graduated from Rutgers in 1948 and went on to receive his Ph.D. in sociology from New York University. He has taught sociology and criminology at the University of Massachusetts, CCNY, Columbia, Harvard, and UCLA and is currently Professor of Sociology at California State University at Northridge. In 1967 he was selected from among 9000 professors in the California State University system to receive the Board of Trustees' Outstanding Professor Award for "excellence in teaching, scholarship and public service." Professor Yablonsky, who lives with his wife and son in Los Angeles, is the author of *The Violent Gang*, *Synanon: The Tunnel Back*, and *Robopaths*, all three published by Penguin Books.

LEWIS YABLONSKY

The Hippie Trip

Penguin Books Inc
Baltimore · Maryland

Penguin Books Inc
7110 Ambassador Road
Baltimore, Maryland 21207, U.S.A.

First published by Pegasus, New York 1968
Published in Pelican Books 1973

This edition published by arrangement with
The Bobbs-Merrill Company, Inc.

Printed in the United States of America by
Kingsport Press Inc., Kingsport, Tennessee

To

The United States of America

Table of Contents

Into the Seventies

The hippie trip is a phenomenon that captured America's imagination and interest throughout the 1960's. The new youth life-style developed in that decade encompassed among other characteristics: an extremist approach to "love"; greater sexual freedom; and a concept of work that defied the Protestant ethic. Drugs were used as a vehicle for pleasure, new levels of consciousness, and internal social change. The movement was essentially a counterattack against formalism, bureaucracy, and robot behavior. The hippie phenomenon involved disaffiliation from the existing society, and at its peak around 1967–68, several million people dropped out. They were dominantly, but not exclusively, young and from the more affluent segments of American society. The people involved came from almost every city and town in the United States. The evolving new life-style and its concomitant activities were mainly centered in large urban areas like Los Angeles, Boston, San Francisco, and New York.

A close study of the movement and its social patterns reveals and mirrors a great deal about the structure and problems of American society in the latter half of the twentieth century. In the past decade the movement has attempted (with some success) to dramatically alter the basic institutions of the family, government, economics, religion, and education in America.

The shape and style of the hippie phenomenon of the sixties has been modified in the seventies; yet the fundamental reasons for dropping out persist, and for thousands of young people the commitment to alternative life-styles outside of the formal system is greater than ever. An aspect of the new scene in the seventies was revealed to me by a young lady living in San Francisco's Haight-Ashbury: "Around 1968, after being in the Haight for a year, I visited my family. My mother screamed at my long hair, my weird clothes and called me a whore. I was home again last week. We rapped and I smoked a joint right in front of her. In fact she took a toke!"

Many hip people agree that the recent greater acceptance of the new perspective by parents and the establishment in general has made it easier to lead an alternative life-style without the necessity of totally dropping out. Hippies can now hold straight jobs and maintain their personal life-styles with less societal persecution than existed in the sixties.

Moreover, many people in the movement now have a greater acceptance of some of the dominant culture's prescriptions for behavior; appointments, certain functional machines, and schedules are more acceptable now then they were at the height of the purist hippie scene of the previous decade. As one young man who participated in the Haight now remarks: "We were too far-out in the sixties. We rejected and ignored many realities about life in America which we have now learned to live with." What appears in the seventies, therefore, seems to be a greater tolerance for the coexistence of divergent life-styles.

Even though the partial drop-out is in greater vogue, there are thousands of hearty bands of hip people in urban and rural communes who are living in the more classic counterculture form developed in the sixties. The purist numbers are smaller, and their publicity is virtually extinct, yet the life-style still flourishes today.

One of the keenest observers of the hippie phenomenon is Dr. David Smith who founded the Haight-Ashbury Free Medical Clinic in 1967. Over the past five years he has lectured and studied the hippie movement in large cities around the country. I recently interviewed him and recorded his current viewpoint on the size and shape of the scene:

> The hippie movement is now about ten times larger than it was at its public peak in 1967. The media image, the flamboyant street scene and the Woodstock festivals are dead; yet the life-style continues. There are mini-type Haight-Ashburys in cities all over the country. Our research reveals over four hundred rural communes in northern California alone (involving around ten thousand people) and there are similar communes in most states around the country. Also, almost every city has a form of urban commune.
>
> There are new operating rules in effect in the seventies as compared to the sixties. Hip people now reject publicity. There is a greater awareness of social realities, so that many hip people have become political. They work for positive change in their community. Generally, drugs are not used as promiscuously as in the previous decade, even

though heroin has infiltrated the situation. In general, recruitment of people into the hippie life-style seems to be growing because there are more open doors in every community. It is no longer necessary to go to New York, San Francisco, or Los Angeles to participate in the hippie life-style.

The scene has opened up widespread social experimentation with cultural alternatives. For example, the Free Clinic idea of providing medical and social help has become an enormous development. There are now over two hundred free clinics around the country handling over two million client visits a year. Communal experiments also now take a variety of new forms. Many are basically political or religious systems.

A large percentage of young people in the United States now go through some hippie phase. And even though most return to a straight life, the experience invariably affects the way they live out their lives. So the hippie culture continues as strong as ever and has enormously affected the dominant society.

In a greater variety of forms, therefore, the hippie phenomenon is more vibrant, relevant, and alive in theseventies than it was at its more colorful peak during the (now nostalgic) 1967 summer of love. The original Trojan Horse has virtually been dismantled, but the philosophy, culture, and people have successfully invaded and blended into American society.

This subtle infiltration of the hippie phenomenon has produced a varied impact on American society. The results are not completely new or different from the American way of life; however, in combination, the total gestalt of the hip culture has significantly affected the society.

Psychedelic drugs (especially marijuana) have introduced a vehicle for pleasure, new perceptions, and in some cases instant personality and social change. "I can't change anything around me. But I can change my perception of everything around me."

Communes of various types, both urban and rural, have become compelling new counterculture forms. "The work of life gets done without anyone laying a heavy power trip on anyone else — and we are all loving brothers and sisters."

A more natural organic way of life has been emphasized and adopted by many people. "I've become super-careful about the food I am putting into my body. We grow things for ourselves."

Pollution and ecological self-destruction have become important causes for action as the problems become increasingly visible. "We can see more clearly the ecocide being committing on our natural resources and it has to stop."

War of any kind is increasingly viewed as a horrendous absurdity. "I will not put my body in any position to be killed or to kill my brothers and sisters."

Anarchism, the absence of all government and rules, is progressively considered a more natural and positive state of being: "Everyone should be free to do their own thing."

All of these issues and others have become significant credos in the social movement that has been spontaneously developed by several million young people around the country. Freedom is the key principle acted upon and a new pattern of life has emerged within the hardened shell of the traditional system.

Counterattacking the Machine

The hippie phenomenon in its most idealized sense is a revolution toward life rather than death. One dimension is that it is a partial counterattack against what many contemporary scientists have recently come to view as a suicidal condition of epochal proportions. This suicidal megaproblem has been recently highlighted by a world-wide panel of seventy-five eminent scientists, industrial and government leaders. The group arrived at the conclusion that human society will suffer, in the next century, a major catastrophy involving mass starvation, wars over dwindling resources, and epidemics brought on by pollution — unless major alterations are brought about in the world's technological growth patterns and life-styles.*

This vision of a deadly, plastic, social machine, perceived by scientists in the seventies, was sighted in the sixties by many of

* Donnella H. Meadows, Dennis L. Meadows, Jorgen Randers, and William W. Behrens III, *The Limits of Growth* (New York: Universe Books, 1972).

the young hip drop-outs of that era. The hippie movement or counterculture viewed in this context was fundamentally an advanced extremist reaction-formation against what young people interpreted as a "doomed" society. They attempted to abandon its institutions, controlled and inhabited by what the counterculture perceived as robotlike people. Their counterattack can be viewed in retrospect as an attempt to move from super-bureaucracy to anarchism; from a group-think regimentation to a do-your-own-thing philosophy; from alienation to total love; from a synthetic, plastic way of life to an organic existence.

One most significant effect of this revolutionary life-style on the so-called establishment has been the appearance of soul-searching on the part of political leaders, people in industrial power, and many parents; because their sons and daughters have, in various ways, joined the revolution, the power structure has had to critically re-examine the fundamental nature of their "advanced," "civilized," technological society. In this regard the revolutionary reaction-formation of young drop-outs has produced a valuable counterpoint to some of the destructive characteristics of contemporary Amercian society.

Their cultural revolution was and still is based on different levels of consciousness about the social system. In this context, hip revolutionaries and dissenters are not "the problem" for society; they are actors or, at times, over-reactors in the situations they confront. They represent a counterattack against a pathology in the dominant system. It is, after all, the dominant society that produces the megaproblems of ecocide, war, potential total annihilation by atomic power, and a general dehumanized existence.

By no means have all the people in the social and political power structure re-examined their values or capitulated to the counterculture's negative viewpoint of society. Around 1968, the big guns of raw power were brought out to contain visible signs of the revolution. In Chicago, at Kent State, and elsewhere, the permissiveness for freedom of expression was grotesquely contained by people in power.

Another facet of the establishment's reactions to the hippie phenomenon has been a strange new propaganda ploy to placate the movement and change the machine system's image.

Through massive media and self-deception, America has donned a more humanistic face, or at least the process has begun. The tokenism of longer hair, flared pants, and anti-war sentiments voiced by Harris polls has anesthesized the gloomier perspective of many people on America as a social machine. The runaway technological system and its unresponsive robots have been camouflaged by some clever (albeit transparent) government, corporate, and mass media strategies: the army now "wants to join you"; the polluters, the new "saviors" of the environment; and "peace" negotiations in the midst of the slaughter of children and civilians. The robot society dressed-up in human drag.

Robopathology and the Hippie Movement

People versus technology in the social machine system is a basic causal factor of the drop-out phenomenon. Another is the growing problem of *people as machines* — or what I have termed robopathic behavior (the pathology of robot behavior).* Robopaths are people who are relatively devoid of such humanistic qualities as compassion, spontaneity, and creativity. A central dimension of the hippie phenomenon is that it is an extremist effort on the part of the participants *not* to become robopaths.

Robopathology is a disease that seals people off from each other to the point where only their surface images touch. The subtle quality of the dehumanized life that has emerged in modern society is not clearly manifest to many people because of the various available means of dulling sensitivity to the problem. Continuing and immediate sensory gratification can be obtained, very much like the soma pills described by Aldous Huxley in *Brave New World.* The problem suffered most by many robopaths is deadly boredom with themselves and with others: an existence fraught with meaninglessness and irrelevance.

The condition Thoreau described as "leading a life of quiet desperation" is the crude equivalent of a "robopathic existence." The surface image of this life-style is often shining and sparkling, like the happy TV commercials and "Father Knows Best" series. The robopathic actors are ostensibly living a full life. Beneath the surface, however, there is nagging unhappiness, enormous dissatisfaction, and simmering hostility.

It is this pattern of robopathology that I believe largely explains

* Lewis Yablonsky, *Robopaths* (New York: Penguin Books, 1972).

the escalation of the drop-out rate among young people in its many continuing forms. Most of these youths, who have access to the affluent goals of the society, correctly perceive the "victorious" end of the road as a lifeless, robopathic existence. They reject the life-style carefully planned by their parents and choose what the establishment views as a hippie pattern of outrageous alternatives, such as communes, dope, and even poverty.

A conversation I had with a young hippie at the peak of Haight-Ashbury's popularity helps to reveal the general motivation for rejecting the idealized goals of the society.

LY — Why are you here in all this disorder and poverty? In a matter of twenty-four hours you could be in a big comfortable home . . .

Young Man — I look up at my old man. He makes $50,000 a year. My Mom and Dad have every material thing you can want in this society. Yet, I know they are both miserable. They don't know how to talk to each other or to me. They probably make love once a month.

In other words, if I'm a good boy and do just what my old man did — go to college, get good grades, run a business, and become a success — I'll become a miserable robot like he is when I'm fifty. Later for that. It's bad out here sometimes — but at least I'm trying something different. I know where my old man's trip leads. I don't know where I'm going now — but it's got to be better.

In recent years this drop-out urge has not been restricted to the sons and daughters of the affluent. There are increasing numbers of drop-outs derived from the older affluent generation itself. The traditional escape routes from a robopathic existence on the part of affluent adults leading lives of quiet desperation in the soft cream of luxury have been alcoholism and prescribed, legal dope. These more traditional patterns are giving way to hippie forms of adults dropping out. For example, recently, I was talking with a hip liberated woman in Haight-Ashbury and used the term *youth-culture.* She remarked, "What youth culture? Christ, I'm thirty-two. I was a housewife and mother with two kids trapped in my kitchen by a chauvinist husband. Now I'm enjoying life; I smoke dope, meet lots of groovy people, fuck more than ever, dance every night, and really enjoy life."

Another example of this situation is found in the rising numbers of men in affluent executive positions who, by all overt criteria, are successfully living the "good life," then one day quietly disappear. In recent years tens of thousands of men from the upper socio-economic strata, in top technocratic positions, have dropped out of the mainstream robopathic way of life. (In many such cases when the family is not part of their social machine problem, the family drops out together).

In general, therefore, a variety of people have dramatically veered toward leading a hippie life-style. Its super-emphasis on "love," touching, living closer to nature, seeing more cosmic realities, and being more spontaneous and creative in human interaction has helped to make the society more humanistic. The alternative life-styles fashioned in the sixties have thus been instrumental in producing *some* humanistic social change as a counterattack to American robopathology in the seventies.

Hypocrisy

The dominant emphasis has thus far been placed on the more positive aspirations and impacts of the counterculture. It must be noted that hippies are also capable of producing and participating in their own peculiar social machines. In the movement there are many robopathic hippies, locked into hypocritical, nihilistic positions, who destroy more than they create. This is most apparent in the actions of some hippies-turned-revolutionaries who have actually killed people and, symbolically, in trying to destroy the plastic beast, have themselves adopted violent and dehumanized patterns. One long-haired hippie recently told me: "We've stopped rapping about killing pig-cops. Not because we still don't want to do it — but because it wouldn't do any good. There are too many of them and too few of us."

In another context, many of the alternative, experimental life-styles developed in the new community have turned into ineffectual and hypocritical efforts. The communal way of life, for example, when closely analyzed reveals some glaring problems that contradict some of the glowing underground and even mass media newspaper reports.

A return to the land by hip people "turned on" to nature is an admirable and adventuresome goal. However, a quick switch from city dwellings to this new way of life can result in assorted and complex problems. The few I have seen try the natural environment have little or no skill for farming or learning how to live on the land. For many, the new organic existence is paid for by government welfare, food stamps, and checks from home. These resources are used to buy the same plastic, ersatz food from the same supermarkets that supply most square Americans.

Another problem in many hip collectives contrasts with the lofty ideal that everyone will help with the basics of living. Instead of leadership, everyone "does their own thing," and chaos often prevails. More often then not, dishes, garbage, and other debris pile up to create health hazards.

In many anarchist hippie scenes psychopathic strong men have taken over disorganized situations for their own egocentric ends. At best, this has involved a degree of predatory exploitation; at the worst extreme, it has involved some grotesque examples of violence and homicide. The best-known example of this bizarre leadership condition is, of course, the notorious Manson family. Here the psychotic fantasies of a sick leader dominated the group's behavior. The pathologic Manson family syndrome does appear in many other communal situations, albeit with a lesser degree of human exploitation and violence.

Another hypocritical condition of the counterculture scene is related to the socialization of children. The hip credo is to let children grow up without "laying any heavy trips on them." Often this means that the parents are too egotistically consumed with their own trip to pay any attention to their child's needs. I vividly recollect a conversation with a stoned hippie mother who was rapping to me about cosmic love. Her five-year-old son (dirty and dressed in rags) came over to us, crying about a splinter in his hand. Without missing a stroke in her diatribe about "love," she turned to the child and said, "Fuck-off kid. Can't you see I'm busy." Unfortunately, her performance was not totally atypical. Many sons and daughters of the hippie movement are currently beset with emotional problems stemming from childhood deprivation.

The question of social reality raises other hypocritical attitudes in the movement. Many hip people talk about changing society simply by altering their perceptions with drugs. Of course, this viewpoint has a degree of validity. Getting high does block out harsh conditions from individual perception. An LSD trip, a joint, and especially a fix of heroin will often eliminate racism, war, and poverty for the user. It also incapacitates the person from doing anything really constructive in the environment, especially in cases where the individual becomes hopelessly addicted to the "reality-changing" drug.

The hippie drug addict is an increasingly visible problem. Many young people, on the scene, who began using drugs for expanding consciousness or pleasure have become traditional drug addicts in hippie clothes. The metamorphosis often involves a spiritual, loving person changing into a lying, often violent, ahuman "dope fiend."

The new middle-class junkie is one of the unfortunate results of the hippie movement. His social reality has become an ambulatory death. The new junkie paradox that emerged from the hippie movement is graphically described in a blistering article by Dr. George and Anne Gay. (Dr. Gay is Medical Director of the Haight-Ashbury Free Clinic, Heroin Addiction Unit.)

> It is no longer buried in black and Puerto Rican ghettos; no longer confined to the "ignorant" poor. Heroin is in the suburbs, and white parents are beginning to know the impotent rage of fear and despair that black parents have lived with for decades; the call from school, from the police, from some hospital somewhere. The call that rips you from complacency and tells you the cold, neon, street-corner truth: your kid has been arrested; your kid is a junkie.
>
> Your daughter, the lovely, clear-eyed child who was going to marry a nice, attractive, sensible, hard-working young man, who was going to give you grandchildren and comfort your old age, well . . . she ran off with a greasy slob on a motorcycle. When he got tired of fucking her, he split, so now she is turning tricks on the street, hustling for enough bread to cop a ballon of dope. . . ."*

Drugs and a group process are often used for the self-deception of social reality. One young man recently told me how everyone in his commune got high one day and all concluded that the revolution for social justice and equality had been won. Un-

*Anne C. Gay, George R. Gay, "Haight-Ashbury Evolution of a Drug Culture in a Period of Mendacity," *Journal of Psychedelic Drugs*, Fall, 1971.

fortunately, the continued use of various types of soma pills or drugs alters nothing but the user's perception for a moderate period of time, and often impairs the person's ability to concretely change the system in a more humanistic direction.

Even though I recognize many positive characteristics in the counterculture, my view of its potential as the exclusive approach for totally "greening" social machine societies is more cynical than the perspective of others. Many parents, educators, and social scientists have unrealistic hopes of achieving nirvana through the hippie movement. This extravagant faith in the curative power of the counterculture is epitomized by Charles Reich.*

One problem, among others, with Reich's exorbitant faith is that most young people in this country are raised in robopathic families, and this majority will most likely occupy roles in the various factories of the machine society. Very few young people will occupy the ivory towers of Yale and Harvard, where Reich was influenced and collected most of his information about hip young people, potential social change, and Consciousness III. Reich's sample of Yale students is a small and unique group of people, who are, in effect, the new aristocrats, supported by the labor of millions of less fortunate, enslaved robopaths who run America's physical and bureaucratic machines.

Despite a certain level of hypocrisy, the hippie movement has had a considerable impact on American society, having raised people's levels of consciousness. The new life-style has served as a refreshing counterpoint to the deadly robot image that tends to pervade and control American society. Many of the young people who struggled through the hippie trip of the sixties have emerged in the seventies as potential leaders of freedom from the robopathic existence that still dominates America. Their hope for the future was optimistically summarized for me by one young person who commented, "Remember, the old robots are dying and more of us are being born."

---

* Charles Reich, *The Greening of America* (New York: Random House, 1970).

The Research Approach

My basic research and personal trip into the hippie phenomenon was primarily carried out in the mid-sixties. For almost two years (1966 and 1967), I devoted my full time to the counter-culture scene. I traveled around the country, lived briefly in several urban and rural communes, and interviewed hundreds of people in the hip life-style. Although my investigations took place primarily in the last decade, I have maintained contact with the scene, its changes and developments in recent years.

Since the book chronicles my personal trip, as well as my sociological observations, I feel it is of value to the reader to know something about my orientation. I have been engaged in "live" non-statistical research for over twenty years. In my two prior research books, *The Violent Gang* and *Synanon: The Tunnel Back,* I relied almost completely in my research on firsthand participant observation. Some of the issues involved in this type of research are succinctly stated by Severyn R. Bruyn:

> We may observe at the outset that while the traditional role of the scientist is that of a neutral observer who remains unmoved, unchanged, and untouched in his examination of phenomena, the role of the participant observer requires sharing the sentiments of people in social situations; as a consequence he himself is changed as well as changing to some degree the situation in which he is a participant. The situation which is created is not unlike that created by the famous Heisenberg Uncertainty Principle in physics where the instruments used to measure the velocity and position of an electron alter the accuracy of measurement. That is, by the very act of observing the position of the electron its velocity is changed, and the more accurately its velocity is determined, the more definite its position becomes. In participant observation the effects are reciprocal for observer and observed. The participant observer seeks, on the one hand, to take advantage of the changes due to his presence in the group by recording these changes as part of his study and, on the other hand, to reduce the changes to a minimum by the manner in which he enters into the life of the group.*

---

* Severyn T. Bruyn, *The Human Perspective in Sociology: The Methodology of Participant Observation* (New York: Prentice-Hall, 1966).

I do not pretend to be completely "objective." In fact, I consider it almost impossible to be fully objective in the study of human behavior. There are simply too many personal and situational variables in the human condition for a student of society to become fully detached. Rather than trying to avoid personal and emotional interaction, in my view, plunging into the human arena you are trying to understand is apt to be more illuminating than striving for an elusive and questionable objectivity.

In my research participation in the hip world I utilized all of the relevant social theories I knew of in directing my research camera. In writing my findings I attempted to blend my personal observations with pertinent theoretical perspectives.

In the project I gathered data, not only through my personal encounters in several hundred interviews, but through the use of over seven hundred written questionnaires. (This dimension of the methodology and the data collected is fully discussed and presented in the Appendix). All of the characters in the book are real people. Some names have been changed to protect the identity and privacy of those persons.

The taped interviews used in this book are highly selective. Everyone presented was chosen from at least ten comparable interviews. After checking the validity of a commentary, I would zero in on a representative individual who could most articulately describe an important situation or a particular scene. After I had sufficient pre-test exposure to the subject, the interviews were carefully directed into avenues that I believed were the most relevant areas of investigation. In this respect I fully admit to my own subjective view of what was significant.

In most cases, my interviews were carried out *in situ* (in live situations). Whenever possible, they were not simply researcher-respondent interactions, but discussions that took place in their natural setting. I attempted to fulfill a principle postulated by my good friend and mentor in the field of sociology, Dr. J. L. Moreno, who described an ideal research approach this way: ". . . research procedure has to be shaped in accord with the momentary potentialities of the subject, so as to obtain a maximum of expression. If the research procedure is not attuned to the live and momentary structure of a given community, we may gain only a limited or distorted knowledge about it."

I placed myself squarely in core situations so that when a vital event or discussion emerged, I could capture the happening in the moment. The tape recorder I had with me most of the time was an unobtrusive instrument that recorded many live discussions, arguments, love-ins, and "parties." The research scene included many situations where dope was freely used and sexual relations were happening nearby.

My personal and professional judgment was a major factor in selecting certain scenes from the overall hippie drama. My decisions and emphasis are certainly subject to criticism; however, wherever possible in the chronicle of my voyage I attempted to openly present my reasons for following a particular line of inquiry, in its actual context. Any possible errors of emphasis in the book are placed as "out front" as I can possibly make them. The reader in most instances, therefore, can see where I was, how I got there, and how I arrived at certain "factual" and theoretical conclusions.

At a certain point in the research I decided it was of vital importance for me to personally experience some core behavior patterns in order to truly tune-in to what was happening. Among other activities, I tried to smoke pot several times; but being a nonsmoker I had difficulty and never did get high. I was more successful with LSD and on one occasion had a remarkable fifteen-hour acid experience.

The philosophical positions expressed in the book are, in my view, as relevant today as they were when originally stated. In recent years the word *hippie*, as well as some other jargon, has become somewhat tarnished and less popular. In the seventies, terms like *youth culture*, or *counterculture*, are more in vogue. In describing the trip, however, I have not modified or altered anything from its original terminology or form. I have, therefore, preserved the book as a historical period piece, true to its original style and meaning. In rereading this account of a colorful, dramatic, and exciting American social movement I received some new insights and intellectual stimulation; and felt a pleasant sense of nostalgia. I am hopeful the reader will share my experience.

LEWIS YABLONSKY
Los Angeles, California
1972

Part One
Preview

CHAPTER ONE

The Scene

A TRIP IN THE HIPPIE WORLD can be more than one or a series of psychedelic experiences—it can refer to a person's total life voyage. In the argot, when reference is made to someone's "trip," the person's philosophy and life goals are implied. The immediate trip of some type of drug experience is only a transitory part of the larger human condition. For the high priests and philosophers of psychedelia, even one's life scheme does not necessarily refer to the Western concept of one birth and one death, but to the Eastern religious view of many deaths and many lives of reincarnation.

My own trip in this kind of eternal context was a short, abrupt excursion. Yet it was for me a dramatic and significant life experience. The impact of the voyage has not yet fully registered on my psyche or life plan. The changes I went through may be detected in this total chronicle.

Geographically, emotionally, and philosophically, I traveled from the West to the East coastlines of the United States. Hippie community tribes (and the term tribes is used literally) are to be found in areas like the East Village area of New York City, a Jewish section of Los Angeles (Fairfax Avenue), Sunset Strip, the rugged hills of Big Sur, and communes in Northern California. I lived for a time among hippie aggregates in all of these areas and places.

I saw, and to some extent experienced, a kind of extended family life and group sex that was probably practiced back in The Beginning. And, on the same scene, I heard the sounds of a highly sophisticated philosophy based on scholarly study and meditation that could conceivably extricate twentieth-century man from the spiritual ravages of the Great Society, overkill, and the super-mechanical world.

In the hippie arena, LSD is ever present, either as a trigger to a new world of cosmic brotherhood or an acid that scrambles the brain and one's chromosomes. It pervaded all of the behavior I witnessed and personally experienced. LSD was used by a large majority of the thousands of hippies that I met as their personal key to cosmic consciousness and universal unity. LSD was also used, as one man put it, "only as an aid to seeing reality more clearly and clearing the ground for the hard work of self-actualization." It was also observed and admittedly used as a kick—"like, man, it's just groovy fun."

Marijuana is the basic black-bread staple of the hippie world. "Grass," as it is mainly called, is an aid to the overall high. It is not smoked in isolation but in a circle of friendly love, passed from one mouth to the next like the traditional American Indian peace pipe.

Both LSD and "grass" are viewed by many hippies as the sacraments of their religion. My central guide, Gridley Wright, described it this way: "As a Catholic at one time, I would have said, 'No, you don't have to have the Sacrament of the Eucharist to know and be a Christian and a Catholic.' But it just seems to be a part of it. And I like acid, it's a lot of fun! It's there. It exists. To decide whether there is a need for it or not is kind of academic. It's a part of it. The whole, taken together, is to me far-out beautiful. And acid is part of that whole. Not THE whole, but part of it. That's what the brotherhood of man and mystical union is all about. That kind of unity, a unity where we are without veils or deceptions or games between us, with only pure truth in life. LSD is a truly religious experience."

Grass and acid are in this way considered religious sacraments by the high priests; however, hippie society has its own brand of "dope fiend." Throughout the hip-land, there are signs in psychedelic shops and on toilet walls that say "SPEED KILLS." The reference here is to amphetamine drugs like Methedrine and various psychic energizers. A true hip believer "puts down" the use of these drugs, which are considered, along with such drugs as heroin, to be a "bad trip." In spite of the addiction danger of these clearly destructive drugs, most have tried them and about half of the new community regularly indulges in the use of these non-sacramental" narcotics.

Sex is not practiced religiously. It is more of a happening. With ego boundaries at almost the zero level from drug use and with American middle-class values slashed from "the life," sex is wide open—but only if you are part of the love scene. It occurs between people who are tuned-in to each other. According to one advocate of psychedelia: "Promiscuity? That's such a cute word. Oh, wow! What is promiscuous, man? Sex without feeling, without tuning in? Indiscriminate sex? Well, people are more or less tuned-in, open to, and grooving behind sex, or they're not. If they're not tuned-in to it spiritually and they fuck compulsively, maybe that's what we would call promiscuity."

I closely observed in many situations and under many conditions that the hip sex scene is not "free love." Many "untuned-in" sailors, students, and "dirty old men" who gravitate to the hip community for sex become angry when they are rejected by the love children. Sex is not free—one must be resonant to the feelings of the potential sex mate. For people fully tuned-in, sex is "free," plentiful, and, from all reports, "a groove" (great) in the hippie world.

Hippie culture is a para-society in the sense that it exists casually beneath the surface of American society. It is not clearly either a sociological sub-culture or a contra-culture, yet in certain respects it is both. A sociological sub-culture loosely translated comprises remnants of the larger society organized in a microcosmic fashion. A contra-culture is one generally opposed to the larger society. In the pure hippie world, neither of these conditions is true. Hippie society attempts to be tuned-in to and resonant with a deeper reality, or a cosmic consciousness of Man that is the pure framework for all societies.

This complex notion of hippie culture was partially expressed by a hip philosopher, Stan Russell, in the following commentary: "The notion that the great plastic society is the only reality, and anything other than that is a drop-out culture is one of the crazy, insane, lunatic notions that is indulged in by its leaders. Another more profound reality existed before American culture existed. Hip people who live in the woods by themselves, have beards, and make their own clothes are very natural people who live close to the land and are part of the reality of nature. Or hip people in the city tuned-in to their community, like in Haight-Ashbury, are not living in a drop-out culture, they are part of a truly turned-on new way of life.

"American culture with all its values, mechanisms, and industrialism is just something that came along in the last hundred years, and it is essentially unsatisfying even to those who are extremely successful. There are millions of people who are not now and never were caught up in this particular plastic society called the United States. What is going to endure is the Universal society of nature that underlies all of this crap we see on the surface. This is one of the important realizations you have under acid." Stan was attempting to describe a phenomenon that I heard about many times on my trip—that there is a natural social condition that underlies man-made cultures and societies. This structure, according to the high priests of the movement, is the fundamental social reality.

The hippie world does not attempt to be contra American society. In some cases people trying to live by the love ethic attempt to embrace the forces that they believe are most hostile. If police reflect philosophically and in violent action society's counterpoint to hippie values, then the following vignette about a police-hippie encounter partially describes the hippie position vis-á-vis society. The incident described by Gridley Wright is an event that happened in a rural hippie community he founded called Strawberry Fields:

"The heat [police] raided us once in our commune and it was a total victory, if you want to call it that, for the community, because we were just so super-cool. It was kind of cute. It was about 2:00 a.m. and I was asleep. Someone came in and said, 'The police are here.' There were about thirty people there, and we had been smoking dope all night. However, we had such a tight ceremony about being cool about roaches [marijuana cigaret butts] and not having anything in the house that isn't being smoked, that when I went to meet The Man I just went totally cool.

"I told everyone to be quiet, that they shouldn't answer any questions, that The Man was there illegally. I asked him for a warrant and he didn't have one. I said, 'Well, you'll have to go.' He didn't go. His men went around asking questions, looking in the ash trays, and shining lights in people's faces. Nobody answered them. Everybody kind of just sat and smiled at them. I told Him again that he HAD to go and then I kind of got them all into a corner and I gave them a lecture, man, about how they had taken an oath to observe due process, to uphold the Constitution. And that they were being hypocrites about that, right? And, 'if that oath means anything to you, you ought to think about it!' The cops said, 'Well, we'll go outside,' which they did.

"We then put on the record player and just started dancing. We had these huge speakers and we put on the Jefferson Airplane's 'Let's Get Together.' You know that song. It says, 'Hey, people, now smile on your brother, let me see you get together, love one another, right now!' We all went out on the porch and SANG it to them! It just blew their minds, man. They just turned on. One of the cops grabbed his bull horn and said, 'Love one another right now!' "

Hippie encounters with the Establishment tend to produce

imprints of change on the larger society. The fact of an increasing number of people living a hip life has already affected the inclusive society's equilibrium. The fact of their new existence tends to point up some of the fallacies and limitations of the larger society.

When I appeared on a television show in Los Angeles called "The Newsmakers," I was interviewed on two subjects: the hippies and the Watts-Newark-Detroit type of riot. A final question posed was: "What similarities do you see between the riots and the hippies?" I replied, "One group is trying to burn down the country, and the other has totally disengaged. One might speculate that they both reflect a massive dissatisfaction with the 'Great Society.'"

The Negro rioters who are attempting (with some degree of success) to burn down the cities are in at least one important respect different from the hippies—*they buy the American Dream*. They still want a "piece of the action" that includes the Cadillac and the white picket-fenced house. The Negro in the bottom socio-economic position has been dropped out *involuntarily*. Most hippies have *voluntarily* dropped out.

Most hippies (according to my data over 70%) come from the middle- and upper-class segments of American society. The hippies have almost all had access to the American Nirvana. As I toured and lived in certain hippie scenes of filth, disorder, and self-imposed poverty on rugged mountain tops and in the city slums of New York and Los Angeles, I couldn't help but reflect that most of these people within a matter of twenty-four hours could return to the America of fine apartments, two cars, and all other standard material possessions and advantages. Yet they voluntarily chose to drop out into scenes that Negroes and other minority groups have been trying to escape from for more than half a century. Americans must examine America in the light of our young people who have had or been offered all of the fruits of this nation's struggle and have dropped out.

Either the hippies are a new breed of sophisticated intellectual dope-fiends "stoned out of their minds," or they are on the path to a new society of Man. I take one of the prophets of the movement, Tim Leary, at his word when he says, "Let's mutate, baby." The goal may be a new higher species through the LSD experience. (Recent research that suggests chromosome "changes" resulting from LSD use gives the Leary comment increasing significance.)

Aside from the immediate impact on the people currently involved in the hip scene, the trip that they have embarked on is of major significance to all members of our society. The pioneers of the movement, the youth who have stepped out into inner space, come from that segment of society which generally produces the core management and administrators of society.

Disadvantaged children (unfortunately), given their level of aspiration and the blockades to their fulfillment built into the society, for the most part would achieve minimal positions of occupational power and position in the society. Their alienation and disaffiliation into delinquency or destructive drugs affects the American equilibrium, but it does not cut a large swath in the important future of American society—at least at this time.

On the other hand, the hippie "drop-out" movement contains a sizable number of future lawyers, doctors, businessmen, professors, and other potential professionals of the next generation of American society. The evidence seems to indicate that these youths are dropping out in increasing numbers. An important issue, therefore, is that American society as it is now constituted and for the near future may be deeply affected by the hippie drop-out development.

A most significant impact of the new scene is that it represents a serious attack on the contemporary values, goals, and "advantages" of the larger society. One can reasonably understand the discontent of the "have-nots"—but if a sizable number of the "haves" voluntarily disengage, the leaders and exponents of American society must take another look at their "hole cards." There must be something drastically wrong with a society whose *achievable goals* are rejected in increasing numbers by youths who have clear access to most of its highly publicized advantages.

By definition, the postures, philosophy, and way of life adopted in the hippie world are for several hundred thousand Americans a more desirable state of existence. What is of even greater gravity is that the hippie way does not seem to be a passing fancy. I have so far observed very few complete drop-outs from the hippie movement.

The True Hippies: High Priests, Philosophers, and Novitiates

Where did the term "hippie" come from? My speculation is that it emerged as follows:

In the 1930's and 1940's, the terms "hep" or "hep-cat" (for whatever reasons) were used to describe people "in the know," people who were "swingers," people tuned-in to the popular swing and jazz music of that period. The term "hep" somehow in the 1950's was changed to "hip." To be "hip" was (and is) to be "in," to have an emotional wisdom about what's really happening on a sensual level. During the 1950's, if you said "hep" you were a square and if you said "hip" you were "down" (wise) and "in" (in the know).

My further speculation is that the extensive use of the term "hippies" in the mass media was significantly fostered by an article entitled, "The Social History of the Hippies" that appeared in *Ramparts* (March, 1967). From that point on, the term hippie has been used widely by the mass media to identify the people of the new movement. Although many leaders in the movement reject the term hippie (they even held a quasi-ceremonial funeral to bury the concept in Haight-Ashbury), my view is that the term has caught on and is here to stay as long as the movement maintains its current basic structure.

As in other social movements and cultures in the hippie social system, there is a hierarchy and a variety of roles.

There are many types of hippies and different behavior patterns in the overall movement. This is partly due to the fact that even though their origins are primarily middle-class, the youths who comprise the hippie world come from all segments of American society. These "searchers" come from various strata in the larger society and are seeking varied experiences and goals.

A representative sample of hippies exists in the urban mecca of the hip world, Haight-Ashbury, San Francisco. At any given time Haight is almost a fantasy land of sights and sounds. Flute players in robes. Micro-minied girls in boots, without bras, obviously aware of a kind of sexual attractiveness, swing down the street. There are consciously dirty teenagers and underfed youths who come from upper-middle-class families. Some seem to be beating their parents up obliquely by literally starving and begging. On the same scene are wiser, older "heads"—erudite philosophers of the movement. These bearded figures (some in their late thirties and forties) smile straight ahead as they walk down the street, many in flowing robes with "hip" crosses around their necks.

All of these people are doing "their thing"—but who among them is a true hippie? The position that I choose to take is that they are all hippies, even when they are obviously only aspirants to true high-priest status, or teenagers "blowing their minds" with drugs and sex. Perhaps the best way to define the role is to first describe the ideal type or true hippie.

The High Priest

The ultimate hippie is a high priest or the philosopher of the hippie scene. His primary distinction is that he claims to have achieved some level of being tuned-in to the cosmic affinity of man. The high priest believes on some level that there is a God in all people and all things, and that he is part of this unity. According to one of these leaders: "Basically, man is God. And this is one of the profound insights that you can have on LSD. You experience yourself as God. You come back down here into this dismal state of reality . . . after being God on LSD. You've seen it. You've experienced it. It's a true feeling. You know it's truth. So, you can't change them, but you can change yourself and you can become God-like, and you can relate to people like a God or like Christ. You can let your light shine. And if you meet somebody else that is letting his light shine, then the two have created a God-like culture and this is the cosmic unity we try to achieve in the new community."

The love ethic derives from this position. According to the high priest, if all people and objects in nature are part of oneself and God, then it is ludicrous and inimical to the God if you are hostile or opposed to anything. In fact, a person who believes in this kind of love attempts to help humanity.

The true hippie priest believes he has achieved his position of ascendancy, in part, through the use of drugs as a sacrament. Here, the selected use of LSD is clearly the key that has opened the door to this holy world and marijuana is a continuing daily sacrament that helps maintain this religious" level of awareness. Drugs are not for the simple purpose of getting high and having fun. They are, in this context, a sacramental part of daily existence.

Work is also part of the high priest's daily existence. It may simply be the work of role-modeling—demonstrating by example—for aspirants or novitiates. On a more active level, the work of the high priest is a very low pressure ("soft-sell") missionary work—turning on as many people as possible.

Some of these leaders have a special creative artistic skill (painting, writing, ceramics, leather work) and may work in their field sporadically. Their essential work, however, takes a religious form similar to that of a priest or minister. They interpret and analyze hippie philosophy. They interact with other learned men, teaching them and learning about their views. In this way, they represent the hippie community to the larger world and learn from it for the advancement of their religious experience.

No true hippie leader would take a nine-to-five job in the "plastic society," even though he might work twelve hours a day at his "thing." (A person's "thing" is what he does, his "bag," his central existence, his most satisfying posture toward life.) Occasionally some of these people will take a part-time job to earn money for the advancement of their community; but a full-time position in the larger society is out of the question. "I would have to give up too much of my body and soul."

In spite of serving in a communication role, or occasionally working in the Establishment, the high priest is philosophically totally dropped out of the larger society. The kind of work position a high priest might accept is partially revealed in the following account of the development of an important hip underground newspaper. This particular scene is described by Stan Russell, sometime editor of *The Southern California Oracle.*

"A group of us started the *Oracle* about five or six months ago. We all had had at least seventy-five acid trips. We all went through very profound changes as a result of being on the *Oracle.* When we began the *Oracle,* we thought that we knew what we were doing. We laid out our trip in the *Oracle.* We all attempted to get on this work trip so that along with the use of more acid we could tune-in to higher forces than we were aware of when we began."

Although some hippie priests and philosophers relate to work in various segments of American society, they consider it fundamentally "plastic," phony, and doomed to extinction. They disagree with its laws, its politics, its wars, and its unnatural view and practice of sex, child-rearing, and education. In brief, the high priests have spiritually disengaged from the "plastic society" and are fostering another mode of existence.

The Novitiate

Following the leaders of the hippie movement are an army of aspirants or novitiates. They have had a number of LSD experiences and smoke pot religiously. They have all had a glimpse of Nirvana under LSD and are true seekers.

They have dropped out of the "education, phony loving family, nine-to-five rat race scene" and are grabbing hard at the "hippie bag." On the surface, some seem purer in their belief and more committed than the priests. Because they are insecure and new to the hippie world, they still contain a heavy measure of self-doubt, related to their "former hang-ups." They act as if they see more beauty and more "beautiful people" than really exist. Their enthusiasm reigns unchecked. The high priests see and admit to many phony and destructive possibilities on the hippie scene. The novice admits to none. He is more vocal and perhaps clutching more desperately at the new ideas and philosophy because he has not yet achieved "the peace of pure involvement" in the movement. Many novices are part of the new left political movement. As very part-time students or non-students they participate on campus in various protest and demonstration situations. They are, therefore, not totally dropped-out.

The novice has not yet achieved the pure seeker position that is characteristic of the completely dropped-out high priest. He has not fully disengaged from rebelling against his parents, or the Great Society. The priests often chastise the novitiate. "Man, you're still fighting your parents and the war in Vietnam. It's all bullshit and irrelevant. You are God and the struggle is in you."

Attitudes toward the police and law may delineate the priest from the novice. The newcomer is hostile and arrogant toward law enforcement. He is "paranoid" about openly smoking pot because he is afraid of arrest. In some measure, on a deeper emotional level, he accepts and is battling in himself the validity of the legal role. The priest "knows" that the laws on marijuana and LSD are ridiculous.

The unparanoid priest claims to and does smoke pot freely. He accepts arrest as a philosophical trip he must take. "Man, if I get busted [arrested], I'll just do my thing in prison like a monk. The Man [cop] is beautiful. Look at him as someone testing how much you're behind your thing. I dig the Man, he tells me where I'm at." This kind of statement, which I have heard often, is usually met with the hippie "Wow!" or "Too much"—sounds of recognition of a remarkable insight or commentary.

Because the hippie priest-philosopher is apparently more secure in his life-position, he is better able to be honestly self-critical. The novice is still most defensive because he is not sure of his position.

Novices and priests are people I would consider to be "true hippies." They are at different levels of pursuit, but they are in agreement about certain hippie values, postures, and behavior.

In the entire hippie world, I would crudely estimate that only about 10–15% have achieved the position of high priest or philosopher. The novice I would estimate make up another 35% of the total. Thus my view is that, in the sense described, the hippie culture is only about 50% "pure."

The "Plastic Hippies"

The other half of the hippie world is a conglomeration of people, mainly young people with varied motivations. There are roughly four categories: (1) A new breed of hippie drug addict; (2) "teenyboppers"; (3) severely emotionally disturbed people using the hippie world as a sanctuary; and (4) miscellany.

There are young people mainly in their late teens and early twenties who are essentially a *new breed of drug addict*. Using a thinly veneered hippie philosophy as a front, they spend most of their energies getting and using drugs. Although some heroin is used by these addicts in hippie dress, the main drugs they use are "speed" (Methedrine and other amphetamines).

Even some high priests and novices refer to the "new breed" as "Meth" or "speed" freaks. They don't reject these youths; however, they view them as going through a self-destructive phase, one that is necessary to purge them of the "game-playing bag that was laid on them by the plastic society that they are trying to escape from." The philosophical view of the leaders is that drug use and abuse is part of the youth's efforts to free themselves from the "social garbage" scene of the larger society. Through drugs, they claim, these youths are trying to unlearn the ego-games and dishonesty they have been taught by their parents and society. They allege that after these youths go through this first chaotic drug phase they will be more "open" and receptive to living in the "new community."

Another segment of "plastic hippies" are the *teenyboppers.* They are essentially teenagers who "make the scene," very often in the most "far out" clothes. They have an enormous involvement with the new music; and with allowances granted by indulgent middle-class parents, they buy the records that keep the industry spinning. They use the drugs on the scene, not for spiritual purposes, but admittedly for fun and kicks. They are the flower children of the overall hippie movement. Their concept of love, however, tends to be very slender and irresponsible. Most teenyboppers are part-time, weekend, or summer hippies. Their superficial first involvement as a so-called teenybopper may, however, given time, circumstances, and drugs, project them into the world of the hippie—drug addict, novitiate, or high priest. They are the raw recruits for the upper world of the new community.

Another category of hippie participant that I have observed is made up of *severely emotionally disturbed people* who seem to find a refuge in the hippie community from institutional mental hospital custody. Many of these hippies, seated in catatonic states, or acting out bizarre patterns of behavior or dress, are shielded from confronting society's definitions of emotional illness by the liberal attitudes, tolerance, and great acceptance found in most hippie communities.

Part of this pattern of absorption of mental illness in the hippie world is related to a *self-administered cure,* the practice of drug use. A hippie is not considered psychotic by his peers, he is simply viewed as freaked-out on drugs. Sometimes this sheltered freak-out, with hallucinations and mumbling speech pattern, goes on for months. In this way the new community has absorbed, made legitimate, and given protection to a large number of people who would ordinarily be classified by the cold larger society, through its administrative psychiatric devices, as "mental patients." Perhaps the hippie approach to emotional disorder, among its own, is a more rational method of treatment. It is certainly more humane than the standard mental hospital approach of the larger society.

A category of *miscellany* exists in the hippie world. Many people gravitate to the festive allure of the scene who cannot be identified as hippies, but who form part of the totality. This would include a range of people like the Hell's Angels motorcyclists, overt criminal drug addicts, religionists (legitimate and cultish), a scattering of social scientists, and a large number of curious tourists, who spend considerable amounts of time "hanging around the hippies." Most of these conglomerations are found in the cities. The hippie rural communities tend to be mainly composed of priests and novices.

Characteristics of the Scene: A Summary

On the basis of my overall trip and research, I would make the following crude estimates regarding various characteristics of the hippie world:

1. About 10–15% of the total "pure" hippie scene comprises people in the role of *high priests* or *philosophers*. In this same "pure" category, another 35% of the overall total are true seekers—people enacting the role of *novitiate* or *aspirant*. Although some of these people may be, in some sense, addicted to drugs (marijuana and LSD), their drug use is, from their viewpoint, sincerely "sacramental" in the pursuit of new religious, spiritual, or intellectual levels of con-

sciousness. The fact of clear emotional disorders, in this upper half of the hippie population, would be difficult to identify because of the mystical and hallucinatory nature of their trip.

2. The other half of the visible hippie scene is composed of "plastic hippies." This category would include teeny-boppers, part-time summer and weekend drop-outs, and a new breed of drug addicts who use the hippie cloak of immunity.

3. In the total hippie world ("pure" and "plastic"), my data reveals that most people (over 80%) have used some "speed." About 40%, however, are emotionally addicted to speed, particularly Methedrine, in some self-destructive way. The bulk of these "Meth" or "speed freaks" come from the lower "plastic hippie" class.

4. Perhaps 20% of the hippies, from all categories, are severely emotionally disturbed young people who have found in the hippie community a refuge and personal immunity from the formal society's approach to dealing with psychosis.

An estimate of the total number of hippies in American society is a speculative sport; however, my guess is as good as any. There are, I would suspect, about 200,000 core visible and identifiable total hippie drop-outs in the United States. Further, there are at least another 200,000 visible teeny-boppers, part-time summer and weekend hippies.

In addition, there are perhaps several hundred thousand invisible "Clark Kent" hippies. These are students, young executives, and professional people who use psychedelic drugs, interact, and closely associate with totally dropped-out hippies, yet maintain nine-to-five jobs or student status. Many of these "invisible hippies" are potentially total drop-outs.

Alongside of these categories, there are millions of hippie "fellow-travelers" in the United States. (A large segment of these admirers of the hippie philosophy are found in the academic community.) Although they have an enormous sympathy and identification with the core drop-outs and their philosophy, these "hippie sympathizers" do not use psychedelic drugs in any regular way or make the scene personally. They help with money, property rentals, and in other supportive ways. In this category of involvement I would also include the families of hippies. They are generally not sympathetic to the movement, and find themselves involuntary participants.

In total, therefore, there are several million Americans rather directly involved with the hippie movement. This fact, plus the real and potential impact that the movement is having on young people, makes it an important issue of concern to all citizens. The vectors in it are both destructive and constructive. Most important, there is a reasonable possibility that this outrageously flamboyant, non-violent psychedelic revolution may have a significant impact on the basic values and structure of American society.

CHAPTER TWO

The Guide

The attitude and behavior of the guide are critical factors. He possesses enormous power to shape the experience. With the cognitive mind suspended, the subject is in a heightened state of suggestibility. The guide can move consciousness with the slightest gesture or reaction. . . .

The role of the psychedelic guide is perhaps the most exciting and inspiring role in society. He is literally a liberator, one who provides illumination, one who frees men from their life-long internal bondage. To be present at the moment of awakening, to share the ecstatic revelation when the voyager discovers the wonder and awe of the divine life-process, is for many the most gratifying part to play in the evolutionary drama.

(From *The Psychedelic Experience*, by Leary, Alpert, and Metzner)

GRIDLEY WRIGHT, 33, WAS MY primary guide during my hippie trip. I literally traveled with him for about six months during the central data-gathering and live-in part of my research. We visited both rural and city hippie communities together, and Gridley, a high priest in his own right, introduced me to many other oracles of the movement. When I went off on several side-excursions of my own, as for example to New York or Haight-Ashbury, I usually returned to digest my findings in discussions with Gridley. He was an invaluable guide, companion, and research consultant to my voyage.

I first met Gridley in 1963, at a community meeting related to an attempt by Synanon, an organization of ex-addicts, to buy property and operate its organization in Malibu. The community was split in half on the issue, and the opposition prevailed. In spite of Gridley's Republican-conservative position he was a humanitarian, and was, like myself, on Synanon's side.

I remembered him then as a super-straight young man on the rise. He was a graduate of Yale University, where he had majored in political science. He was a political conservative in the image of William Buckley. Gridley at that time was working as a stockbroker. In that period of his life, Gridley was generally in Brooks Brothers type clothes and, along with his Vassar-girl wife, he defended the rights of minority groups to live and work in the Malibu community.

Several years later I met Gridley when I lectured to a group of probation officers at a juvenile delinquent camp. At that time he had a job as a deputy probation officer and worked as a counselor to delinquent youths. As he later described it to me: "This was my partial drop-out scene. I worked three straight days and was off for four. About that time I began to turn-on to pot and acid, and the job was perfect for my needs."

From this partial drop-out position Gridley moved all the way into the center of the hippie scene. When I began the book, he was intensely involved in the new movement. His hair was very long, he had a magnificent blonde-red beard, and his clothes were denim and leather with psychedelic patches. He wore Indian beads, a headband, and bells on his buckskin boots. Gridley made the total transition to high priest, including the wearing of a simple muslin ceremonial robe at love-ins or on special hippie religious occasions. Gridley literally adopted the new scene in a religious fashion.

His commitment, I was fully convinced after many long philosophical discussions, was deep and sincere regarding the religious implications of the movement. This religious issue and a drug-offense charge against Gridley became a *cause célèbre* in the national hippie movement. The case was tried in greater detail in the mass media than in court.

The legal happening emerged in the following set of circumstances. In an appearance on a local radio station, (May, 1967) Gridley discussed his new-found "religion" in great detail. He asserted that the use of LSD and marijuana were sacramental vehicles to religious grace. To make his point on marijuana use, he freely admitted to having smoked marijuana immediately prior to his radio appearance. When he returned to his car the police were waiting for him. They found a jar of marijuana in the car and arrested Gridley. When I met him he was free on bail until his trial, which took place during the period he served as a guide to my research.

I knew of Gridley's prior arrest during our research period. In many conversations we had together he seemed unconcerned about the trial and its outcome. "If I have to go to jail, I will do so like the Buddhist monks. I will meditate and learn from the experience. It's all part of my trip and no one ever said it was going to be easy."

The trial became a carnival. Gridley dismissed his lawyer and took over his defense—as his own attorney. The first report of the trial, carried in the L.A. *Times* (Tuesday, October 3, 1967), presented Gridley's flamboyant position at that time with great accuracy:

HIPPIE CHALLENGES MARIJUANA LAW
IN SUPERIOR COURT TRIAL

> A hippie leader who threatens to smoke a marijuana cigaret in court went on trial Monday, charged with possession of marijuana.

> Bearded, long-haired Gridley Wright, 33, a one-time stockbroker, told newsmen prior to the beginning of the trial:
>
> "If they find me guilty, and give me some cop-out sentence like a suspended sentence or probation, I'll light up a joint right there in court."
>
> Fifty supporters followed Wright to the eighth-floor Hall of Justice courtroom of Superior Judge Mark Brandler, and as many as could crowded into the courtroom.
>
> Wright, a Yale graduate and when last employed a deputy probation officer, asked for and was granted permission to act as his own attorney.
>
> He sat before the bench at the counsel table dressed in a tattered denim jacket and levis. Before him was what he called his law book. It was a small copy of the New Testament.
>
> He said he would ask prospective jurors only one question: "Do you believe in God?" . . .
>
> Many of his followers trooped behind him to the Hall of Justice.
>
> Their clothes, gypsy bright and of obvious rummage shop stripe, marked them apart from the somberly clad Hall of Justice regulars.
>
> The men were long-haired, and many wore picturesque beards. Most of the women seemed innocent of hairstyling, make-up and some of rudimentary underwear. One woman nursed a 2-month old baby in the back row of court as the court session began.
>
> Children—who seemed to have no last names—sat quietly in the courtroom with them. In the hallway outside other hippies squatted, childlike, against the walls.*

As the trial gathered momentum, over a period of several weeks, Gridley switched his defense over from "the insanity of the laws of marijuana" to his rights to religious freedom, covered under the first amendment of the Constitution. Simply, his position, as presented in the trial's closing argument, was that he was a leader in a new hippie religion, and that marijuana was a sacrament of this religion. Gridley produced, among other witnesses, a Unitarian minister in his defense. The minister's testimony was reported in the L.A. *Times* (Tuesday, October 16, 1967) as follows:

*Courtesy of the *Los Angeles Times*, October 3, 1967.

In support of his argument last week, he [Gridley] called the Rev. Ernest D. Pipes, minister of the Unitarian Community Church of Santa Monica and a Harvard Divinity School graduate.

Mr. Pipes was asked if he thought psychedelic substances could induce mystical experiences.

"Yes," replied the minister. "I have read extensively in the literature, and there seems to be little doubt that the use of psychedelic substances brings about a state of mind very similar to, if not identical with, the traditional mystical religious experience otherwise come by."

"Do you consider that the use of these substances within a religion, within a commitment to spiritual growth is a valid use of these substances?" asked Wright.

Mr. Pipes replied:

"Yes. All that I would want to add to it is that I see many approaches, many pathways to religious experience, esthetic religious experience, of which the pharmaceutical way is one." *

Gridley's trial involved me personally and professionally in an unanticipated way. The trial took place near the end of our research association on the book. We had come to know each other well as a result of being traveling companions for many months in our trips around the state. During the trial, Gridley would show up at my home at almost any time of the day or night to discuss the situation. Most of the time he was elated about the trial. "This gives me an opportunity to test these insane drug laws. Also, people have to begin thinking about drugs in a religious context."

In this connection Gridley asked me to testify, to further validate his sincerity about using marijuana as a religious sacrament. In all of the time I had been with him, Gridley and I had had long talks about this issue and I was firmly convinced of the sincerity of his beliefs. In ruminating on testifying for Gridley on this issue I found the following statement of his religious position in a taped discussion we had during a trip we made to several hippie communities in Northern California.

"Now I am more and more every day just overcome with

*Courtesy of the *Los Angeles Times*, October 16, 1967.

the metaphysical, religious character of the trip. When it's carried to its logical conclusion . . . all the feelings, or all the words that are used to describe the mystical experience, all those feelings are things that I am experiencing all the time. Now there isn't one religion, that I know of, that says this kind of a trip is supposed to be easy. And, well, my reality on the dope scene is that it is what religion is all about. Probably the great majority of the people that are on the scene are not yet on to the religious part of it.

"I would say that ours has every characteristic of any religion, especially the secret type of religion—one that is persecuted as the early Christians were, as small cults of secret societies have been all through history. . . . The thing that we have that is secret about ours, from the Establishment, are the rites in which we use the dope. Those are not allowed to be observed by non-members. That is what it actually works down to.

"I see the whole drop-out process as simply being the religious process. Once you start being completely open in your self-awareness and in the expression of yourself in communication with others, you start on a process which, when used with psychedelic drugs, will inevitably lead to mystical experiences. There are people more or less advanced along that path, as in any given organization. I think that the longer our new community exists, the more it is going to be oriented toward what you would call religion. Now that doesn't mean that they're going to have a lot of rituals, and services, and dogma, and talking about 'this is religion.' But the way of life that will be lived is one which can only be described by using, semantically, words which are historically connected with religion."

I told Gridley that I would have no reservations introducing these statements as a witness at his trial. I further told him very candidly that the D.A. or the judge were sure to question me regarding my general views on drug use. Given my anti-drug-use position, my testimony was more apt to hurt rather than help his legal cause. In addition, I informed him that although I could testify with complete honesty about his religious sincerity in drug use—my testimony about whether drugs actually achieved religious goals would take another direction. In spite of my reluctance, Gridley subpoenaed me to testify.

Gridley's performance as an attorney did not succeed in getting the testimony he wanted from me into the record. The human-legal interaction in the court produced the following scene (reported in the L.A. *Times*, October 11, 1967):

> A Valley State College professor took the Fifth Amendment nine times Tuesday when asked by a judge if he based his observations about marijuana on its being smoked in his presence.
>
> "I refuse to answer on the grounds that it might tend to incriminate me," Lewis Yablonsky replied to the questions put to him by Superior Judge Mark Brandler. . . .
>
> Yablonsky testified that Wright had helped him research a book he is writing, "The New Community—The Hippie Scene."
>
> In the process, he said Wright, 33, had traveled with him to several hippie communities in California.
>
> He also testified that the "subculture" of hippiedom is "characterized by the prevalent use of psychedelic drugs."
>
> Wright, who is acting as his own attorney, sought during his examination of the sociologist to establish that Wright used marijuana because he considers it a religious sacrament and that his use of the drug is neither injurious to society or himself.
>
> Yablonsky testified that he had found Wright docile during their travels and had heard the defendant discuss marijuana in a religious context on visits to hippie communities.
>
> Most of the questions at which the professor balked resulted from Judge Brandler's asking if Wright had smoked marijuana during these discussions and travels. *

I invoked the Fifth Amendment against self-incrimination for several reasons: (1) I did not want to drive another legal nail into Gridley's conviction; (2) according to a California statute, it is a misdemeanor to be in the presence of someone

*Courtesy of the *Los Angeles Times*, October 11, 1967.

using illegal drugs; and (3) I have a firm belief in the rights and privileges of a research sociologist to be on any scene (even an illegal one) in the legitimate pursuit of acquiring social science research data.*

Gridley was not particularly disturbed by my testimony and in later discussions he told me he believed it helped his cause. In any event my testimony did not negatively affect our continuing research association.

At the conclusion of the two-week trial, the Judge called Gridley a "false prophet" and convicted him for the possession of marijuana. He appealed the case, but the conviction was upheld. Gridley was sentenced to five years on probation and was fined $300.00. A stipulation of his probation was that he would cease and desist from using and advocating the use of drugs. His probation was later revoked and he imprisoned.

Gridley's militant philosophical position on drugs at his trial enhanced his status in the hippie world. His status in the "psychedelic revolution," however, had already been firmly established by his past almost legendary role as a founder and leader of a hip community known throughout the hippie world as "Strawberry Fields." The community lasted about six months and ended when an overturned candle set fire to the main building and reduced the place to ashes.

Gridley was my primary guide into psychedelia; consequently, his life experience, viewpoint, and position are cru-

*The last reason was the most significant one for my refusing to admit to an act that any reader of this book will know I observed many times. Of course, I was in Gridley's presence on many occasions when he was using a substance that was apparently marijuana. I say "apparently" because I never had the substance chemically analyzed. I chose not to admit to this situation at that time because the role of witness in a trial is an inflexible one that would not provide me with the necessary and proper opportunity to present all of the scientific reasons for the validity and necessary privilege of live-research. In brief, I am adamant about the rights of a social researcher to investigate live situations as they are happening. This position is more fully presented in a paper I have written on the subject for a professional journal.

cial to understanding my whole trip. My later experiences on the hippie scene further validated that Gridley was a philosophical leader who was nationally known in the overall movement. The following collage of his positions on many issues (prior to his trial and conviction) are essentially taken from an interview with him in the August, 1967, *Southern California Oracle* and from tapes I made with him myself. The dialogue portrays Gridley's trip and provides, I believe, an excellent introduction into the land of psychedelia from the viewpoint of one of the movement's high priests.

STRAWBERRY FIELDS FOREVER

"I was pretty much living by myself when I completely dropped out. I was a probation officer, which is a pretty dropped-out kind of a job to begin with. I worked in a camp where you work three days and then have four days off. Well, you can drop a lot further out on those four days than you can on a weekend, if you're working a five-day-a-week job. I had started taking acid about eight months before I quit work and it just occurred to me that it would be interesting to see what would happen if I just did what I FELT like doing all the time. You know, get up when I feel like it, wear what I feel like wearing, go to sleep, think, say, do whatever the fuck I felt like. And you can't do that if you're working for somebody else. So I did! I was thirty-three years old, and it was the first time in my life that I ever did really feel free. I'd had vacations before, but always, even in the vacations, you're thinking about what you're going to do after the vacation is over. I was on unemployment for about ten months once. I couldn't really enjoy that because I had a certain amount of guilt. You shouldn't be drawing unemployment. (YOU SHOULD BE THIS, YOU SHOULD BE THAT.) But I was able to accept the freedom, and I seem to be able to accept it more and more all the time.

"Around October, when I quit work, a bunch of us from various places started getting tighter and tighter and closer and closer together. We had hit on the game of pushing each other to be open about our feelings all the time. We found that the more we were together in this kind of atmosphere, the more we opened up, the more we enjoyed each other and life. At the time I was renting a house in Malibu Canyon and it just started filling up with people. At night it was wall-to-wall with people. It was in a pretty residential neighborhood and things were getting hot. We were using a lot of acid, staying up all night with music and motorcycles coming and going and so on. One of my partners heard about some property out in Decker Canyon. We decided to move in there and at the same time decided to let anybody else that wanted to come there, come. I kind of laid down that there would be no structure. There would be complete acceptance of everybody's trip, simply because I found the more I had been able to accept MYSELF and people around me, and they were able to accept me, the higher we got. I wanted to see a whole community where this could happen.

"The word just spread all over. Half our population came from the San Francisco area. The average number of people there was about thirty to thirty-five. On the weekends it would go up to over a hundred. And I'd say probably anywhere from fifteen hundred to two thousand people passed through.

"We got the name Strawberry Fields from the Beatles' song. Actually I gave the community two names: STRAWBERRY FIELDS and DESOLATION ROW. Everybody remembers Strawberry Fields, it's a lot pleasanter.

"It was pitch black and horrible, and the depths of misery. Yet it was also the fairest, lightest, purest thing. Everybody, including myself, had some images and expectations as to what it would be. It *was* everybody's image and expectation, and the opposite. It was all things.

"It was a beautiful place where people could go and take acid in a relatively paranoia-free atmosphere of trust about the community. It was a place of accelerated evolutionary change. A way of people seeing themselves and, as a result, seeing life. It was accelerated to a degree that, to my mind,

I have never before experienced. Evolutionary change is a process which is a result of being open, being trusting, and not being defensive.

"I feel that the reason an infant begins to close up, the reason that it needs to build ego defenses, is because it is threatened by the hypocrisy and lies of the civilization into which it was born. This is represented usually by its parents, later on by the school, and later on the police. The defense is against the fantasy that is laid on children that they are not perfect. That they are slightly imbecilic, that they are definitely inadequate until they become SOMETHING sometime in the future. They should grow up intelligent, mature, respectable, ambitious, and successful, with no underarm smells, or bad breath, or shitty diapers. This is, of course, a lie. But the lie is enforced by threatening vibrations communicated to the child.

"At Strawberry we used drugs to break these threatening repressive fears. We believed that psychedelic drugs, given and received in an atmosphere of trust, enable man to know his God nature and his unity with life.

"The only ritual about taking acid was that people at Strawberry were asked not to leave the property. If they wanted to freak out and take their clothes off, yell, scream, on the property they were safe.

"I think that our community did the community-at-large a tremendous service by having a place where people could go, take acid, and could freak out without harming themselves or the community. REALITY is that more and more people are going to use acid. Whether we like it or not. Unethical, immoral, depraved, call it what you want, sick, whatever! REALITY is that more and more people are going to use it. Repressive laws, paranoia-producing laws are going to cause more flip-outs. Our place was as paranoia-free a place as has ever been where there is a lot of dope.

Sexual Freedom and Children

"A principal of our religion was that dynamic spiritual

growth happens in an atmosphere of complete acceptance of infant and childhood sexuality. Which means, to get right down to it, that eight-year-old kids should play with each other sexually. And you let them do it because that's what they feel like doing. At one time we had thirteen kids at Strawberry Fields. They had complete sexual freedom.

"Of course, some adult under these rules could try to lay his trip on a young kid. . . . I wouldn't dig fucking a prepubescent female. It may be somebody else's trip. I would hope that adults would be tuned in enough not to impose this on the kid if the kid wasn't behind it. In an open community it's difficult to think of someone that would impose that kind of trip on a kid. That was the only negative 'no no' raised about sex in our religion. Obviously if you're going to have free infant and childhood sexuality, it's implied that there is complete acceptance of adult sexuality.

"A lot of people feel that sexual freedom is a very bad thing. This culture accepts that little kids want to play with their penis. It's all right for LITTLE kids to masturbate. But somehow after a certain age, say around three, sex isn't supposed to happen. This is a fantasy because it's an anthropological fact that we alone of the creatures on this earth, our species is capable of sexual enjoyment, play, and pleasure from the day it's born to the day it dies. That is the one place that evolution has brought us that is different from every other species of animal.

"The first time I ever saw this idea in print was in a book by Philip Wylie called *They Both Were Naked.* The whole book is pretty absurd except for this one rap where Wylie delivers that whole scene about kids and sex. I saw that this is the way it IS, man, out at Strawberry Fields, because we had kids there. One time we had twelve kids; the oldest was thirteen.

"I never saw people go through such rapid changes as those kids did where everybody's accepting them. Where, when an adult is trying to lay their game on them the kid can say, 'Fuck off, man' and not be afraid to say it. No human being has reached enlightenment till they can say 'fuck off' to their mother or dad.

"We only had one casualty to the Establishment. One of our kids was taken from the community. The petition filed in behalf of the child by the Establishment stated that the child was in danger of leading a lewd and immoral life. But in our community the words 'lewd' and 'immoral' have been thrown out. [In the case cited, the five-year-old child was regularly smoking marijuana.]

. . . "I remember one time, I guess I was twelve or thirteen, I was living with my aunt and uncle. And my aunt was always rapping about how you had to be a certain way because you have to be thinking about what people say. I just said to her, 'Who the fuck CARES what people say!' I guess that's when you start dropping out, when you see your identity doesn't have anything to do with what people say.

Confronting the Establishment

"Just let your light shine! That's about all you have to do. One of the things that a far-out righteous cat named Krishnamurti says is that you don't change the world, you change yourself. The world is a projection of yourself and you change the world around you, and this is, like, so fucking true, man, it's incredible! That's how the world gets changed. And that's how it is happening with the acid movement. It's not a political movement. We don't have lobbies in Sacramento, man. It's just a thing where people are going into their center, their light is shining, and people are saying, 'hey man, what's going on?' Like the sheriff coming up to our place to see what's going on.

"People who get hung up in protest stuff are, here again, looking OUTSIDE THEMSELVES for things to change. They've been doing that ever since recorded history, man, and we're no better off now than we were then. It's a circular bag, and people don't get to change very much inside it.

"People have reactions to policemen clubbing people. Part of the load that has been laid on them is that there is such a thing as justice, that there is right and wrong. In fact there is no such thing and there never has been. People have been clubbed 'unjustly' since the first club went into somebody's hand. And yet we've been brought up to believe that this is the land of the free, with liberty and justice and all those fantasy concepts. The only source of peace IS FROM WITHIN. When one is confronted with the lie about justice, it seems to stimulate a sense of great frustration. Frustration is just being disappointed because something didn't fulfill the image you laid on them in your head. And so people shake their fists, and they say, 'we shall overcome,' and 'let there be justice and equality!' and 'it's all THEIR fault OUT THERE and if THEY will only change then everything will be cool!' It's never gonna work that way, that view will only compound the sense of frustration! Because anything, man, which gets people outside of themselves for identity is just reinforcing the whole cycle. We're going to have to realize that very soon. There are going to be a lot more clubbings.

"But the trip isn't supposed to be easy. It never has been. A lot of holy people have been in jail. Christ spent forty days in the desert. And if you want an easy trip, just forget it! All the energy that is being wasted by people in putting down the Heat and putting down the Establishment and their families and looking outside of ourselves is far more grave a sin than anything the police are doing. We wouldn't exist if the police didn't exist.

"If there were to be another confrontation with police violence, I know what I would like everybody at a love-in to do. Immediately be quiet and get down on their knees. If you had five thousand people, man, getting down on their knees, it'd be all over!

"But that's a mind trip. It's not WHAT a person would do at a love-in, because if a person is straight, and they're tuned-in, that isn't even an issue. Whatever they DO will be absolutely harmonious and will effect change and they will be protected. If everyone got down on their knees it would be just a holy righteous thing. But it would be hard for that to happen unless everyone there was open to the collective consciousness of their brothers and sisters, and were aware of the confrontation of dark and light.

"There are a lot of beautiful hymns being written by our people. One of them that I think would be particularly appropriate at a confrontation with police violence is the Jefferson Airplane's 'Let's Get Together.' Now if you and me and all our partners got together and decided that the next time that we are confronted by the police devil, we'll get down on our knees and we'll sing him a hymn. Man, you've got five thousand people at a love-in and if a thousand of them started singing, it'd be all over. Why couldn't we all do that?

"That's one of the things about a love-in; everybody should just be there in one big squirming mass. As it is now it's getting to be like a Hollywood show. You go there and there's the platform and people get entertained. I think it'd be so groovy if we just started doing stuff together, singing together, everybody holding hands. Get everybody to shut up for just a minute. If everybody'd shut up and then they sang one of those songs like 'Let's Get Together' we could turn love-ins into religious services. If the police started breaking people's skulls open who were on their knees singing to them, we'd go to the United Nations with it. Don't think we couldn't. Don't think we couldn't get a lot of allies! What do you think is going to happen to the police chief when the actions of his police force are brought up in the UN? Let those fuckers know we mean business, man. I'm kind of slipping into a kind of game status here where it's like my team versus their team. I think it's a very respectable thing to call the other team 'fuckers.' I guess it means that I'm feeling intense about what I'm into. The police are holy purifiers. Last week I was in jail, in the glass house, the city jail; they don't allow you to have paper or pencil or anything. I asked the guard if they had a Bible, because I know that when I worked in Juvenile Detention facilities we always had a Bible. The guard looked at me and said, 'What do YOU want a Bible for?'—you know, you dirty, communist, beatnik, pervert, hippie, creeping scum. And I said, 'Well, I'd like to read it.' So I told the man it's a beautiful book and I learn a lot about myself when I read it and this would be a good place to do that. He didn't say anything, see, and he just looked right at me and then one of the other guards comes along and says something to me to the effect of, 'Ha-ha, look at this, where are your apostles?' And I said, 'Well, brother, I just really don't know how to answer that kind of question.' Then the other guard said to him, 'Say, just leave him alone, man.'

"Every brother and sister should carry a Bible and when they go to jail say, 'I want my Bible out of my possessions.' You know, things like that, because it blew this guard's mind, see? It opened him to a new dimension of reality about our people. And those guards, man, want to KNOW, because they're in that jail every day and nobody is comfortable when they get into a sadistic game, which is an awful big part of being a guard in jail. Some of them are probably, because of what they are in, probably close to potential for enlightenment. If every brother and sister who is confronted by The Man looks him in the eye and just is open to him, they're going to change. I probably had fifty- or seventy-five encounters with The Man in the last seven or eight months and he's been changed every time we've parted.

"Another thing that I'd like to see is a bumper sticker which says, 'Love the Local Heat.' The Birchers have 'Support Your Local Police.' Support, man, support! No, man, 'LOVE Your Local Police.' That's where it's at! Put them through changes.

"Like when they had these demonstrations on the Sunset Strip. Man, those demonstrations would have been a thousand percent more effective if instead of saying, 'Stop Police Brutality' the signs had said 'Love the Police.' Because, you see, a policeman has a response to the word 'love.' That has a reality to him. He wants to love. If he's ever loved or ever had flashes of love, he feels good, right? 'Stop Police Brutality.' Man, the policeman doesn't think he's brutal. HE THINKS HE'S RIGHT! You're not communicating with a person unless you are TALKING to the person and they understand and listen to you. A policeman can't listen to you if you're saying he's brutal. You have to accept another person's reality if you're going to be able to communicate with him, 'cause otherwise you're just playing a word game. I never talk to the police about what THEY'RE doing, you know. I answer his questions about me. They're not necessarily the words that he's using, but just feeling out the tone of where he's threatened and of where he's not threatened by you, and where he's open to you. It's just like communication with anybody.

Love and Hate

. . . "I have a very strong negative reaction to the movement being characterized as the Flower Children and the Love Children and love-ins and love trips, because all that is saying that hate is bad, which is a lie. It's a refuge in another fantasy. There never has been a man who didn't have hostile feelings. There never has been a man who hasn't had the feelings of grief. Hate is righteous, if you can accept it, and you express it. When it doesn't become violence. But if it's repressed because you 'OUGHT' to repress it, and you HAVE to, and it's NOT NICE to express feelings unless they're acceptable to somebody else, then it builds up to where violence can eventually become the expression. But I know that some of the most far-out feelings of love I've had have been when I've been confronted in relationships with hurtful experiences, reacted to them, expressed my hate as vehemently as I could, and almost instantly I became suffused with far-out feelings of love and acceptance.

The Demise of Strawberry Fields

"I kind of took on more than I could handle with Strawberry Fields. I got pneumonia and hepatitis, which I think is my body telling me that a lot of things aren't quite in harmony. I think a community, unless it's going to have an awful lot of money behind it, is going to have to be restricted to productive people for a while. It would be righteous if there were a community that was so far-out that it could accommodate people who are still in a state of being slobs. You know, some people have been told what they HAVE to do for so long, man, that they get into a place where they're free and they just don't know what to do. They just sit around in their own filth. Which is where they're at, at that time. It would be righteous if there were people who could be on a trip to pick up after them and produce for them, and provide them with food and clothing and things like that, but there doesn't seem to be the money right now, or, more important, the people. Most communities are going to have to be pretty restrictive. There was a community up in Gorda, near Big Sur, which has just been closed down for the same reason. It just got too big and became like a refugee camp.

"You have to have a leadership with a broader base than just one or two people to even begin with. You'd have to have a council. Then if somebody wants to live in the community, they could rap with the council. Presumably the council will be comprised of tuned-in people who can tune-in on the person that wants to come in. Maybe we'll take some grass or acid with the applicant and really get down to it. They won't have to have an application blank or references.

"I had an image when Strawberry Fields started as to what it should be. I would like to see it be a more or less self-sustaining commune where there would be such a complete atmosphere of freedom and acceptance that creative people could really get right into the expression of their creativity. What happened was that it turned into kind of a retreat or a refugee camp. The people who were around were kind of tired of the cities, and run down physically, and kind of up-tight. They would come out there and stay and take acid and smoke grass and kind of get their heads straightened out a little bit and split.

"We never got to the point where we could produce anything or be self-supporting. Success? I don't know. It was a success in terms of MY growth. I went through more far-out changes in the six months that that place existed than I have in any other period of my life. For me it was a success.

The Movement

"For me the 'hippie' movement is the most far-out, unique, revolutionary thing to happen in the history of the species! And I simply say that because it's been that revolutionary for me. I'm projecting my image on the whole world, of course. A year ago, if someone had described a person who feels the way I feel now all the time, I would have said impossible, nobody could feel that way, you're putting me on!

"Most of the time I feel the way I felt when I first started taking 250 micrograms of acid. That's the way I feel ALL THE TIME! How do I feel? Describe an orgasm to a virgin! I can't tell you how I feel, man!

"Strawberry Fields helped me get where I am. I guess in a way Strawberry Fields ISN'T, now. There isn't an organization, there isn't a geographical place that you could say is Strawberry Fields. I guess you could say it's just an idea, something that's in the air, that has become a part of the psychedelic movement.

THE PSYCHEDELIC CREED

Gridley's "commentary" included many concepts I later heard from many other hip people, at other times and in other places. In a sense it was a hippie position paper. A summary of these notions is a useful guide to the trip. The following may be viewed as the idealized principles of the new movement:

1. The hippie movement is a spontaneous evolution. It is not a "heavy" worked-out plan.

2. Drugs are a key to the God in men. Drugs are sacraments for a greater knowledge of the universe. Drugs are a vehicle to a cosmic consciousness.
3. There are spontaneous leaders in the movement. They are not "pushy" leaders, who are self-appointed. They are selected by hippie constituents, because they are "spiritual centers."
4. Sex is free, holy, and should be naturally acted out without guilt—for pure pleasure and communication.
5. The establishment and the police are not the enemy. They are a constant reminder that the trip into the universal unity of man was never meant to be easy.
6. Communes are places where people can "do their thing," use psychedelic drugs, seek their personal freedom and identity with a minimum amount of "hangups" and interferences.
7. Violence is a result of frustrations and repressions.
8. "You can't change anyone else—you can only change yourself." A true hippie believer would not get "hung-up" with heavy game playing, the new left, war protests, or civil rights battles. He simply would strengthen his own perceptions of honesty and truth.
9. Children should not have the "heavy trips" of their parents put onto them. They should have the freedom to "naturally" evolve in their own line of growth.
10. People should stop playing "heavy games" in their life—as in work, marriage, or the general plastic society. They should, as Leary postulates, "turn-on, tune-in, and drop out." In this more natural state of reality—with the aid of drugs—they will find their true spiritual condition.

In my many encounters with Gridley during my trip, I noted inconsistencies and considerable conflict with his effort to live by the creed that he accepted. However, one observation I had about Gridley throughout was that he was clearly "behind" or believed what he said. In brief, he was truly tuned-in and honest about his trip. I could be completely candid with him about both my positive and negative feelings, and he would attempt to answer or get an answer for any question that I would present. These characteristics of Gridley's experience, personality, and behavior provided me with an invaluable guide for checking out the many complicated issues that emerged along the way.

Part Two

The Trip

CHAPTER THREE

Tuning-In

MY LONG VOYAGE INTO THE hippie world began with my first really personal encounter with a group of hippies. It happened in the unusual setting of a Jewish restaurant in Santa Monica called Zucky's. While encircling a plate of salami and eggs, I observed the arrival at the next group of tables of Jesus Christ, several apostles, and three Mary Magdelenes. Jesus was like all of the pictures I had seen of him. He was tall, had a reddish-blond beard, and sky-blue eyes. This version of the Savior had bells on his leather boots and looked most beatific.

Along with other patrons in the restaurant, I was somewhat amused by the group's orders of such foods as "bagels and lox," "lean corn beef," and "Matzo ball soup." Some patrons were hostile to the band of people they considered to be intruders. Sounds like "disgusting" and "go to work" were muffled in pastrami sandwiches. The hostility was met by the beatific group with comments like "Nice to see you, partner" and broad sincere smiles.

I was somewhat surprised when the leader himself approached my table with a pleasant smile and greeted me by name. "My name is Gridley Wright. Don't you remember, we met when you gave a talk to a group of probation officers? I used to be a probation officer." I wasn't sure at that moment that I had met Gridley before; however, in his other life, I might have known him. Intrigued by the incongruity of a probation officer turned hippie, I invited him to sit down and we began to discuss his new scene. In short order, I became aware of my past associations with Gridley and expressed my great surprise at his new appearance.

He told me about the new movement he had become a part of over the past year and his "tribe" at Strawberry Fields. He invited me out to visit him and all of his "brothers and sisters."

At that particular time I thought of visiting Gridley's "new community" but I wasn't motivated to actually make the trip—until I began to work on this book. At that point I felt it was most important for me to visit his commune.

The directions to Strawberry Fields Gridley had given me at the restaurant carried me through many desolate twisted roads in Malibu Canyon. Finally, at a local fire station in Malibu, I picked up his trail from a hostile fire chief. The chief informed me how the residents of Strawberry Fields had burned the commune to the ground. He had a negative position on Gridley and Strawberry Fields. "Why do you want to find those bastards who burned themselves up? You don't look like one of them. They're all crazy, running around those hills nude. Naturally they finally burned the filthy dump down. They say it was by accident—an overturned candle—but I'm not sure that they didn't do it on purpose. There's still two of them living there now—a crazy fifteen-year-old girl who calls herself Moonglow. She's living in a tree with some young boy. They're both crazy on dope. Just sit around and stare out in space."

After some further discussion on his negative views, the chief gave me directions to where Gridley was now located. He was living with part of his tribe in a house in Malibu. After much circling and directions from a sheriff's man who ran a prison work camp and delivered another diatribe on "the degenerates," I arrived at Gridley's outpost. It was a small Spanish-style house isolated from the main road.

My first view of the scene was two attractive young girls who were both, to use a crass "plastic society" term, "topless." I later determined that Cass was sixteen and Wanda was seventeen. They were both "heads" (had used LSD) and both were as dropped out as they could legally be for their age. Cass was Gridley's girlfriend.

Gridley's large dog came barking up to me and Gridley shouted what I later found out to be one of his gag lines—"Kill, Kill, Kill." He seemed pleased to see me.

The inside of the house was in better shape than most of the hippie converted pads I was to encounter on later trips. As we were settling into some discussion, another attractive girl entered the room. Gridley and the girl who had just arrived hugged each other ferociously. (I later observed this most loving greeting take place many times on my trip. It was much more fervent and effusive than any greeting of affection given in the straight world. It involved a tight encirclement of each other—some swaying-searching smiling looks directly into the partner's eyes, and final comments like "too much." The hug is sometimes held for several minutes, does not usually involve a kiss on the mouth. It is as appropriate for two men or two women as it is for a mixed couple. A loving recognition of mutual views of the world is affirmed by the greeting.)

The girl seemed familiar. We looked at each other in surprise. She was a student from my college. I quickly learned she had moved in with Gridley's group for the summer, had not had acid yet but smoked pot, and apparently from self-admitted and later observed behavior, led "a completely free sex life."

Ginger later abandoned her "middle-class provincialism" and appeared as topless as the other girls. As she bobbled around the room serving coffee, I had the feeling that she shared my sense of slight discomfort in her act of nudity.

About this time a hippie named Gus came out of another

room wearing nothing but his long curly hair, a beard, an Indian headband, and a big smile. We were formally introduced by Gridley. I felt that all of the nudity was candid and sincere, with the exception of Ginger's. She seemed to be making a declaration with every bobble—"look how uninhibited I am."

I had the feeling that the group was all high. My later experiences clearly revealed that every member of the group—most of whom had lived at Strawberry Fields—stayed as high as they could get at all times. This was especially true of Gridley, who seemed to smoke as much pot as he could every day. I later found out that he used some LSD about every four days.

Some of my stereotypes about drug use and its impact on behavior were changed, especially by Gridley. No matter how high he was he could maintain the trend of a conversation. As he once told me, he could no longer distinguish between his drug high and his "spiritual high." This seemed to be true of most of the high priests of the hippie movement I was later to meet. The youngsters were giggly and silly on drugs; however, the intelligentsia of the movement were usually coherent, often eloquent, whether they had recently used drugs or not.

Many questions about the movement were stirring in my head. After some preliminary discussion about the book I planned and how he could help, Gridley suggested that I "get my tape recorder out of the car and we'll rap." I had not mentioned that I had a tape recorder. This was one of the first signals of sharp perception I had from Gridley. This pattern of quickly tuning-in to my inclinations was later repeated in my dialogues with many other people of his status in the movement. Most of these people were really "tuned-in." They seemed to leap past oblique questions, and confronted me head-on with discussions of my central interest. They really were as they described it, "open people." Whenever I would fence, or in their terms play an "ego-game," they would cut through to a center of relevant interaction.

The directness and the tuned-in quality of our interactions was refreshing, and enormously speeded up the research process throughout the project.

Following are some selected excerpts from a three-hour taped discussion of various preliminary hippie issues I discussed with Gridley and his tribe that afternoon. (G is Gridley, as distinguished from Gus in the following. I am LY throughout the book.)

G–I have had over a hundred acid trips. Ninety-five percent of my trips were taken with other people around. There are some times when I would go off to get by myself, but most of the time there's been other people around. Sometimes as many as sixty, seventy people.

It's beautiful to take acid with other people with whom you're close and don't have game shit going on. It's just so beautiful to be there with them because *they* are so beautiful. The visual changes that people go through and your perception of them is just so far out and new in nature. . . .

Making love under acid is really beautiful. So much crap has been laid on me about making love in my life. All the pornography and the flashes that you have sometimes when you're making love. Pornography, "nasties," and "no-no's," and things like that. A long time ago I'd have flashed on pornography like that right in the middle of making love. But when you take acid, see, your mind is empty of everything but exactly what you're dealing with; and there you have a woman and you're a man and you make love to that woman. And you have nothing else in your head. It's a beautiful thing. Your whole body has an orgasm. God, it's unbelievable!"

Coming out of middle-class left field, I raised the question of hangups between "beautiful love-makers." What about adultery, cheating, and the like? Fortunately, or unfortunately, Gridley and his girl Cass and Gus and his wife had experienced a love mix-up several days before and we discussed the matter in that personal context.

GUS–I made love to Gridley's woman. It was really involved. Gridley and I really had a heated battle, but we continued to love each other even though we hated sometimes during those days.

LY–Why did you do it?

GUS–Well, first of all, there was a total lack of communication amongst all of us and it created a confusing situation. And I just reacted to the situation.

LY–Was there something like this? There's this groovy chick and you were stoned good and you were in a position, so you did it? Or were you going to get even with him? Or what?

G–It was the former thing, that's what it was, man.

GUS–It was what former thing?

G–You know, you guys were together and you felt like fucking and you fucked.

LY–I'll tell you what I feel is a better question. Why would it bother you, Gridley? You are a member of the free-love clan. I know that if somebody balled my wife, in the value system that I'm living in, I would be furious and hurt. But why were you even bothered by two beautiful friends who happened to make it?

G–I am still up-tight with the system, it fucks my head up.

LY–So you think that in time you'll become unencumbered with that kind of morality?

G–If I were totally enlightened, nothing would fuck my head up.

LY–Then you wouldn't be bothered by someone balling your woman.

G–Right. In fact, I could sit and watch it if I were totally tuned-in and right with myself.

LY–In part, what I'm trying to explore is whether there is a new morality here, or is it amorality?

G–I think we are probing toward a new morality.

LY–In other words, right now your girlfriend is kind of your chattel or property.

G–My reaction is this. Just let me talk about it for a while and don't ask me questions so I can get into kind of a flow on it. I'll just kind of give you my whole theory on sex and kind of fit this incident into it if I can. I really got my mind blown by a passage from the Philip Wylie book that made the point that we homo sapiens, alone of all the species on the face of the earth, are capable of enjoying sexual stimulation and pleasures from the day we are born till the day we die. That is reality. That is truth. That is what twenty billion years of evolution has brought us to.

Society says that it's not nice, you know, so they lay down a bunch of shit on reality. These circumstances fuck people up. Now in my head *I* say, "People ought to be able to fuck whomever, wherever, however, they want to—including my woman and me." Now, my feelings aren't anywhere near that. They're open enough so that I can confront the situation without blowing myself apart over it, you know. So that we can sit around and get into it, and find out what's happening, and *why*, and everything like that. And the conclusion that I've come to is that it doesn't matter what ought to be, there's only what is. What is, right now. And what *is* will change, as long as we're open to change and see that change is the only answer.

So, well, a year ago, Gus fucking my girl would have blown my mind totally and I wouldn't have been able to confront it. Now I can look at it and come up with some things on it. And, operationally, what we've kind of come up with is that it isn't necessary to fuck someone else's woman if it's going to be that big a thing to them, because you have different values. Like you have the value of your relationship with your partner, and they have these values, and if it fucks it up too much for people to be fucking other people's old ladies, then pass on it.

LY–You've been up and down the coast quite a bit, and

you've been in other situations with hippies, pursuing whatever's happening. Is your position on this pretty typical?

G–My behavior?

LY–No, not that. Your general notion of sex. Let's look at what sociologically might be called "group marriage." This is the way a group's sex life was probably like back in the caves in The Beginning. There men and women were probably all balling each other indiscriminately. Then it probably began to get compartmentalized around economic things, and possessions and families emerged. There may have been more involvement in a woman, not as a sexual thing, but because she cooked your dinner and you kind of wanted her to keep doing that.

I understand there are around twenty-five hippie communities or more going on in California. What is the sex life like in these situations?

GUS–I can't speak for that—but I can speak for myself. My wife Mary and I are still together as man and wife, but I refuse to tell my woman that I'm not going to make love to another woman. I think she would actually like me to say that I . . . No, she would like me to *feel* that I would not want to make love to another woman. She doesn't want me to promise anything. She's pregnant now. Yet she doesn't want me to promise anything . . . like take care of the baby we're gonna have, or anything. She doesn't want any future promises or anything. She wants me to continue to feel—she would like me to continue to feel that I want to be with her. I had a thing once, Gridley. The day I walked out to show you the trees and stuff—I had a flash. I was stoned on everybody's loving everybody else. I'd like to watch somebody *make love* to my wife. What happens, in our culture, is that too many people are fucked . . . I think too many people *do* fuck and like it's groovy to fuck and make love at the same time, you know, that really beautiful thing going on and that's fabulous, man. I don't want to push my woman into it, but if it happens, I really feel that it would be a beautiful thing.

LY–If something happened—if she cut out on you—wouldn't that be a blow?

GUS–Well, right now, if she split, man, I'd be . . . you know. I probably would be [laugh] . . . Let's see, right now if she *did* split, I don't know.

G–Sure are a lot of groovy chicks around, Gus!

GUS–To tell you the truth, man, it wouldn't bug me that bad.

G–It wouldn't bug *me* that bad either (ha, ha) because I superlove Cass, man. I love her more than anyone that I've ever been with in my life, and yet, every day you see beautiful people and every day you see *more* beautiful people.

When sex isn't a big issue any more, then sex happens more than it ever happened in your whole life. When you stop grasping for something, it begins to happen more than you thought it would or could ever hope it could happen.

I was particularly interested in the friendly spirit of hostile encounter that appeared between Gridley and Gus. I began to pursue the handling of aggression in the hippie world in general and at Strawberry Fields in particular.

LY–You were apparently "wide-open" at Strawberry Fields. What if someone moved in and simply would not cooperate. How far would he get with this position? Let's say he didn't want to help clean up—work or anything. If somebody rubs him the wrong way, he says he's going to punch his head in. What did you do with a guy like that?

G–Listen, we had people who would hit the kids. I really had strong feelings of rejection and reaction to people hitting kids. Probably the strongest—in hitting kids and animals. Man, that really bugs me more than anything else. And so, this cat would hit the kids, and I would talk to him about it, and other people would talk to him about it, but he was never forced to leave. I said to him, "You know, if you have to hit kids I wish you wouldn't be here, because it bothers me to have people hitting kids."

LY–Here's what bothers me about your position. There seems to be a proposition in the hippie world that no one tries to modify behavior. But apparently you were there trying to modify this guy's behavior. Weren't you?

G–I'm there to be whatever I can be to help people tune-in to themselves. I know that inside everybody is God. And so, any manifestation of someone's telling me by their behavior that they're not aware of that is not going to fuck my head up that much. I don't want to modify behavior, because behavior is simply a symptom.

LY–Are you opposed to the system that is trying, in your view, to push people in directions where they are being twisted out of shape?

G–Right. Yes.

LY–Okay. Then you do have some ideal-type individual that you're pushing toward. And so, as laissez-faire as you say you are, there's a push toward a certain kind of conformity. This is a paradox in the hippie philosophy that I can't seem to resolve.

G–Well, to me the goal is total acceptance. . . .

LY–If you're ridiculing the guy who is hitting kids, for example, aren't you trying to get him to tune-in to some other way of life? You're not accepting his behavior.

G–I'm totally accepting his behavior, man. I'm also accepting my reaction and my feelings on it and I'm expressing them.

Now he can say "Fuck off, man, this is my trip. You take yours." And I'll say, "Righteous, man, take whatever trip you want." But part of my trip is running my mouth, and if I . . .

LY–I thought you left people alone to do what they wanted to do. His thing may be hitting kids.

G–You're taking a really weird example. First of all, anybody that ever came to Strawberry Fields wanted to and usually did change. In some ways we got the dregs of the psychedelic world, and most of them changed. I feel each man and each woman has a hundred million different ways of being. And life is so groovy. There's so many ways to go through it, you know. And it's really neat to try them all, good or bad.

Actually there's no bad or good. Everyone just has his own trip. If someone else's trip bugs me, I tell him. I don't care if he changes or not then. He's going through his thing and I'm going through mine. That's where it's at.

LY–Since Strawberry Fields closed, where did everyone go?

G–All over. Venice and Haight-Ashbury mainly.

On our later trip Gridley and I encountered many people who had been at Strawberry Fields. All of them became enthusiastic and loving with Gridley. The clear nostalgia was that Strawberry Fields had truly been a kind of hippie Garden of Eden, at least compared to the scenes they had encountered since it closed.

About this time we were disturbed by a car pulling up in the driveway. In spite of many comments I had heard about hip people using dope openly, there were some furtive glances out the window to make sure it was not the "heat" [police].

It was the farthest thing from the "heat" possible. Two people, a Negro around forty and a young white girl around sixteen, entered. A few minutes later a young man around twenty arrived. This was the first time I heard the standard hippie greeting I was to hear repeated many times. "Do you have any dope?" The young girl produced a marijuana cigaret. And a ritual occurred that I was to witness at almost every future interview session. Someone would light the marijuana cigaret and then it was passed around the circle.

This was the first time I had ever been at a pot party. I was rather nervous and "up-tight." I could see the headline —*Professor Arrested at Marijuana Party.*

In spite of my inner feelings, I maintained as best I could

an outer illusion of "cool." Thereafter, although I consistently refused the pot offered me (except once, and I'll relate that experience later), I was somewhat more relaxed. My tape recorder mike may have had more pot smoke blown into it than any other one in existence.

The new people were apparently visiting L.A. from a hippie community in Gorda, Big Sur. I was intrigued by their discussion of the happenings at Gorda.

LY–How many people are up there?

JOE–Oh, probably two hundred living around in the hills. We have around thirty in the big stone house. All of us wanted it to be an open community, but it couldn't be too open. Even though we have guests all the time.

LY–How many guests show up each day?

JOE–It turns out there is getting to be about thirty guests a day. It's really kind of a drag because you don't know who they are—and things get pretty disorganized behind them. People are living in seven other cabins permanently. Some lady gave us a few hundred-pound bags of grain and stuff like that for food and we're doing pretty good.

Another car pulled up and another young man came in. He eyed me and my tape recorder suspiciously. Gridley detected this and informed him, "Man, this is my partner, he's writing a book on the scene." The group was getting high on the marijuana cigaret that was being passed around.

The young man, John, mentioned his appearance at the Century City L.A. peace demonstration (summer, 1967) that resulted in a small riot. He turned to me and asked me somewhat belligerantly, as if I were responsible for all the trouble, whether I had gone to the peace demonstration. I told him that I hadn't. Somehow he identified me as a member of the opposition. Gridley began to "put down" the young man with his view of protests.

G–Man, to me all that bullshit about peace and war and integration and all that is just part of that other plastic world, man. You wouldn't catch me dead at a fuckin' peace demonstration.

Gridley then changed the subject back to the commune up at Big Sur. He asked Joe if they had room and Joe assured him it would be "out of sight" if Gridley visited Gorda. Gridley invited me to drive the group up on Saturday, and I quickly agreed.

My hurried agreement changed to anxiety in the several intervening days before my trip north with the gang. I felt an enormous paranoia about driving several hundred miles with a group using illegal drugs.

I wanted to do honest first-hand research and at the same time I had a realistic fear of being arrested with the group on an illegal drug charge. After much ethical mental gymnastics, during several sleepless nights, my motivation to plunge into the research finally dominated my fears. From that point on, I had very few internal battles of anxiety and went along with the most available and relevant avenues open to my research voyage.

CHAPTER FOUR

Big Sur

WHEN I PICKED UP GRIDLEY, Ginger, a youth named John, and a man who called himself Turtle at Gridley's Malibu retreat, there was a festive air about the group. They were all elated about going up to Big Sur to visit the community and some "old friends."

Gridley set the male hippie style with his Indian headband, beads, and bells on his leather boots. Turtle was one of "the beautiful people." He was about thirty years old, heavily bearded and long-haired. He talked a great deal about time spent in various jails. He was clearly a close associate of Gridley, since he had been one of the central people at Strawberry Fields. He was a very heavy pot smoker and was very "far out" most of the time. The girls were all free from any middle-class beauty-parlor accouterments, wore plain cotton shifts and apparently little else.

As we put sleeping bags and baggage into the car, I noticed Gridley place a small black pill box in his levi pants. I later found out that he had about ten caps of LSD in the box. I made some casual oblique remarks out of my nervousness. My comments about the LSD were immediately and correctly sensed by Gridley as my concern about getting arrested. He assured me that if he saw a black and white car with the "heat" in it, he would swallow the pills or give them out in a hurry, and there would be no evidence of the drugs. He also made a comment which I couldn't prove one way or the other at the time. "There is very little LSD in the capsules and the little there is would break down under police analysis."

It was a completely beautiful, clear California day. As we sailed up the coast highway with a marvelous view of the Pacific, my spirits soared. The worries I had about dope use on the trip and the fear of arrest had left me. My anxiety came roaring back when about ten miles up the road I notised Gridley dispensing the LSD capsules to the group. He took several himself and gave the rest out during the trip.

I was somewhat surprised at this small continued dosage use of LSD. My model for an LSD trip was what I had heard and read about. It was a notion of an intense type of trip that would last eight to twelve hours from one large dosage. Gridley later told me that the reason he took several caps at a time was because he wasn't always sure of the drug's strength. He would take some, feel it for a while, and if it was not "heavy" enough, he would take some more.

The tone and pace of the trip accelerated when we picked up a hippie hitchhiker while stopping for gas. He introduced himself as Pan. This model of Pan was about 5′ 6″, roughly twenty-two, very slight, with a frozen smile on his face. His hair was long and went in all the right directions to cover his ears. Pan had psychedelic designs and several testimonials for pot embossed on his worn-out levi pants. He had just left a car full of hip people with whom he had hitched a ride. It was kind of a truck-car that had penciled on its side, "Keep America Green, Grow Grass." He told us that he had just come from Hollywood where he had stayed at the Los Angeles Diggers' headquarters in Hollywood.

When Pan got into the car, the usual business of establishing communication ensued between the group and Pan. Each asked the other whether they were holding any dope of any kind. Gridley responded with some LSD and Pan said, "Gee, man, that's beautiful! I haven't had any good acid in days. You're all beautiful people. Man, it's beautiful to be with your brothers."

Pan was a typical novitiate in the movement. He also seemed to be high on speed, prior to his ingestion of the LSD. He didn't stop talking. His stories were lengthy, frenetic, and rather humorous. His monologue included tales of the following kind about his brief tour as a drug addict in New York. It was the kind of story typical of a "speed-freak"—long, unrelated, and pointless.

"Out of sight, man. I had a doctor—let me tell you about my doctor connection in New York. I was there for two months. I worked for him. This cat, a beautiful dude, gave drugs to anybody who wanted it. And, of course he 'used' himself. But he was such a 'heavy' user—no dope really got through to him. One day, he was lying on the bed nude and I picked up this needle. His veins were all gone from using. But I see one vein sticking out in the back of his leg. I fixed some demerol and before he could say anything, I had popped him in his one little vein. He just turned around and thanked me a million times because it was the first flash he had in five years. [Laughter.] I really dug that cat. He was just beautiful. Hey, man, let me tell you about the day I came down the road from the mountain in Big Sur, and there was this big truck. Did you ever see a half-ton truck full of grass [marijuana] all in one place? Well, man, this truck had like big bales of grass sticking out like alfalfa. The most beautiful sight I ever have seen in my whole life!"

The group seemed amused by Pan and his antics and this encouraged him to continue his high pace of frenetic commentary. He told us about the community in Big Sur where we were going and about all of the "beautiful people." Gorda was also his destination.

"The most beautiful people are there. The most beautiful brother I've ever met in my life is Jack Miller. Jack is one of the great men up at Gorda. Jack is beautiful. He has fewer hangups than anyone I've ever met in my life!"

Pan went on to talk about his past life. "Man, I wasn't always like this. I was a bad cat. I spent seven out of my twenty-two years in prison. I was with the Youth Authority for seven years, man. They kept me locked up in those cages. I'm on parole now but I've really broken loose. Acid has just 'blown my mind' [opened up new doors of perception.] I'm a new person. I see life real different. In fact, would you cats like to hear a poem I wrote?" Before our amused group could respond, Pan began to recite the following poem, which I later had him write out for me. (The misspelled words are not corrected.)

POEM ON THE ROAD

you want to look you want to see
you almost catch a glimpse.
you can not have this other wurld,
Except at great expense.

This wurld will cost you nothing.
Except for all you own.
you must stand up and be a man
and walk this path alone.

you must give up your Hangups.
Its humble to be poor,
And God will give you all your need
you can not ask for more.

you finally opened up your eyes
you only have to ask.
O Wow its really out of site
my God it happens fast.

you finally see the things you want
youve grabbed it with both hands.
your made your move and won the stakes.
Which were the sex and land.

You know its not a gamble
you only have to ask
and once you find your a "head"
you never will be lost.

you know you really want to be
you know you love the land,
you lay there with the sun and sea
and gently love the sand.

The sea will fill your stumich
you make your bed of grass
and then you finaly stop to think
my God I'm home at last.

And once you had a house in town
it neve was a home
Ther were so many people there
and still you were alone

And when you wirship to your God
your Church is where you be
you can not hate you only love
I know we're truly free.

Pan

When he finished reading the poem, he was almost kissed by everyone. "Too much." "Out of sight." Pan was a smashing success. "You know, I still have a little ego in me, in spite of my new life. One of these days I hope to get this published."

I zeroed right in on Pan and said, "Done!" He looked surprised. I told him I was a writer and that I would publish his poem in the book I was doing on hippies. His face beamed. Gridley, from the back seat, told Pan, "Dig, man, when you look for something you never get it. It just happens to you. Isn't it beautiful? Dig, you're going to get your poem published."

During the trip Gridley began to get obviously stoned. His face was beatific and with his beard and thin features he increasingly resembled pictures I had seen of Christ. The problem with the Jesus Christ image for me was that this one was necking with a young girl. Ginger was responding to his loving. When we reached the Big Sur area, Gridley had me pull the car over to the side of the road.

After we parked off the main road, Gridley and Ginger walked into the woods. Out of the corner of my eye I couldn't help noticing her legs thrown into the air as Gridley and she fell down completely onto an old coat. Their sex scene was private, but yet not hidden from the rest of the group.

Turtle, John, Pan, and I gazed seaward from the beautiful hill at Big Sur. In spite of the hectic emotional nature of the trip, I began to sink into a calm, meditative mood. The ocean, the mountains, and the trees were truly magnificent. The meditation of my "partners" was very pronounced and visible. My own view of the natural beauty around me was enhanced by their subtle way of calling it to my attention.

I noticed a significant contrast between the hippies' awareness of the scene and the vacationing middle-class campers whizzing by on the highway—unconsciously avoiding the natural wonders of Big Sur. The combination of the Gridley-Ginger sex happening, Pan now writing a "new poem," and Turtle's obvious meditation had a total affect. Perhaps, as they told me, the Universe can be seen in a grain of sand, a blade of grass, or looking at the sea.

Gridley and Ginger returned from their tryst. As if to emphasize the casualness of their love-making, Ginger commented, "God, I hope I don't get any poison oak on my ass." She then threw her now dusty coat onto the floor of the back seat.

Gridley called for another stop on the road to Gorda. This scene was also beautiful. There was a waterfall, and a tree with its roots at the bottom of a clear pool. I was out by the road and when I heard Gridley call me, I went to this idyllic scene. Ginger was wading in the pool stripped from the waist down. I suspected she had also "made love" with Turtle, who was now squatted in his standard position of meditation along side the rippling stream.

Our next stop was at the foot of the mountain in Big Sur where the Gorda hippie community was located. We parked the car on the road and began to follow Pan on foot up a rugged mountain trail. It was a two-mile hike up the mountain. I could sense the excitement in the group.

My own reaction was apprehensive. Possibly these people *were* on to a new, more meaningful way of life. On my trudge up the mountain I began to review my own world. True, I was happy and satisfied with my own way; however, I had thoughts about the LSD trigger. Maybe there was a more cosmic view than the general provincialism that surrounded most situations. On the trip I had rediscovered the more natural world, at least in a partial way, and perhaps these "dropped-out," "tuned-in" people did really know a better way of life. I had a vague feeling that I was about to enter a kind of Shangri-la.

Gridley came alive on the walk up the mountain. His energy seemed to flow stronger. He led Pan and me by a few feet, as Ginger and Turtle fell into the background. It seemed that the farther up the mountain we got, the more vitality Gridley appeared to have and the more saintly was the smile on his face.

We finally hit a plateau and some human images appeared that were new and hauntingly strange to me. It was either a scene from Man in The Beginning or a small troupe of human stragglers who had survived the desolation of the earth by atomic destruction. I could see about eighty people moving around in the strange foggy mist that hung over the mountain top.

On one side a young twenty-year-old boy with an Indian headband holding in his long hair sat in the center of a hole in the middle of a blanket staring straight into space. The crowd blended with the surrealistic scene. Several children dressed in ragged clothes pranced about, evidently part of the family.

The clothes were bizarre, but not casually bizarre. There were many leather garments, buckskins, and Indian headbands. Several young girls wore long colonial-style dresses.

It was a quiet and casual scene. Tired from the walk, I sat down on the remnants of a sofa that really didn't fit into the scene. It had a piece of cloth thrown over the exposed springs. I said hello to the girl sitting next to me who was staring out blankly at the mountain. She smiled and said, "Hello. Where are you from?" "Berkeley." "Are you a student there?" "No, I live there." "I dropped out of an art school in Oakland." "How long have you been up here?" "About a week."

A young man about twenty wearing ragged, torn pants greeted me with a smile. He had a horrible hacking cough. My paternalism stirred in me. I bypassed the whole scene and told him he really should do something about his cough, "like see a doctor." It sounded like an advanced case of T.B. He gave me a warm smile and walked away, hacking into the fog.

Gridley sat down, squat style, with Turtle and the others. They seemed to have a prayerful, meditative look. I lay down on the ground (which seemed the thing to do) near Gridley and a scraggly-looking blonde-haired girl, wearing a long denim gown.

Pan, who had been "visiting around," returned to our group. "Brother, things have changed up here. It's not the same. I even hear that Joe, the leader, is going to split. I'm going to Nevada City (another hippie community). This is terrible." On this note of gloom, he continued to inform us of the "bad changes" that had occurred in this community since his last visit.

At this point I became aware of a pungent odor. A group gathered around a large pewter pot were cooking some kind of soup that smelled of bad onions and old vegetables. People began to gather around the cook-out in a predatory way. There were some regular soup bowls, but mainly the diners used old plastic containers, tin cans, and the like. People began to dig into the soup. They ingested it mainly by sucking on the hot substance, since there were no spoons available.

Suddenly I felt completely out of place, as if I were dressed in a full dress suit. In spite of the fact that I had on an old sweat shirt, cotton slacks, and sneakers, I looked and felt overdressed for this primitive scene. Compared to the others, I must have looked like Fred Astaire in the movie *Top Hat*.

I was rather disoriented and followed Gridley around, on the assumption that he knew where one goes in a scene like this. I increasingly became aware of the fact that, in addition to the eighty or so people in the immediate area, there were perhaps two hundred more in many other small camps within a radius of several hundred yards on various ledges of the mountain. Many campers were literally dwelling Indian cliff style.

The camps consisted of hastily set up fireplaces and tents. There were boxes of Carnation powdered milk, Campbell's tomato cans, and the incongruous appearance of standard supermarket packaged sugar, rice, corn flakes, and other middle-class suburban foods.

Gridley, Turtle, and I squatted around one of the camp sites where a young man around twenty-five and a Nordic-looking blonde girl were cooking brown rice mixed with tomato soup. Another fellow—long-haired and in denims—was seated Indian style around the same fire. We sat down and listened to his chant: "I'm cutting out, man, I'm going to that other mountain. There've been all sorts of bad things happening here. A buddy of mine got stabbed last night. Some guy went crazy and started wielding a knife around. We took the knife away. I don't know where he got it, but he came back later with a sword. People are all losing their goods, too. It's really out of sight, man."

Gridley replied to the incantation of the cliff dweller with a venom and a self-assurance I had not expected. "*You* fucking people are disgusting. Here you have this beautiful mountain, you have no hassle with the county, no hassle with people trying to bust you—you got it made, not like in Strawberry Fields where we were hassling all the time, and here you want to split. Why can't you get together?"

Gridley's charisma, power, and commitment to the overall movement registered with me and the others present. He easily defined himself as a leader to this man he had never met. His assertive behavior implied to me that these were all his people and that they were all part of the same large social movement.

The young man's reply confirmed my assumption of Gridley's charisma. "You're right, man, we should stick with it. I'm ashamed of myself. We'll think about it. Maybe we'll stay." He shifted his position immediately in the face of Gridley's diatribe.

About this time Pan reappeared out of the mist and voiced his apprehension once more. "Brother, this isn't my home anymore. Something's happening here, I don't understand it. I hear Joe is really going to split." Gridley chastised him for his gloom. Pan (at Gridley's suggestion) said, "I'm going to get Joe and the others. Let's have a meeting." The people there all agreed. "Cool, let's have a meeting!"

People began to assemble around the camp with Gridley in the center. In addition to about fifty adults, there were several children. One attractive blonde-haired girl had her little four-year-old boy on her lap. Cats and dogs also came to the spontaneous meeting. (Most of the people were dressed in typically hip style.)

The group began its random dialogue. At first it became a gripe session. "People are stealing around here, man." "We are split up, there is no unity." "No one helps anyone else do anything." "I'm cutting out tomorrow." Gridley intervened at various points and it became increasingly apparent that he was truly the leader of the moment. To Pan he said, "Don't quit, man. Make your light shine. Here is where it's happening. It's happening all over. We felt like this many times at Strawberry, but we stayed with it. You can hang on here, too. Let's not quit now. There's nothing better over the ridge. Do it here where you are, Brothers."

Pan and the others seemed to take heart from Gridley's monologue. "Brother, you're right. We gotta love each other. Man, this is our home. Out of sight, too much. We really gotta stay here. This is it!" Others began to join in with the more positive viewpoint sparked by Gridley. One man seated in the center of the group said, "Let's do a chant! That's what we should do. We oughta have one of our religious group chants right now." Gridley suggested that a prayer was in order. Everybody said, "Too much. Let's pray."

The group bowed their collective heads in two minutes of silent prayer.

After the prayer, the rather perky girl next to me with the four-year-old son between her legs said excitedly, as if to give the group courage, "I hear Gridley Wright's coming here." Gridley looked over and smiled and said, "I'm Gridley and I'm here." She said, "Too much, out of sight. We're glad you're here. You'll help change things."

During the meeting I noticed the blonde's son holding on to a cat—which obviously wanted to run off. The boy kept retrieving and holding on to the cat. Finally in a burst of anger a fellow, seated next to me, admonished the four-year-old. "Hey, man, let the fucking cat go. Can't you see it wants to run off. Let the fucking cat do its own thing, man!" The child continued to clutch the cat.

Pan also began to emerge as a group leader. He began incanting Gridley's chant of "Let your light shine, brothers and sisters. We all have to love each other." At one point he became practical. "We gotta help Joe, so he won't leave. We should rebuild the kitchen. They broke the stone house kitchen—they destroyed it."

Gridley grew angry and went into a diatribe on this point. "They, they, they. They are part of you, man. These are your people who destroyed it."

Another man related a theft that had happened the night before. "This cat came up and began to make away with my sleeping bag. And I told him, 'Brother, you do that and I'll split your head open with an iron bar.' Two of my brothers joined me and the cat left."

Gridley gave his view of the theft and the fellow's response: "You fucking people are out of sight on that. Those people who are stealing are part of you. If someone wants something I have, it is not my property, he can have it. Let him take it. It belongs to all of us—it's part of you." This totality view had great impact on the group. They began to chant: "Out of sight. Too much." The fellow who had related the theft incident expressed regret at his position:

"Man, you're right. I'm never gonna do that again. That thief was my brother and I truly treated him wrong."

Someone asked Gridley, who was now clearly the center of the total discussion, "What were the rules you had at Strawberry Fields?" He replied, "We just had two rules: no drinking, no shit [heroin], and no Methedrine. We really wanted to have no rules, but a lot of Meth freaks came to clean up and we really couldn't handle them—too well."

Gridley then went into a diatribe on how the group on the mountain had lost their purpose. He told them for one thing that food was holy and they should at least have a kitchen as a center of their activity. This notion was picked up again by Pan. "Well, are we gonna build the kitchen tomorrow?" The group assented: "Crazy, cool. We'll build the kitchen tomorrow."

One member of the group suggested that 9:00 a.m. would be a good time to meet and work on the kitchen. Another member of the group warned, "Let's not get into the same fuckin' organization bag we dropped out of. We'll all show up some time after breakfast and everybody will do what they can." Other apparently "over-organized" members of the group wanted to give out work assignments. Another one disagreed. "Everybody just do their own thing and it will get done. It's pretty hard to watch somebody work. The crowd will join the act." Somebody else repeated, "Yeah, it's real hard to watch somebody work." Gridley said, "I find it very easy to watch someone else work." Everybody laughed and said, "Too much, out of sight."

The group seemed buoyed up by the meeting. Pan was elated. His face was shining. "Out of sight, man! This mountain is my home. I'm gonna take care of it. We're gonna build the kitchen tomorrow. Should we build it outside or inside?" Someone replied, "It's more sanitary outside, because food gets all slopped up on the floor when you do it inside."

Someone asked Gridley, "How did you handle distributing the food at Strawberry." "People would line up, go in, and take their turn. We had some big dude standing out in front and he would see to it that no one got in out of turn. People went in turn; otherwise, some people would fall on the food and eat it all up in no time flat." "Beautiful, man. That's what we'll do. We'll have someone standing at the door." Gridley disagreed: "No, man. People should learn to control themselves."

At one point in the discussion, Gridley made a demonstration of one of his viewpoints. Someone asked him, "Can I have one of your cigarets?" Gridley fumed, "Fuck you, man. Don't you know that these cigarets are yours as well as mine? When are you going to learn that brothers share everything." The man said, "Too much. You're right. That's right. Your cigarets are mine." and he took a cigaret and lit it up.

By this time darkness had fallen. And, except for the flickering fireplaces, the group was sitting pretty much in the dark. There was an occasional flashlight, which reminded me of the outside world of good steaks, clean apartments, and "materialistic junk."

The group was ready to adjourn. Someone made the point that the meeting was useful and they should have others. "Man, we should just have meetings when we feel like getting together. Let's not get in that organization bag. Man, why don't we have a committee?" Everybody roared with laughter at the ludicrous possibility of a committee. The group was in agreement with a young man who commented, "Yeah, we're falling into the Establishment bag of setting up committees of people and . . . this is too much, man—we have to do it spontaneously."

Several people said, "Beautiful, that's the way to operate—spontaneously!" Pan got up and once again made his speech about "the beautiful people are back. I found my home again on the mountain. It's wonderful, brothers! I love you all." The groups incanted with delight. "Too much, out of sight."

At this point, Gridley said, "I want to talk to Joe." He rose and left. This officially closed the meeting, and the group began to drift into the darkness.

I followed Gridley to the stone house, where Joe was supposed to be. The stone house was an area about 30′ by 30′. Apparently at one time it had been a building. At the moment there were the remains of the wall of an older, firmly constructed building and several lean-to boards. One window looked out over the mountains onto a beautiful view of the sea. The stone house did not have electricity. The room was lit by several candles.

There were fifteen or twenty people sleeping wall-to-wall, on the floor, in one corner of the room. In another part of the misty room another group was gathered around two candles listening to someone playing a guitar very badly. The guitar "tune" was joined by a harmonica that sounded even worse. Another person joined in by humming loudly.

Someone yelled to Gridley, "Hey, man, here's Joe." The two leaders, Joe and Gridley, spontaneously embraced hippie style for about two minutes. They slapped each other on the back and almost danced around together. They then settled down quietly by the fire to meditate on the scene.

The spontaneous musical entertainment became worse. At a certain point, Joe and Gridley rose to leave. I told Gridley that I might leave at any time since I had other things to do. He said, "Cool, man. Go when you feel like it. But if you want me to, I'll fix it so you can sleep here tonight." I said, "Well, no, I'll see to it. I may leave or I may not." "Cool, that's the way to look at it." He strolled out with Joe, probably to have an upper-level management discussion about the problems on the mountain.

It was then about 10:30 in the evening. In addition to the people sleeping on the floor there were around thirty people in the stone house sitting and staring into the darkness. There was no conversation, only the dissonant music, and some random snoring. The boredom annoyed me and I felt a strong compulsion to leave immediately.

I asked a fellow directions to the path to the main road. He said, "Cool, man, follow me," and showed me the path.

He asked me whether I wanted him to walk me down. I just wanted to get away and I told him I could make it all right on my own.

As I stepped out onto the path alone, a strange and unexpected fear hit me. Up to this point I had been "tuned-in" to and living life along with Gridley and the rest of the group. I was identified by the other members of the tribe as a hippie myself. Even if I was pseudo and part-time.

The stories and vignettes of people "freaked-out" on LSD in a psychotic manner came to me now. Other thoughts crowded in on me. There were reported cases of violence, including homicide. Were these people sane? Or were they using the hippie role as a legitimation for their insanity? More unexpected panic hit me as I walked and partly fell down the strange mountain path.

People alone, and in groups of two and four, passed me on the road with a cheery, "Hi, brother." Others merely stared at me as I passed them.

For the first time that day I drifted sharply back into my forty-year-old-professor role. What a weird place for me to be. It was absurd.

I suddenly realized I had about $110 in cash in my wallet. I clumsily tried to think of a place to hide it. I thought of putting the money in my shoe. After all, Pan and at least a dozen others I had been with had records of armed robbery and prison in their experience. Foolishly my panic quickened and I literally began to run down the mountain into the pitch blackness.

When I reached my new Chrysler at the bottom of the mountain, I got into it fast, spun it around, and went speeding down the highway toward home.

As I drove, my mind raced into various reflections. The recent sounds of the people in the meeting who were leaving one mountain peak to go to another reminded me of the old colony of British criminals in Australia. When homicide, cannibalism, and disease ran rampant in the main criminal colony, people broke off into smaller groups and took to the hills.

In the hippie group on the mountain, I felt there was a search for civilization. A humorous thought hit me that they would probably discover fire and the wheel before too long. The question that I couldn't answer was, why were these people, who had all that American society could offer, so driven to start all over again?

Part of the paradox was that they were using remnants of the Establishment, which they claim to hate, to start their new civilization. This was, in certain respects, a "cop-out," predatory and exploitative. The Campbell soup, polished brown rice, flashlights, candles, and most of their clothes were all from the industrial society that they rejected. Their use of Carnation powdered milk symbolically reflected for me their exploitative and somewhat dishonest use of American middle-class ingenuity.

Perhaps the mechanical-man, robot, plastic-world bomb had already dropped and what I had witnessed was part of a kind of social fallout. The people on the mountain were mostly young, potentially vibrant members of American society. Why had they returned to the primitive position of the cave? They were not rejects. They were for the most part young people whose paths of American opportunity were wide open. The central question disturbed me. Why were these thousands, perhaps hundreds of thousands, of youths retreating to a primitive position?

Big Sur: Post Discussion

My panic and negativity about the mountain scene diminished after several days of eating good food at home and sleeping on my king-sized bed. I really was not familiar with the philosophical basis for the new community. In my role as sociologist, it was unfair of me to draw any conclusions on the basis of one trip.

Perhaps I was suffering from what one sociologist called

"culture-shock." The way of life I had briefly viewed was so at odds with my soft "creature comforts" situation that I had recoiled too quickly. I needed to know much more about the scene, especially the philosophy.

Gridley had lived both ways; perhaps he could elaborate and enlarge on my narrow vision. Several days later, I visited him at his house in Malibu. Compared to Big Sur the hippie way of life here was more civilized and pleasant—if not distracting. As usual there were some new people present. Several of the girls were almost completely nude—wearing only bikini panties. Probably due to some pot-smoking, there was much giggling and joking among the eight or ten people on the scene. The environs weren't too conducive to research; however, Gridley and I finally settled down to tape a discussion on the Big Sur scene we had both experienced the week before.

LY–To be candid, Gridley, I was expecting a better organized, happier community than the one we witnessed up at Gorda. In fact, I found the whole situation rather disconcerting. About the only positive thing that happened was the meeting. What were your impressions?

G–I felt that people had a higher emotional tone after the meeting. A lot of the people were carrying around a lot of shit [dissatisfaction] and some of them got a chance to talk about it.

LY–What about the so-called stabbings and the story of the guy trying to steal this guy's sleeping bag and his grabbing an iron bar and so forth. I was surprised to find this violent behavior among "love people."

G–To get hung up about people stealing things is to get into a circular bag, for me. It takes two people to steal something. Someone to steal it and someone who'll let it be stolen. So there isn't anybody going to come in here and take anything from me because I'm just too fucking pushy. I mean, I'm not going to hit him or do anything like that, but I'll rap [talk] them out of stealing from me.

LY–What if the potential thief persisted?

G–I'd say, "Look, man, you obviously need it more than I do."

LY–You would back off at the point of violence?

G–I wouldn't know that I would back off into conceding that he could have it, but I'm sure I wouldn't get into a violent thing.

LY–What about you, Turtle?

T–Material possessions aren't that important. If I couldn't argue him out of it, he would just have to steal it. When stuff starts gettin' stolen, you usually wind up with just about what you need anyway. The rest is extra baggage.

LY–It would be useful to me if you would free-associate or describe your observations of that scene up on the mountain.

G–When I first got up there, it was a real romantic kind of picture. Man, it was kind of foggy. There were these really beautiful people—men, women, kids, dogs and cats, and campfires. It seemed quiet and stable. And I really felt like love was about me. I thought, "This is the place, man. It was happening. I don't have to do it. I would just kind of fit in and do my thing and that would be like a groove."

After we were there about fifteen or twenty minutes, I heard the people bitching and moaning. I listened to it for a while and circulated around to hear more about it, and, man, I couldn't believe it. Here they were secure in their land—beautiful land, where they could be free—and all these people were doing was bitching and moaning. I thought, 'Oh, shit, man! Do I have to go into this kind of shit again, where I gotta step in and get heavy and get ratty and get people to start talking? Do I have to get them to be open and get in some dialogue and get some communication going and organization? What the fuck's wrong with the leadership here, that this kind of state of affairs is happening? And why do I have to do it again? Man, I'm through with it. I just got through with hepatitis and double pneumonia and . . . fuck it! Then I really felt bad.

LY–Speaking from a square practical position, I wondered, for example, where the food was coming from.

G–I know you can always get food. You can always get food, man! Nobody has ever starved or gone hungry or not had clothes in any of the communities that I know about. Somehow the food always comes to us.

T–One thing . . . every supermarket in the United States throws away two hundred pounds of perfectly good food a day.

LY–Well, what was wrong with the scene among those people?

G–About 99% of the people up there have had LSD. An awful lot of people who are taking acid are, in a sense, fucking up. I mean they're only doing what they're doing 'cause where life has them. But they're taking acid without using any knowledgeable approach to what it is they're doing to their minds, their souls, and their bodies. They just know, man, that all the bullshit that they've been taught to believe is where it's all at, isn't where it's all at. It's lies and hypocrisy and it's shit. And they hear about acid and they see other people who have taken acid, who may be feel better, and they hear about communities and so they say, "Wow," ya know, and they go for it. They go to a community of their brothers and sisters.

LY–Okay. They're up there. Then what?

G–They're up there and they're taking acid, but there's no leadership.

LY–Well, here's where I fall into a bit of a quandary. They began to move toward a bare minimal kind of organization and leadership at which point somebody said, "Well, let's not get into that organization bag," and "Let's lighten up." There's a kind of a paradox there. You need organization and yet you put it down. You use the word "leadership" in a way that I can't understand. Most hippies I've talked to reject the usual concept of a leader.

G–Most people see the whole leadership issue, I think, unconsciously as being tied in with a dependency thing—depending on a figurehead. That isn't the way I see it. I see leadership, man, as a process whereby people come to be divested of their dependency, so that they are effective. So, I think people's negative reaction to leadership is a carry-over from what they have seen as leadership before in their straight life.

LY–Is there another word than leader that applies?

T–Teachers.

G–Teachers, yeah.

LY–In other words, someone who is in a certain scene, living it and setting kind of an example of the way to operate, or the way to live it.

G–Yeah, that's a part of it. And also whose trip is communicating this and sharing it with others.

LY–How do you get around this one? Forgetting whatever reactions I have to it, and yours are probably more extreme, let's look at this example. Here's a man experienced in setting up a restaurant. He knows how to set up a kitchen right. He really knows how to do it. He does it by barking orders at people in the usual ways. He could have that kitchen they discussed at Gorda set up one morning in an hour. But yet this efficient leader would be in conflict with your philosophy.

T–Dig, man, the only way that I can possibly look at things . . . is things that I can't handle, man, I leave them for some other cat that can handle them better than I can.

G–If you've got some cat who's pushy behind organizing a kitchen and getting that thing done and that's his trip, well, that's righteous. If other people don't like it, they can complain, pitch him out, or they can leave, you know.

Man, the whole emphasis is on love. If you got two cats behind the kitchen thing and they're both strong cats, I see no reason why they can't get together on it. And I think this is a big difference in what's happening here and what happens in other types of organizations. Here there's something bigger than any two or three people happening. They don't necessarily feel that they have to compete, or be one up or that their way has to prevail.

LY–The group up there seemed very fragmented to me. Weren't they?

T–Different groups with different opinions is what the whole thing is all about.

G–There was no form. There were no group meetings where they could get a purpose. People just came and they were there. There was no one to meet them, no one to tell them what was happening . . . just nothing.

LY–Here's another thing that troubled me. Whenever I've talked to you or Turtle in the limited time we spent together, we've gotten into some philosophy or ideas. I found Gorda an intellectual wasteland. Most people were staring out into space. I didn't see anything that was at all interesting—except perhaps the beauty of Big Sur and the potential. I didn't experience any dialogue at a deep human level.

T–It was there. It was there in some of the people that were there. But most of them seemed to be just keeping completely covered up to keep it from becoming polluted by all the bullshit that was going on. That's what I felt.

LY–But did you pick up on any groovy conversations? Or have any?

T–No, but I'll tell you I found some very groovy feelings.

LY–You did?

T–Not vocal conversations, but on another level there were good vibrations.

G–Well, I think there's a lot to what you say, in that a great deal of what's happening to these people is intensely personal and it's so new that there are no words that they can use to talk about it. They don't yet understand characteristics of religious experiences or mystical experiences. They're not familiar with Eastern religions or with what any religion is really about. And they have no framework in which to put their experiences. They have not yet integrated it into their daily life, so that they can communicate about it. That's why I say they need teachers.

LY–In other words, your impression was that the raw possibilities of the scene were there but it wasn't properly tuned-in or focused.

G–The whole community itself, admittedly, had no structure to it at all. It was kind of like doomed that way from the beginning.

LY–That's where it hit me. I had a really negative reaction.

G–I feel that what is happening there is that the people who are getting there have been told all their lives what they have to do, or what they should do in order to be acceptable to themselves and to the people that they think love them. So you're getting people there who for the first time are in a position where no one is telling them what to do. They're in a vacuum. They don't know how to handle that. For a community to get somewhere it has to be started by a few people who are out of that bag. People who've gone through just doing nothing to the point where they have opened up enough to themselves to tap into their creativity so that it will come out in their daily lives and they will be productive.

LY–So your feeling is that they didn't have any guidance or direction?

G–*They're really refugees.*

LY–That's the impression that I got.

G–They're refugees not from physical oppression, man, but from the psychic oppression of American society. And they're as depleted as any refugee can be from anywhere. And it's pitiful and it's tragic. It's tragic that there can't be a rehabilitation center for these people—run by hip people whom they would trust and respect. People who could take them through the process and truly into themselves.

What I found is that to be with people, the way I am with my partners in our own communities, is the supreme value. I don't think this is the way it is in the Establishment world out there. It certainly wasn't that way when I was out there. People's relationships were almost entirely game-type relationships. And so there were substitutes like nice clothes and cars and things like that. But more and more people are finding that in order to get those things you have to sacrifice yourself. You have to sacrifice time and a way of looking at things. In other words, you have to be competitive to get them. And all this doesn't seem to have much to do with loving people and being open. That's why we're willing to settle for what people call primitive circumstances. And that's where Gorda and other communities are trying to go—toward learning how to love and live in a new way. These people are desperate and they are willing to start anywhere.

In later discussion with Gridley I made the point that most hippies were still in the cities and not in the country communes. He denounced the city hippie scene as short-lived. "Eventually we will all be with our partners in the country—the city hippie scene is mostly transitory."

Now that I had viewed and reviewed at least one rural hippie camp, I decided that the next leg of my trip would be "the life" on the city scene. Next to the Haight-Ashbury section of San Francisco, New York's East Village contained the largest concentration of hippies in the world. This would be the next stop on my trip.

CHAPTER FIVE

Galahad's Pad: New York City

THE BEATNIKS OF THE 40's AND 50's disengaged from a "society of oppression" in order to create in some art form. They were little concerned with searches for a Utopian society or the "Brotherhood of Man." They sought freedom to express themselves creatively, or the right, if they chose, to sit in the fetal position. Although they were angry with the larger society, they seldom took up arms against its hypocrisies; nor was the way they lived their lives part of a serious protest.

According to the hippies' philosophers, they have disengaged from the games and ego involvement of the "great society" in order to tune-in to the cosmic unity of man. The articulate high priests of hippiedom view the "plastic society" (their term) as a clump of cultural gargoyles signifying nothing but massive hypocrisy and dishonesty. They want no part of it and seek to move forward into what may appear on the surface to be a more primitive society, but one that is honest and closer to the natural state of man's reality.

New York's East Village is the hippie center of the East Coast. From the old west Village "the people" (including some former beats) have moved east to checkerboard a substantial portion of lower Manhattan. Washington Square and Tompkins Square Park belong primarily to the established hippies, including their spiritual kid brothers and sisters, the teenyboppers. As one of the oracles of the new hippie scene described it: "Ninety percent of the teenyboppers and part-timers will become full fledged hippie drop-outs when they grow up."

Tompkins Square Park is dominated by brightly clad hippie boys and girls gaily parading around every day in the week and especially on Sundays. Their appearance seems to be a continuing source of irritation to the local residents, especially the firmly entrenched minority group populations that have lived in and claimed the area for several generations.

The East Village, running from Third Avenue almost to the East River, is a massive poorhouse of old tenements and cluttered lots. Here the hippies have taken over various small apartments to set up their tribes and city communes.

Tuning-in to this situation was for me, at first, a difficult problem. I wandered the streets of the Village for almost a full day before I could get close in to some hippie pads. The time spent roaming around did, however, give me a tourist's view of the situation.

I first made direct contact on a Saturday morning on St. Marks Place, the orbital center of New York's hippie movement. I accosted a young man, properly wearing Indian beads, who had started into an apartment building which was emitting the loud noise of a rock band. I asked him the classic question, "What's happening up there, man?" Without missing a step, he invited me up to the party.

In a brutally hot fifth-floor loft, made more sweltering by shaded closed windows, I walked into a loud and phony psychedelic scene. A light show was flashing, a five-man rock band was jamming, and about thirty people were dancing. The party was a strange combination of bona fide hippies, some teenyboppers, and a management team of Abercrombie-Fitch-type sophisticated administrators who had obviously put on headbands and beads for the occasion. I learned from one of the Madison Avenue fellows, who offered me a sandwich from a totally unhip catered corned-beef-and-potato-salad lunch, that this was a commercial party "to push the band for a recording date."

I followed the acrid smell of marijuana smoke to a wildly dressed young man who told me defensively, even before I spoke to him, "Man, if you're the heat, fuck you. I'm no longer paranoid about smoking pot. I'll do it here, in the park, on the street, anywhere." I assured him that I was not a cop and then told him precisely who I was and what I was trying to do.

He first offered me a drag on his "roach" (a smoked-down marijuana cigaret). I declined as gracefully as I could, and asked him if he could put me in contact with one of the hippie community "pads" (apartment/life situations) in the East Village.

"One place you ought to check out is Galahad's pad—that's over on East Eleventh Street. It's always changing, but there are a lot of people there, mostly young kids. They had a picture of the place in that big *Time* magazine article on the hippies. You know, kids sleeping on mattresses on the floor and all that shit. Like man, that poverty isn't for me. I just like to smoke pot and groove with my own scene. I work once in a while and got nothing against making some bread [money] for my dope." I ignored his hustle, thanked him, and was glad to get out of the loft situation.

Even though it was the middle of a sunny day, I felt a touch of fear walking across Tenth Street, past Avenue A. Around Third Avenue and beyond there were belligerent old-fashioned American drunks staggering around, begging for wine money. There were Negro hoods engaged in their Saturday crap games and ferocious young Puerto Rican gang kids. I felt them eyeing me, a man with a briefcase, suspiciously. (I carried my compact tape recorder in my briefcase throughout my trip.)

"Galahad's pad" was actually a large tenement building with about ten apartments. It was named after a man called Galahad who had the reputation of being a hippie patron saint. He was out of town that week and I never did get to meet him. His legend was one of supporting hippies and then, as one of his charges told me later, "He got all ground up in the publicity bullshit about hippies and he forgot the people."

Seated on the stoop of the broken-down building were about seven youths. All wore the hippie trademark—either beads, an Indian headband, or a bell on a leather thong around their necks. They quietly blocked the entrance and, in spite of their love commitment, appeared to be suspicious and hostile.

One youth about nineteen asked me directly what I wanted. When I told him rather candidly, he said, "We've had swarms of reporters and photographers here and it's a bunch of bullshit. They just come in and make money off us." I told him that if "I could get into the thing," I would be glad to give some money to the cause.

This opened the gate, and the youth whose name was Chuck invited me into the building. I later learned that he was kind of a coordinator or, as I later called him, the "Mother Superior" of Galahad's pad. He tried to see to it that food was provided for "his people." He settled disputes and generally played the role of "house mother" to over one hundred nomads who moved through the ten or more apartment cells of Galahad's tenement each week.

This scene, as I later confirmed by seeing almost thirty other buildings of this type on the lower East Side, was typical of the "garbage pile" buildings that the hippies inhabited. Almost all of the buildings that the hippies invaded deserved to be condemned and some were. Pipes were leaking, toilets flooded, windows broken, filth everywhere. Rodents and roaches swarmed all over the mess.

This building was very much like the one in which a notorious hippie drug-party murder was later committed in the fall of 1967. A couple, James ("Groovy") Hutchinson, 21, and Linda Fitzpatrick, 18, daughter of a wealthy Greenwich, Connecticut, businessman, were beaten to death in the basement of a typical hippie apartment building several blocks from Galahad's pad. *Time* (October 20, 1967) described the dismal apartment and the incident this way.*

Flanked by a sleazy bar and grill and a dusty antique-and-junk shop, the tawdry tenement at 169 Avenue B on Manhattan's Lower East Side is typical of the area. Decaying plaster and peeling paint festoon its dark blue hallways, and a flight of creaky wood stairs leads down to an oppressively low-ceilinged cellar that reeks of dog droppings and rancid garbage. A single naked light bulb illuminates the grimy heating pipes, the cockroach-scampered walls, and piles of loose, whitewashed fire-bricks from the building's boiler. It hardly seems the place for a tryst, yet into that foul tomb last week walked a pair of hippie "love children" intent on the pursuit of passion. Instead they rendezvoused with death. . . .

Groovy and Linda apparently entered the cellar—which often served as a clandestine exchange point for drug sales—late at night. They may have been high on speed at the time, or "dropped" (swallowed) it later, preparatory to making love. Three or four other persons were also in the cellar. Possibly they were customers of Groovy's; all of them were turned on. Since Methedrine is a super-pep drug whose "flash" generates an instant demand for action, it is likely that the onlookers demanded to "make it" with Linda. Groovy tried to defend the girl and was smashed with one of the boiler-wall bricks, his face crushed. Linda was raped four times and bashed with a brick. Their nude bodies, faces upturned, were found on the dank stone floor; their clothes, including Linda's black panties and Groovy's beat-up jacket, were neatly stowed in a corner. . . .

Drug-induced violence is nothing new to the neighborhoods where hippies live. . . . The deaths of Groovy and Linda carried an added burden of horror. They sent a chill through all of hippiedom.

Groovy's closest friend, Galahad, who once ran a communal crash pad (dormitory), muttered about revenge and then, at the funeral in Pawtucket, R.I., played a turned-on taps on his dead friend's harmonica.†

*Throughout the book I will quote *Time* Magazine and other mass media reports on the hippies. My purpose is twofold. One, the news clips I will use are relevant and help illuminate conditions on the new scene; and second, the fact that so many of these stories are newsworthy reflects the mass American public interest in hippie happenings and events.

† Courtesy TIME, The Weekly Newsmagazine; copyright Time Inc. 1967.

This description of Groovy and Linda accurately describes the love children I met in Galahad's pad. Although I am not certain, I believe Groovy was in the group I interviewed that afternoon in the building on Eleventh Street.

Loud noises were heard from various pads in the building as Chuck, my newly hired guide, and I walked up three flights of stairs. The apartment was typical for the scene. It consisted of two 9′ x 9′ rooms that were full of nothing but wall-to-wall greasy mattresses. About five hippies, three young men and two girls, were sleeping fully clothed on the mattresses. Several other youths were sitting around smoking and staring straight ahead into space, obviously loaded on something.

Chuck and I sat down on the floor near the sleepers and young zombies and became acquainted. I learned that Chuck was from California, liked to travel, had used acid and pot, and was a zealous believer in the new hippie communities that were emerging.

Chuck especially interested me because, unlike other young hippies I had met, in spite of his commitment to being a drop-out, seemed to have a sociological interest in the movement. He was fascinated by all of the happenings he encountered. "What you're doing as a sociologist is what I love to do. Like man, I really like to find out what's happening, not only for me, but in general." We talked for about an hour and I was more than pleased to conclude that I now had acquired a very articulate and knowledgeable research assistant.

I agreed to pay Chuck a nominal fee for his time and help, and he quickly agreed to assist me. I soon learned, from reactions to him by other youths, that Chuck was known by and knew almost everyone of importance on the East Village scene. His help and approval immediately lifted the resistance and suspicion about my being a cop and expedited my tuning-in to a variety of significant situations. Chuck was a most vital guide for me on my New York trip.

I noticed as I talked to Chuck that people were coming and going all of the time. Sleepers awoke and others lay down and dozed off. It was a young people's flop house. Most of the boys and girls were between the ages of fifteen and twenty.

I also noticed some incongruous-appearing "old-fashioned" heroin addicts on the scene. They were dressed in "straight" (regular shirts and cotton pants) clothes. I later learned that these "old-fashioned dope fiends" preyed on the "love children" for any money, dope, or cigarets they could get. They "beat them" for money by manipulation, or when necessary by force. The "love children" in turn apparently fed off of their generally affluent parents.

I asked Chuck if he felt it would be all right to tape the discussion I began to stir up in the group. The group agreed with Chuck that I could record their commentary. The following selected excerpts are rather slow moving, but pertinent since this group and their views were very typical of many others I encountered in the East Village. The discussion is representative of the younger "flower children" teenyboppers I met in "the movement" around the country.

Mike was eighteen and from a middle-class background in Rochester, New York.

M–I had never seen drugs before I got to New York, although I read a lot about it. Everyone thought that I was on drugs back in Rochester because of my long hair. This is my first time down here. You see, I had been all around the East Coast but I had never been to New York City.

LY–Have you used LSD?

M–Twice.

LY–What did it do for you?

M–My first trip was pretty good, but my second trip—I was feeling bad when I took it and I took it to get happy and it didn't work too well. The way I felt when I took it was like jumping out of windows and everything. Like I was the Almighty or God. Right now, I don't know what I want. I have problems, I know. I should go back to Rochester. I think that I have a big problem living here.

LY–What's the problem about living here?

M–Well, when I left Rochester I left my apartment with all of my clothes in it and everything that I own. And I came here just with a little money and a plan to go back. I just came down for the weekend and was going back. Plus when I came down here, I brought an under-age girl down here and her parents found her and I don't know what they did to her. Plus I don't have any real friends. Because when you are down and out on the streets like I am, it's real bad.

Oh, I could probably go back to Rochester. My father would probably send me the money to get back there. When I got down here, at first I liked this kind of living—and then all of a sudden it started getting boring here and the good people started leaving. And the people around here act like "Oh, I don't care what happens" and you start living in real filth. [The "good people" are always leaving almost every scene I ever visited in the hippie world.]

LY–Well, what do you think about the commune idea here at Galahad's pad?

M–It's a great idea. The only trouble is that Galahad wanted it just for publicity and now that the publicity stopped he is gone. Also, people found out that there are other communes that are better than his so this one started deteriorating. The first commune that was here was really great. Then it all of a sudden started to slide slowly down the drain.

I talked to several others whose remarks were very much like Mike's. They came into New York City with high hopes of a good life and, at the moment, they were disillusioned.

LY–You and I have talked, Chuck, but we haven't talked about this scene. What is happening here?

C–In the whole Village I think that all of the tribes are going to start to get together after everybody gets tired of going around to all the different places that there are. I think that they are going to decide that society is still rotten. Some people will probably go back to the straight society with hip ideas, and the rest of them are going to go to tribes.

The whole scene is going to fold into tribes that live out in the country and grow their own food, and become independent. And you know, it is going to be more of a brotherly love thing. And it is going to be a peaceful thing. It is going to go back more or less to like Indian tribes and without war or anything.

LY–What percentage of the younger people do you think are going to get into it?

C–Just about all of them. Some may go through college but they are still going to come out a lot different than they were before. The ones that don't want to work are more or less going to be supported by the ones that work for the good of the communes. The communes are becoming like a socialist government.

Suddenly there was a loud, frightening banging on the door. I thought it was probably a police raid. Pot was being smoked and there were other drugs in the room. The group became somewhat panicked. Cigarets and things were flushed down the toilet. When the group settled down Chuck innocently asked, "Who is it?"

Two names that I don't remember were blurted out along with some raucus, hysterical laughter. It was the kind of laughter I had learned to identify with a true psychopath from my *Violent Gang* research.

Chuck apparently knew the two people and opened the door. Two frightening-looking characters burst into the room. One was a tall, muscular Negro and the other was a squat Puerto Rican. They were both in their early twenties and obviously high on something.

They apparently did not expect to see someone like me with a tape recorder in the room. They were slightly panicked by my presence and one of them bluntly asked Chuck, "Who is this motherfucker?"

Chuck tried to explain why I was there. "He's doing research for a book on the hip scene."

"He looks like the fuckin' heat to me." Their attitude was increasingly menacing. The two "intruders" got into a conversation about taking my tape recorder and said, "Let's throw his ass down the stairs."

I tried to assure them I was a writer. Chuck joined in on my side and this seemed to cool them off somewhat. He finally got them to leave the room.

Outside the door I could hear remnants of their continued conversation. "I don't care if he's the heat or not—let's get the recorder and throw his ass out." After a while, they apparently left.

I never did find out exactly who these fellows were or the nature of their connection with Galahad's pad. They were not dressed like hippies. They were probably old-style drug addicts, who had some hook into the scene and pushed dope to the young hippies.

The group was not, at least visibly, as shaken by this threat of violence as I was. The episode was probably commonplace to them and most of them seemed to know the fellows involved. In any case, after a brief period of readjustment and discussion with the group about what happened I was able to get my interview back into a reasonable groove.

LY–What's wrong with American society? What's your beef with it? Why not live in that world?

16-YR-OLD-BOY–It's just a large machine and you don't know who runs the machine or what. It's just there. It is just cutting out more people from the same machine. Even the cream of society, they become machines, you know. The way I look at it is that they treat human beings as puppets. They are not on their own. I don't know; it is too indifferent, you know. You're not going to learn anything by punching your clock every day when you go to work and then punching out again when you go home. And you know, you never get any good feeling about it because there is nothing there. Bob Dylan wrote a song called "Masters of War" that kind of says it for me about this big machine called Society.

As we were talking, several girls came in and out of the room. They were all teenagers and wore similar uniforms—plain cotton shift dresses, long, uncombed hair, no shoes or bras, and a vapid stare in their eyes. I engaged one of them in the discussion. She was seventeen, and came from a middle-class home in upstate New York. Her name was Carol.

LY–How long have you been away from your home?
C–Well, how long have I been away from my home physically or mentally?
LY–Both.
C–Physically, I've been away a few months. Mentally, I've been away two years, I'd say.
LY–Do you like what you have found here?
C–Yes, it's better than home.
LY–What's better about it?
C–I have a lot of friends. I came here because I just couldn't stand being at home anymore. I'm dropping out until I find something else to drop into. But I know that it can't go on indefinitely. You just can't live like this forever, even though I would like to. Society will eventually get me as a runaway or something.
LY–What's wrong with living in the outside society?
C–There is too much put on what other people think. Like my parents and everyone are concerned with what other people are going to think of you. I'm more concerned with what I think of myself. I don't care what other people think. That's one of the things wrong with this society.

Another girl, called Barbara (about sixteen), joined in the conversation.

B–The thing that I like about this community is that we are trying to work out things as a team.

LY–What are you trying to work out?

B–Just that there are a whole bunch of people trying to work out things, like the people that live here are trying to work at not hassling each other too much.

LY–What kind of family scene do you come from?

B–I come from a middle-class Jewish family in Queens.

LY–Do your parents know that you're over here?

B–Yeah, they don't like it, but now it's no sweat. My father doesn't mind and my mother is at the point where she says, "Do what you want to do."

LY–Well, doesn't she want you to marry a nice Jewish boy and settle down?

B–No, they're not really typical Jewish parents. They never say anything like that.

LY–Do you plan on getting married some day?

B–Yeah, some day.

LY–Well, what about hippie communes and tribes and things like that? Do you go for that?

B–Yeah, well, that's what I'm sort of doing now. I'm only sixteen.

A young man named Dwayne joined the discussion. He was sixteen, dressed in a very hip beaded outfit. Dwayne walked with a limp.

D–Mostly you'll find around here that it's pretty friendly. I didn't know people were that friendly, 'cause like I came into town as a square and I didn't know anybody. And before you know it, I was shacked up here. You know like the kids here—they're really great. We all help each other out.

LY–Do people love each other here?

D–Yeah, I love everybody. You just can't help but love everyone especially when you're high. Then, they're beautiful. Here's a girl sitting down now that loves everybody. [Laughter.] Paula, come here and give him your two cents.

LY–How come you're on this scene, Paula?

P–Oh, I like some things. I like it because it is free and you can do whatever you want but I don't like the other things, you know, like the dirt and everything. And I don't like it that you can't walk out on the street by yourself. The people [Puerto Ricans] around here scare me.

LY–Do you feel safe in here?

P–Yeah. Some people think that this is a place where they can go and get any girl and have sex with them and anything. This is not true. Last night I was sleeping on the mattress and this guy was sleeping there and he tried to put his arm around me and feel me up. At first I thought it was Mike, you know. Mike's my boyfriend and at first I thought that it was him but then I realized that it was this other cat. And I don't like this. And that's what some people have told me, they expect free sex because you are staying here and everything. But that isn't true.

LY–Well, isn't it freer here than on other scenes?

B–It's freer for people who are friends, you know.

About this time an eighteen-year-old Puerto Rican youth named Frank entered. He wasn't dressed like a hippie. Frank was husky and belligerent-looking. I later learned he had spent a considerable amount of time in several mental hospitals because of violent acts. He was fidgety but talked freely when his friend, Chuck, told him what I was trying to do.

LY–Where are you from, Frank?

F–My parents live up on 125th Street. I'm hanging around here living with a bunch of poor people. I don't really have to be here.

LY–Well, why do you choose to be here?

F–Well, I like to know a lot of people. Also, I have been pretty bad to the hippie kids here.

LY–How have you been bad?

F–Well, getting into arguments and fights and especially with girls. I shouldn't have been doing this kind of thing with them. I think that girls don't have as much strength as men do, and I really feel sorry and I feel that I should change for the fact that the women—they get nervous and all that and a man should understand. See? And now me, the other day I slapped a girl across the face a couple of times because she was cursing at me. But every time she cursed at me she mentioned something about my mother and I didn't like it. And I hit her for it.

LY–Is it one of the girls here now?

F–She's not here right now.

CHUCK–It was a misunderstanding. The word was "motherfucker," and that has nothing to do with your mother.

F–Yeah, well, just a word. But you see, a lot of people, they like their mother and whenever they have some trouble they should keep the family out of it, you see? And not put the family in it. But a lot of people, they like their mothers a lot better than they like the rest of their family. And there are other people that just don't give a fuck. Now, if you're walking in the street and somebody mentions something about your mother and you are walking with your mother, you aren't just going to let them come up to you and say something about your mother—like your mother is this, or your mother is that. Would you like it? [Frank was getting very jumpy and belligerent toward me.]

LY–No. What was your past life like, Frank?

F–Well, I was an alcoholic. Yes, when I was younger, I was drinking a lot, getting into fights and I was in jails. My mother, she tried to talk to me to behave myself and all this but it didn't work. So they got a psychiatrist to come over and speak to me 'cause they were so worried with me.

They caught me at violence, you know. So they had this psychiatrist come and speak to me and I went into a mental institution and I spent four years . . .

LY–Where were you?

F–I was in Rockland State Hospital, in New York. And then I came out and they gave me a year-and-a-half probation. For a whole year I stuck it out and then I messed up again. I got sent back in and then I stayed there for a few months and I was about to come out for good to get a discharge. Then from there I got transferred to Central State Hospital in Long Island. I spent two years there and I came out. I'm not on probation now, but I still got to go for my check-ups.

LY–Let me throw this in. . . . How many people here have had their parents or somebody put them into some psychiatric scene at one time or another? . . . That's one, two, three, four, five, six. So, about half of you have had some contact with psychiatry.

[One boy responded further to the question.]

B–Well, where I come from in New Jersey they think that anyone with long hair or wears these kind of clothes is a dope addict and no good. Like where I come from, they all dress different and all that. I was the only one in my college that dug this scene. Everybody thought that I was out of my mind and so they investigated it and all this kind of junk. They thought that I was absolutely losing my mind. And I got sick of the whole thing. Every place that you go they say, "Get a haircut and wash your clothes," and all that shit. And I just thought, the hell with it.

LY–How often do you have personal discussions like this one in this pad?

C–We have some personal ones with a few people, but not in a group thing like this.

F–Well, once in a while we have a meeting of certain things in groups. We like to get together to try to help and try to get money to pay rent and try to help other people besides us. And over here on the block, like I'm Puerto Rican and like we got more Puerto Ricans around here than anything. We have trouble. I try to keep things cool between these people and the Puerto Ricans.

LY–What would you call these people here? Would the Puerto Ricans call them hippies?

F–Yeah, they call them hippies. Or sometimes they say that they're white men and beatniks and no-good things like that. Well, I try to get along with everybody and I like to know a lot of people. I don't know much about life. And I want to find out about life. The hippies are explaining to me, like how life is and all that.

LY–Do you think that the people here, like Chuck, can help you?

F–Yeah—well, Chuck, he has given me a lot of information about how to act and how I should act. Instead of going around beating on girls and trying to be a big man 'cause that's what I been doing lately when I was here.

LY–Have you beat up a lot of girls in your life?

F–I had trouble with four hippie girls here. I hit my sister once and I knocked her out. [Laughs.] She was out cold. I slapped her across her face 'cause I didn't want to hurt her. But I tried to get her to get along with her boyfriend, who was a Puerto Rican himself. He is older than me. He is twenty-one years old and I had to fight him. I had him on the floor and I had the chance to kill him but I don't believe in killing.

Frank's discussion began to make me uncomfortable. I felt that he was obviously psychotic and very possibly dangerous. I had no interest in provoking him into action. So at this point, as smoothly as possible, I took him off his *kill* discussion and changed the subject.

LY–Why is this place called Galahad's pad?

C–Galahad started it. Galahad did a lot for everybody 'cause none of us would be here if it wasn't for Galahad. Like when I first met Galahad, he was a person that I could really talk to. I talked about, like why I was here. And he would ask, like why did I come and—I don't know, he was just like someone to talk to.

F–Well, Galahad is the right kind of person where if you ever need some help and you have problems or anything and you can't sleep or anything, you could come over to him and he would straighten you out. If you are a runaway or something like that, he won't turn you in to the police. He'll try to help you and get you back home. Sometimes he'll take you back home himself and he'll talk to your parents.

B–I don't like him at all because he has done certain stuff and certain people have changed their minds. Well, for one thing, he had a lot of great ideas and he started a lot of stuff but when he saw himself starting to go down, he started doing some corrupt things that a lot of people knew about. We were stupid not to tell him right out. We were throwing money into the pot. We didn't know where the money was going to and stuff like that. And nobody really could speak up against it because if someone had spoken up, people would have found out our problems and maybe this place would not have gone on any longer. Also, a lot of the regular people got to leaving and we started bringing in people who were, like really bums and the other people didn't want to have to watch out for them. Like before, we used to be able to raise our rent money in about two or three days but lately we haven't been able to get it up at all.

LY–Well, where is the money going to come from to support the scene, if nobody wants to work?

C–We'll worry about that when the time comes. Most logically, from the publicity. One place got all of its bills paid off by publicity people. Like movies have been shot in here and things like that. *Time* magazine and *Look* started taking pictures in here at Galahad's and CBS news was here, too. But we never got any money for any of that.

LY–Okay, Chuck, do you want to put a cap or an end on this, and then maybe we'll go over to the park?

C–Well, some people here are starting to create. They're starting to draw, and to write; they're starting to talk to other people. It's getting better compared to what it was when Galahad had it, totally. There is mass confusion and we're still having trouble organizing and paying our rent. Food is scarce, too. But now, people are starting to straighten out and get their own ideas. But still, freedom is what everyone is after—love, understanding, and freedom.

Chuck and I left the scene to visit a newly formed "tribe" called the Rising Sun. On our way over to their pad (which I later found to be much like Galahad's) we unexpectedly met several members of the Rising Sun Tribe walking up Avenue C. Chuck introduced me very directly as a sociologist writing a book. A leader of the Rising Sun named Steve was very cordial.

"If you would like to come to a meeting, we're having one tonight at around 8:00 p.m. We got some beefs with each other that we have to straighten out. Then we can talk to you some more about what's happening. . . . I was just with a real stone nut named Cal you might want to meet. He sees visions and everything. He was with us for a while but he went off to start his own group."

Steve gave us the address of Cal's cult.

I felt that I was now clicking and flowing with the hippie scene. I agreed with Chuck that Cal's situation would be worth investigating. Cal's commune, like Galahad's pad, was located in a large tenement building.

In the smelly tenement hallways on our way up to Cal's apartment we were given hostile looks by neighbors in the building. One thing was becoming increasingly clear to me. The hippies were the objects of an intense hatred on the part of the Puerto Rican, Jewish, and other minority groups on the lower East Side. A non-hippie cab driver who lived in the neighborhood put it succinctly: "We have to live in this shit. They don't. I don't understand these young punks."

A burst of nauseating fumes struck me as we entered Cal's pad. The front door opened right into the kitchen where several people were cooking some soup mixture in a large pot. There were about twenty people in the squalid, small, one-bedroom apartment.

Cal, a man of about thirty, was stripped to the waist. Thin and rather fragile in appearance, he looked somewhat like a rabbi with his deep, black beard. Without too much of an introduction from Chuck about my credentials, he went into his "rap," which was obviously a standard speech he had delivered on many occasions.

"It's all very simple. There are twenty of us now. In about a year there will be two thousand. We'll eventually settle in the country. Drugs and sex are all personal matters. We have absolutely no rules. We'll be moving to a bigger place in about a week. I saw the place last night very clearly in a dream."

From that point on Cal's "rap" turned into the psychotic word-salad ramblings I had heard from patients at many mental hospitals. But in this case, Cal was free, and was the self-appointed leader of a tribe of young hippies.

After delivering his rap, he introduced me to his tribe. One fellow was spastic. His head kept wandering around on his shoulders. Cal propped him up and told me, "This man was a major in the Air Force and was a war hero." The poor fellow insisted to me through dripping saliva that his name should not be revealed at this time, as he and Cal were to be on a national TV show to announce their tribe. I listened attentively and sympathetically to his story.

Another fellow, a man of about thirty who had no hippie garb on, was extremely drunk. He appeared to be a standard Third Avenue–Bowery alcoholic. He smiled at me and then glowered. I felt at one point that he was going to swing at me. Cal smiled at the drunk and told him to sit down. "In our religious tribe, within a matter of weeks, this man's light will shine and he will put down alcohol."

While the interview was in motion, I noticed in the next room a young couple stroking each other. The bed was soon squeaking as a rather bizarre background for the new religion. Cal noticed my gaze and reiterated, "All patterns of behavior will be part of our new way of life. What you are seeing is youth in action. Isn't it beautiful?"

After further rambling discussion, Chuck and I said our good-byes and left. Rather suddenly I had a strong motivation to leave the entire East Village scene immediately. I excused myself from Chuck after some brief discussion and we agreed to meet later that evening at the Rising Sun pad.

I hailed a cab and returned to my comfortable Fifth Avenue hotel room and an excellent room-service steak. Somehow everything felt and tasted better compared to the intellectual and physical poverty I had just experienced.

Again, as in my reaction to Gorda, I was turned off by the movement. It was no brave new world; it was violent and depressing. I felt that my hotel room was a sanctuary from the community insane asylum of New York. The cloak of hippieism, tribes, and new country communities seemed to me at that moment to provide a pseudo-social role that gave many of these youths immunity from being in a mental hospital.

My overall research so far and my first encounter with the East Village led me to believe that many of these youths (some of whom had *been* in mental hospitals) had developed a new syndrome for emotional disturbance. The hippie role-disguise enabled them to wander freely in the society. At this point of my trip I felt that the popular image of the loving "flower children" projected and "sold" by America's mass media was a gross misconception and distortion of the truth.

CHAPTER SIX

Tribes, Teenyboppers, and Loving Dope Pushers

AT EIGHT O'CLOCK THAT EVENing I met Chuck at the Rising Sun Tribe's pad. If anything, the chaos and the filth in the two-apartment headquarters of the Rising Sun were worse than the scenes at Galahad's and Cal's.

The meeting was held in a 9′ x 9′ room—with the usual wall-to-wall greasy mattresses. When we opened the door to the room for the meeting, we found a young couple, Pete and Jay, who had admittedly just finished "making love." Steve, the leader, gave them hell. "I told you to use the 'ball room'; this room is for our meeting."

The tribal meeting went on for about an hour. It consisted primarily of various diatribes leveled one at another for not helping to paint the upstairs apartment and not participating fully in the tribe.

In one case a young fellow was chastised for sleeping out every night with a girl who had been, but was no longer, a member of the tribe. The young man, Brian, was almost voted out of the tribe for his misbehavior. His defense was somewhere in the philosophical area of "love thy neighbor." He was a persuasive lawyer and the group finally agreed that "balling anyone was a person's individual decision" and not a tribal issue.

After their formal conference, I interviewed the group about various personal matters: their views of the world and their tribal association. Six members were present, including my Galahad guide Chuck. With one exception—Tony, who was in his twenties—they all could be characterized as teenyboppers in the overall movement.

Steve, the leader, was an eighteen-year-old Jewish boy from the Bronx. He wore levis, a beard, and an Indian headband around his long hair. Steve had been in a mental hospital for two years. He led the group in its meeting discussion.

Jay was a cute, sixteen-year-old, pugnosed blonde who could have been perfectly cast in the old Andy Hardy movies. She was a runaway summer hippie. Her parents were both school teachers in Pittsburgh. She was constantly referred to by tribal members as a "nympho." She dressed as a pure hippie girl in a loose fitting mini-dress. Her hair was long and stringy.

Pete was rather short and around sixteen years old. He claimed to be "completely dropped-out," but given his age and the law he was probably destined to be a summer hippie—at least until he was old enough to permanently drop out.

Tony was twenty-six, had been in the Army, and "made many scenes—but the Rising Sun are my people now." He seemed serious about his commitment to the group and its development.

Brian, eighteen years old, was a tall, blonde, "clean-cut"-looking young man. He was apparently from a wealthy family in Georgia. He had been a rioter at a "Beach City" uprising and had now become a "serious" hippie. He claimed he was completely dropped-out and part of the movement. Jay had once been his girlfriend. "But man, you can't be possessive about a nympho."

As I talked to the group I was most aware of the incongruity of the situation. They didn't seem to fit together as a group. Steve from the Bronx and Tony from East Harlem mixed up with Brian from Georgia was a strange combination. Yet there were apparently some important dimensions of their *life protest* that made this diverse collection of youths a group.

LY–How did the Rising Sun Tribe begin?

S–I was sitting on the floor one day with two people—a guy and a girl who I had just met—when a guy named Jim came over to me . . . and approached me and the other couple with the idea that he'd like to start a tribe . . . just like that. I said okay.

LY–Where had you been living before that? Were you with some other group or by yourself?

S–I was living at that time in Galahad's. The other couple wanted to think it over. They finally decided against it and said that it would take too much responsibility to start and organize a tribe. At first I had a few hippies who did not contribute. For the most part they were just goof-offs. So I kicked them out. Later on I brought in Cal, the guy you met. I quickly found out that he was not "real" and had certain crazy ideas.

LY–Brian, how did you get to this point—here in the Village? What's your family like?

B–My father lives in Georgia and has a charter-boat fleet. He is a wealthy man and leads a prosperous life. He wanted to make something out of me that I didn't want to be. I met with some people and talked with them and I found out what I wanted to be and this is it. I think that this tribal way will be great some day and I want to be able to say that I helped start it. Personally, I think that I can live better and be ten times more happy a person.

One thing about tribes I like is that I can use drugs freely. It's really a beautiful thing. I mean why should I go out there and ruin myself by intoxicating myself with liquor. I can become addicted to it. I could become an alcoholic. I could ruin my health. I could tear my body down. That's what my father did to himself. If you smoke grass then you're not addicted to it and it is a pleasure to smoke it. You don't have to stay with it if you don't like it. It doesn't tear your body down any, and in most cases people become more peaceful than anything else. I think that I am more peaceful and a better person to get along with. When I drank, I became very hostile and looked for the first thing to smash up.

LY–Jay, do you feel that you are really dropping out for good?

J–Well, I'm just trying to be happy and I hope that this works. Because if it works then it will be beautiful. And I'll hang around and I'll do my part and I'll try to make it work. Life didn't work for me back in Pittsburgh with my straight parents.

LY–How about you, Pete?

P–I think that I have dropped out of society, if that's what you want to call it. I got sick of LBJ's society—I just don't see how what he is doing is of any use. My father is a sergeant in the Army and fought in Vietnam. That's not for me—definitely.

LY–Tony, how do you see the new scene?

T–I don't feel as if I have dropped out. It is for me just a sort of natural movement that has come out of society as it is. I feel this society has been shot since the end of World War II. It is in a big rush to go nowhere and it is completely chaotic now. We hippies, if you want to call us that, have kind of an insight into the troubles of society. We're saying that society is all wound up with hostilities and worry. We see through this rut. We say that the only solution is to find a better life and to show people a better life and eventually a workable solution would be to change people over to it. It's our only hope for the future.

LY–Do you use drugs?

T–Yes. I think that, as far as pot goes, it is a nice high and it's groovy and all that. As for acid, I think that acid is very good for finding out a few things about yourself and the feelings around you. I would say that some people don't need it but that everyone should try it once, because there might be something hidden within themselves that they could find out. I would say that the people could use it and could benefit by it if they're guided.

I have been on my own for quite a few years. I come from an Italian family in Harlem. For some reason they seem to think that I am going to make a success of some kind of myself. Why, I don't know. But they would give me a bed if I need it. They wouldn't do anything bad to me at this point.

LY–Let me ask this question of the tribe. This is always a delicate subject with people. Maybe it shouldn't be. I'll just ask how much screwing really goes on around here? Is there more sex life around here than, let's say, back at your high school?

B–Oh, wow, ha, ha . . . I don't know that, I think there's more at my school. It isn't hidden that much here. Back at school, sex is a taboo thing. I mean the teacher's don't talk about it, the students ain't supposed to talk about it, the moms and pops don't talk about it. Nobody talks about it. If you do anything you do it behind everybody's back. Up here it is open, it's a thing, it's part of life, and I think that it's beautiful. I enjoy it very much myself. Here, what happens is that the girls don't play so many games. They play a few, but they don't play so many. You just ask a girl and she'll say yes or no.

There are girls around here that hit on guys—two or three different guys a day sometimes. It's much freer here. When you are in a group and you and a girl want to ball and there are some guys with you and you want to get rid of them, you don't try to explain to them. Like if you were at school or something, you know, like "Would you do us a favor—go out and get us some ice cream or something?" But here you just say, "Now look, I'm going in that room and that room is the 'ball room,' you know, I'm going to do 'my thing,' excuse me for a while." The way it is back home, everybody knows that girls are getting screwed and that guys are having a good time. I mean, everybody knows that. Ninety-five percent of the girls in the school I went to were not virgins. Everybody knows that. But the first time that the fact comes out that a girl has been screwed in school, automatically she becomes a whore. Here it is different. Like I mean, back home there are lots of girls getting screwed in school, you know, and everybody secretively knows it. But the first time somebody comes along and says, "Hey, Mary got screwed last night," everybody starts on the big thing that Mary is a whore. Now here, like Mary got screwed last night and she went and did it, well, gee whiz, good enough—wow, I mean what's it to me? I mean, wow, that's the way it is here.

LY–Is there any possessiveness here between partners?

B–Sometimes there is a possessiveness or there tries to be a possessiveness, but it never works. I'll guarantee that from my own experience. It is really better to have a girl of your own, it really is. Now I had a nymphomaniac and I tried to convert this nymphomaniac to be my girl and it didn't work.

LY–Why?

B–Every time I turned around she would be balling somebody else. [Group laughs.]

LY–Why do you find this so funny?

B–Because Jay here is the nymphomaniac that I was talking about.

LY–What about the side effects of pregnancy and all that?

B–Girls can get free birth-control pills at Bellevue Hospital. Open free sex has been going on for a long time around here so the girls are pretty well equipped for it. The only girls that get pregnant or get screwed up around here are the ones that come down for the summer, you know, just goofing off. They find a scene where there is a lot of sex and just enjoy it and have a good time. They get screwed up sometimes and end up by going home pregnant or with a clap.

LY–Is there a lot of V.D. around?

B–There is lots of V.D. going all around the whole hippie community. There is V.D. going all around the lower East Side and the lower West Side. Most hippies take care of their disease. If they get it, they go and get it cured. If they get it back the next night, they go and get it cured again.

LY–What about the love ethic here? Isn't there a lot of violence in the East Village?

B–We are loving people. We really are. We don't want to fight and we don't want to hassle anybody. We would love to go down to the park, move aside, and let the Puerto Ricans have a ball game right where we have it. We are not "up-tight." We don't feel that we have to prove our virility.

The Puerto Ricans have no other heritage and they have to constantly prove that they have manhood by screwing our women or by fighting or whatever. And we think that this is a big burden that most people have and we have dropped it and that makes us a lot greater.

LY–What does your tribe do? Who is it for?

B–People who have dropped out and need something. They need a common cause, they need something to do. They need things. They are a lost people sort of, when they first drop out. The tribe is really for people who want to live together and who want to enjoy themselves together and believe in one common cause.

As long as there are people that drop out of the common society, as long as there are people who want to get away from it all, even these people that just want to take one summer and say, "Wow, screw you, the rest of the world, I want to go out and live like I feel." They may know in their hearts that as soon as the summer is up they are going to go running back to their groove and get back in it. Then maybe they go back out again next summer. The next summer they will be a little better because next summer they will be a little more hip to what's going on. Maybe they will be accepted easier or something like that. But I feel that this tribal movement is a beautiful thing! And as long as there are lost people and as long as there are people who believe in this thing, and people who want to have a beautiful world, there will be tribes.

LY–What about the logical conclusion of everyone dropping out? Mr. Jones would say, the presses would stop running, the buses and cars would stop running, the electricity . . .

B–Yeah, we would turn the buses and the cars upside down and make flower pots out of them. Jim said in one of our other meetings, machines are a great and wonderful thing. You can't do without them, you know, I mean they are a great help. They are a help.

LY–But who would run them?

B–We would run them. We wouldn't mind running them. People like to drive cars. Some people like to ride buses, some people like to drive trains, you know. They like to do this. It's just there would be less need to ride things. There would be less need for many of the things that we would have.

You wouldn't need most things like the stock market and the downtown financial districts. You could forget about it. You really don't need brokers. You can do away with them completely. And uptown you can dispense with insurance companies and all of these services, because people would take care of these things by themselves.

LY–Isn't your scene here kind of primitive?

B–Yeah, well, I think that primitive man had the right idea. Nobody is really human anymore. They don't take interest in other human beings. They only take an interest in all the material values of the world. They don't worry about how they can help some man out on the street. They are worried about how much money they can haul in the next year to benefit themselves. Or how to put on this diamond ring while someone is out on the street starving. They think of more material values. In my opinion, material values don't mean a damn thing. I've had it all. I don't see honestly how somebody could put on a four- or five-thousand-dollar diamond ring. They have everything from gold belly-button brushes to mink toilet seats in my home and the homes of my old friends.

LY–How far did you go in school, Steve?

S–Well, I went through the tenth grade but not for reasons that I was doing wrong in school or anything. I had a ninety average in math, and did pretty well in my other subjects too. I was pulled out of school because I think from the very beginning I objected to the society and the way it was.

They labeled me as confused, mixed up, and sent me off to the Bellevue Mental Hospital. I was there for two months and then they sent me to a state hospital and I stayed there for two years. When I got out I moved directly into the hip scene because I knew what I wanted and I found it here.

LY–Well, what about leadership? Steve, aren't you the leader here?

S–There are no leaders. We're trying to move away, more or less, from leadership. People sort of act as guides, but not as leaders. If there is something that has to be done it usually ends up by getting done because of the fact that someone looks around and sees that something has to be done and does it. If they have to be told to do it, there is no sense in trying.

LY–What differences do you tribal people see between the so-called beatniks and the hippies?

B–The beatniks just dropped out. They just dropped every thing and just sat around and they wrote and read poetry to amuse themselves. They painted to amuse themselves. But they didn't want anything. They didn't want to be bothered with anyone outside of their own group or community. But the hippie community is trying to get involved anywhere they think that they can help.

LY–Does LSD make the difference?

B–I have changed in a lot of ways. Like at one time I really was an all-out, super-straight person, I mean, wow. Anything that my pop said was right in there, boy. He was the man. And the President, wow, he was the head of our country; whether he is right or wrong, I had to speak up for him.

I mean, I can't say that acid ruined my mind or anything, but I mean after a while I began to see things differently. One day at school about two years ago, somebody came up to me with some funny little pill and they said, "Wow, this is really groovy stuff, you know." And right away I said, "Oh, you dirty old dope addict, get the hell away from me, you rotten thing." This happened to be a chick and she talked me into it. And ever since then it has just been really beautiful. It has just changed my thoughts I mean, not physically—it hasn't changed my brain cells or anything. It makes you aware of things. Like after I dropped my first acid, I went home and listened to some of the things that my father was saying and I got to thinking, "Wow, what an ass, even if he is my father."

LY–How about you, Chuck?

C–I just started when I was fifteen and a half or sixteen. I had a groovy sister. We found out ideas about our lives and dope, the more we talked. She was just about the only person that I could talk to.

LY–What's your sister doing now?

C–Probably smoking grass. She is shacking up with some guy in Hollywood. The guy is a professional gambler and it works out okay for them.

LY–Well, we're getting near the end of our time—any other comments?

B–Next time when you come by, if you want a good meeting, why don't you bring a briefcase full of tabs [LSD]. It is expensive and hard to get here and the California Diggers would give it to you free if you were going to donate it to some poor people like us on the lower East Side.

LY–Are you putting me on?

B–No, I'm serious. They used to give it away in the streets of New York. Now they sell it.

S–We intend to have a project for giving it away. There is a major project going on about lowering the price of acid, about getting it down to where it costs very, very little and giving it away.

The Rising Sun seemed to me to be doomed to extinction by the end of the summer. The teenyboppers involved were "sincere" enough at the moment, but no doubt the impact of the laws regarding minors and their lack of leadership would cause the group to dissolve in due course.

Even their partial group existence, however, was significant. They were comparable to at least fifty other tribes that I learned about on the lower East Side and hundreds of others I found out about later in Los Angeles, San Francisco, and other large cities.

This feeble attempt at family commune or tribe with its thin pseudo-philosophy seemed to be a crude effort to substitute for a family and society that had failed these youths. Perhaps they should be taken literally at their word that they have dropped out from a "plastic," "machine-like," "unloving" society and were trying to tune back into a more natural, loving, American Indian tribal way of life.

A Loving Dope Pusher

One thing that intrigued me about the Rising Sun dialogue was a concept of the new "friendly," "loving" drug pusher who gave drugs away. The old-fashioned heroin dope fiend world that I knew about contained rather vicious peddlers, most of whom were addicts. They were not at all concerned with their customers, who were very apt to become victims of their predatory business dealings.

Were the purveyors of the new drugs really cheerful and loving sellers of happiness? I asked Chuck about this issue over a cup of coffee we had together after we left the Rising Sun meeting. He told me that it was true up to a point. The old-style drug pushers had not fully disappeared. However, quite a few had been replaced by younger and more benevolent drug salesmen. Chuck told me he could introduce me to one of the new breed, a fellow named Dave.

We found Dave (nicknamed Boo), a twenty-year-old pusher, among the swirl of hippies that hung out around the coffee houses and luncheonettes on Avenue B and 10th Street.

When Chuck first introduced me to Boo he was rather uptight and reluctant to talk with me. He later gave me the usual reason: "I was sure you were the heat." After a while he warmed up to Chuck and me and permitted me to tape our discussion. He clearly informed me, "If you use this in the wrong way, I could be in very serious trouble."

Boo was Jewish, sported an oriental short beard, and had very long hair. His beads and the single bell around his neck were definitely orthodox hippie. Although only twenty, he had been turned on to drugs for two-and-a-half years and had used LSD for two years. He was, I later found out, a well-known figure on both the East and West Coast.

His parents enjoyed "a good income from the nightclub business." Boo had been back and forth across the country traveling the hippie circuit. His primary allegiance was to a hip community in northern California. I got the impression that he was on leave from his post as a leader in this community to visit New York City and "make some bread dealing" (earn money selling dope). He was representative of several young benevolent dope pushers I met on my trip.

LY–For openers, Boo, do you yourself use drugs?

BOO–Okay, well—two years ago I said that I'd never take LSD. Then later I got very curious about it and one night I decided to take it. I took it with a girl and it was her first LSD trip, too. And we sat down and we waited and we waited and I thought that it wasn't LSD that the person sold me and I smoked some pot.

After a while I started to feel it and I knew because strange sensations went throughout my body. It was a normal LSD experience. At first I couldn't control it. I thought that I was going to go crazy or kill myself or kill somebody else. And finally I just sat down, and I said whatever is going to happen is going to happen. And I had total peace of mind. And I saw everything for what it was and that's when I sort of died and was reborn.

I learned from my LSD experience that this society is all built on objects, material objects. You are born, you work, and you strive to collect things that are meaningless. Instead of really trying to fulfill your life, you just go along being materialistic. You don't know who you are; you are a number, or a machine, or just a nine-to-five worker in it.

In place of this shit, we have the freedom of the tribal thing. People are getting together and they're living in communes or tribes. Like I myself have a tribe in California with about a hundred people and I support them when I'm there. I work and they are my family. And all the girls are my wives and the guys are my brothers and the babies are mine and this is love—it is a true love. Everybody loves each other. And there is no jealousy, no hostility, and no up-tightness. Everybody is part of a oneness. It's a unification.

LY–What happens in an average day in your commune?

BOO–On our farm, people wake up in the morning, somebody would make up a big batch of pancakes and everybody would sit around eating pancakes, and people would drift off slowly. Some would take pot and some would take acid. And they would go swimming nude and running around the woods sun bathing and making things and working and plowing the field and just grooving and dealing totally with their "thing." Nobody has to do anything, but see, you do it because you want to. Everybody does what they feel is right, and it has to work out. Everything has to work out.

LY–What rules do you have?

BOO–None. For instance, nobody will tell anybody what to do. But there will be feelings. If the major part of the group doesn't like something, we won't tell somebody that that's wrong, but they'll know it. And if they're really really into it, and they are with us, in our family, they'll know it's wrong, they'll sense it and they'll stop.

Let me give you an example. We got lots of cats up at our farm. Well, this guy got very up-tight with these cats and he was going to put them in a sack and take them down to town and let them go. And these are our prize cats. Some of the people are really hung-up on them. Like this one cat, Dalilah, she has seven toes on one foot. So he started to put them in a bag and one of the guys said, "Wait a second, just wait—just let me see what you have in that bag." He was really serious. It was a major event. Everybody crowded around and he pulled out Ernie and Dalilah, the two favorite cats of them all. So he says, "Oh, you're going to take Ernie and Dalilah." So he takes Ernie and Dalilah and he looks at them and he looks around and he looks at all of us and he just knew that it was wrong. Nobody had to say anything. He just knew that it was wrong. And he said, "Okay, okay," and he gave the cats back.

LY–There was never a time when somebody refused to cooperate and you had to throw them out?

BOO–No.

LY–Well, what about the sex scene in your commune? What goes on? Can anyone "ball" anyone else?

BOO–In a real commune, in a free-love society, people don't just run around balling everybody constantly. It doesn't happen that way because you do what you want to do. Sometimes you might feel like it and sometimes you might not. There has to be some sort of communication first between the people. Like you just don't walk up to a chick and grab her and start balling her. It's not like that.

LY–Well, if you have a broad and someone else gets her, does it bug you?

BOO–Well, it might bug some people but everybody realizes that first they are an individual and that everything after that is secondary. First you are an individual. You can't control somebody else's thoughts or actions, not even by marriage. Well, for instance, I had a habit of walking down the street smiling at people. I smiled at a chick that was walking with her husband and her husband was ready to kill me.

LY–What about the hippie children?

BOO–Hippie children are beautiful. Quite a few hippie children are turned on to acid and pot. I know this girl, Lisa, and her three-year-old baby boy is an acid head. She turned him on. He is taking acid and he looks like he is five and acts like he is five. He has a funny thing. He doesn't like to turn on and smoke pot with a group of people because everyone sits around and watches him. So he is kind of up-tight about turning on with other people. So he turns on by himself. Isn't that wild?

LY–You say you've traveled around the country. How would you compare the scenes?

BOO–California is much freer. In New York you have to be a little possessive and up-tight. In California everybody is going with the same trend—you can live with people and you don't have to work. Here, you should work 'cause you have to have money and you're closed in. You're in a city, a big industrial city, and you know everything that's going on and you have to sort of keep up with it. California is really on top. It's much freer, it's more alive and there is much more happening. . . . It's happening all across the country. You feel it. You sense it. When you turn on, you sense the vibrations in people and you sense feelings. Like I could look at somebody and almost instantly tell if they're a cop or not. Because I can sense it.

I sense the tightness there. With people I can sense how free I can be with them just by the vibrations that I get from them. Just by the way they smile or by the way they walk. By the way they do everything.

I support as many of these people as I can with my money, food, and dope. They're all my people. I'm a dealer. I only deal pot and acid. I wouldn't touch or give "speed" to anyone. A lot of people have misconceptions about dealers, you know. Even some hippies don't understand. They think that we are in it just for the money to make what we can. They think that it's part of the capitalistic society.

It's wrong. We support our own people. We pay a lot of people's rent and we feed a lot of people. We get them stuff to turn on. I give away a lot of it. I give people their first trip free. You know, it's not like you keep tripping and tripping and sell it. I've given dope away to many people that I've never seen again, just so they could turn on. So they can see what it's like.

LY–How does the distribution of LSD operate?

BOO–LSD is a synthetic. Some of it is made by chemists. They get a batch of lysergic acid and they make LSD. Some other people get what would be like grams of LSD and they bufferize it by adding a powder. Then they put it in capsules and wholesale it. Very little of this is done in New York. California is a very, very big acid state. It is the acid capital of the world. ________ is about the biggest name in acid. He made the little tiny white pills and really started the whole acid revolution. It is a very fine acid. It's the finest acid in the world.

LY–What is the chain of distribution?

BOO–There are wholesalers and retailers. Some people will deal with just the people with money and get some acid together and take a percentage out of it. Sometimes they don't even have to touch the acid in order to deal. Some people sell on the street, five, ten caps at a time. And some only sell one at a time. Some buy fifty kilos and sell it five at a time. Some will buy one kilo and sell it for a nickel [five dollars] a bag. Sometimes smugglers bring in a thousand kilos and have a dealer sell it for them.

The distribution is different than in other drugs because you can carry a gram of acid that's only two or three inches high in a little bottle. That's about four thousand doses.

LY–You seem to feel that you're making a contribution to the people rather than trying to make some money.

BOO–I'm doing my thing. It's fun. I get enjoyment out of seeing lots of people turning on. Like let's say that it'll be dry for a while and there is no pot or acid, and I'll show up and then everyone will turn on and be happy.

The teenyboppers on the lower East Side were thus "tribing," "pushing," and using drugs. They seem to share in all parts of the scene with great gusto. All of the Brians, Jays, and Boos "do their thing" in Tompkins Square Park, which seems to serve as the spiritual center of hippie activities on the lower East Side.

CHAPTER SEVEN

The East Village: Love and Violence

THERE WAS USUALLY AN IMportant hippie happening in Tompkins Square Park on Sunday. The park had become a symbol of love and at the same time the shrine of violence against the hippie movement. On Memorial Day the police had moved in force against a love-in being held in the park.

The East Village Other, an underground newspaper, brought out an extra edition on June 3, 1967. The lead paragraph of one of the articles presented the hippie view of the happening.

> On Memorial Day, May 30, several thousand neighbors on the lower East Side watched a clear-cut incident of police brutality, where the police attacked passive "hippies," hospitalizing three and roughly handling a pregnant woman; arresting 36 others, overacting on a simple noise complaint. . . .
>
> Sadistic glee was written on the faces of several officers. Women became hysterical, the police slugged one man and dragged him off bloody and crying, "My God, my God, where is this happening? Is this America?"

The scene in the New York hippie world became as significant an issue as the Texans' remembrance of the Alamo. It also symbolically reflected the potpourri of cultural forces at work in the East Village.

New Cultural Conditions

The police attack reflected the response of the general community to the hippies. The park and the area were not the exclusive property of the hippies. This was also the center of activity for many minority-group families that lived in the neighborhood. Puerto Rican, Polish, Ukrainian, and German groups had lived in East Village and had developed a cultural milieu for at least 50 years prior to the psychedelic revolution. The hippie invasion, however, was not totally rejected by the larger community. The reaction was marked by ambivalence. Some of the hippie cultural contributions to the East Village scene were colorful additions to the drab lives of the older residents and their families. Love-ins, hip clothes, store-front cultish organizations all combined to give the East Village a new flavor.

Part of the hippie cultural injection into the East Village was intellectual rather than visual. The hippies enlarged some older developments and produced new ones. One such group, called the Free University of the Streets, attempted to promote a free-floating, informal type of education. Operating out of a small store, they attempted to stimulate open discussion groups in their store, on the streets, and in the parks of the East Village.

Another hip cultural group in the area is the "free love" Keristan Society. Their motto is "Love Conquers All." In one of their books, the *Kerista Speeler*, they state: "To know what you prefer, instead of humbly saying 'Amen' to what the world tells you to prefer, is to have kept your soul alive." The Keristan Society and its "free love" principle is heartily endorsed by the hip poet, Allen Ginsberg. The Keristans take the position that it is one's duty to accept love from whomever offers it. To refuse to have sex ("make it") with anyone who asks is considered an act of hostility.

At a higher intellectual and creative level exists the Group Image. This hippie tribe is comprised of people in the arts. Some are excellent painters, writers, and craftsmen. An unusual hippie wedding attracted wide attention in the press. Following is part of *Time* magazine's (August 25, 1967) tongue-in-cheek version of a Group Image wedding.

> Beautiful.
>
> Manhattan's Palm Garden ballroom was really turned on. The flowers, Tim, the flowers. They were in people's hair, on the floor, swarming over two huge screens from the color-slide projectors. Lights flashed everywhere, bounding off the Day-Glo lunarscapes along the wall. And when the phosphorescent beams caught the dancers, it turned the boys' white shirts purple, along with their teeth and eyeballs. The electronic band made the floor jump, and everybody was happy, sniffing the incense, smoking pot. It was a real love-in.
>
> Then in came the beautiful people on four motorcycles, right into the ballroom, oozing with flower-power. It was the signal for everybody to get ready for the wedding and gather around the sanctuary, an arbor of aluminum beams and reflecting plastic panels. There came the groom, Artie, 24, carrying a guitar and wearing baggy trousers, a white Nehru-collar tunic with a red trim and cowboy boots. "My wedding suit. Nancy made it," he beamed. And there came the bride, Nancy, 15, her long blonde hair glistening, silver braces on her teeth (she'll take them off next year), and happily, joyously pregnant.
>
> The members of the wedding belonged to the same tribe, the Group Image, one of the new, first-name-only hippie groups, of which Nancy is the den mother, sewing and cooking, and Artie the lead guitar. The tribe has about 25 musicians, artists, and psychedelic experts in it; they decorate clubs, design posters, and teamed up to do TIME's hippie cover (July 7). "They're different from the usual hippies," says Nancy's mother. "They're working and planning something for themselves. Their philosophy is a very loving and tender thing."*

*Courtesy TIME, The Weekly Newsmagazine; copyright Time Inc. 1967.

Provo is another type of East Village hippie cultural center. It is housed in a small store-front situation. The name comes from an Amsterdam youth movement of nihilism called Provo (provocateurs). Anyone can enter the New York branch store and is generally welcome. When I visited, two young men were in charge. One was in hippie costume. The other was dressed straight, in sport shirt and pants.

Bill, the straight-looking "proprietor," gave me a release on the local Provo position as written up in their "Journal." The paper, admittedly, was published whimsically and seldom came out on time. Provo's view of the world was embodied in the following article:

> I dig love—I like to walk down the street where the vibrations are good. Those who go around hating are nowhere. But when the flower contingent tells me that the only way to survive is to clean up, look respectable, and love the cops—well, I just don't know about that.
>
> We can all play the *Time-Life* game, and make the mass media, and keep on reconstructing bourgeois culture in its own image. But where is the psychedelic revolution at? The old society and the old values are corrupt—obvious examples like Vietnam aside. And all of us have found that even if you drop out—if you change your life and your values—you're still somewhere in American society. The nitty gritty of American society is a power structure, built on guns and money. And there isn't really a question of co-existence, because all power structures demand complete allegiance. That's why no utopia has ever succeeded in this country.
>
> Like the Diggers, Provos believe that the community should re-absorb the powers and functions that the State has taken for itself. But Provos go further, because we see that the community must develop new ways of dealing with all of technology and mass society. Everyone is faced immediately with the power structure. Provos seek to provoke clear understanding of the power structure. *New York Provo proposes spreading psychedelics widely now, massive non-violent resistance, and Merry Prankster provocationist politics, to reveal to everyone how cruel and asinine the power structure is.* [My emphasis.]

The Banana Be-In

One of Provo's sponsored "Merry Prankster" provocations was a Banana Be-In. I was informed about the event by Bill, one of Provo's "executives." He was a strong advocate of the immediate legalization of all drugs. One of his plans was to have a national dope-in. On a given day all drug users would go out into the streets nude "smoking pot or dropping acid—doing their thing." After the mass arrests that were expected to follow, each user would do the same thing immediately upon release from jail. "This mass protest," Bill assured me, "would change all the laws of the land in one fell swoop." Being a realist, he felt the major hangup in the idea was "the lack of courage of most drug users." He characterized them as "too paranoid to carry out the plan."

That afternoon I went to the Banana Be-In. It was considerably different from Bill's advocated Nude-Dope-In, yet it was provocative in its own right. About 200 hippies and an additional 300 onlookers gathered in a corner of Tompkins Square Park. I sat in the middle of the happening and watched it flow around me.

Hippies generally have two sets of clothes—day-to-day buckskins and levis and clothes for a festival. The festival clothes were brightly colored and fantastic. The holiday influence was seen in the headbands, beads, and gowns worn by both men and women.

I sat next to Bill, who was busily rolling the brown dried banana substance into cigarets. We were among a group of people who were giggling and apparently having a good time. I accepted one of the "mellow yellows" Bill offered me. The banana shavings were rolled along with regular tobacco in a "Psychedelicatessen"-labeled tobacco paper. (The Psychedelicatessen was a local psychedelic store. The free distribution of the paper was their way of advertising.)

I lit up and took a few drags on the acrid-tasting conglomeration. It was bitter and gave me no particular high that I could detect. It did produce a slight headache. (There has been some actual research that revealed that banana smoke produced no high, and was, in fact, a national joke and "put-on.")

From time to time I detected an unmistakable gust of marijuana smoke in the air. I would crudely estimate that in the crowd of several hundred legal banana smokers (including myself) there were about fifty illegal pot smokers.

A humorous sight to the hippies was the police (plainclothes and uniformed) darting in and out of the crowd hunting pot smokers. They would confiscate a cigaret from a hippie who would laughingly protest, "Hey, man, this is just a banana." As nearly as I could determine, no one was arrested.

The Banana Be-In was later reported in the *East Village Other* (August 1–15, 1967, issue) as follows:

> Several hundred people gathered in Tompkins Square Park July 16 to demonstrate their support for the legalization of marijuana. . . .
>
> . . . Negroes, hippies, Puerto Ricans, and undercover police spent the afternoon smoking and making music, first on the concrete then on the grass. Participants sang a familiar mantra, substituting "Marijuana" for "Hare Krishna."
>
> Sponsored by New York Provo, a group of psychedelic revolutionaries, the event was intended to bring together and to turn on people from all groups in an atmosphere of peaceful defiance.
>
> In spite of the fact that the promised rock band couldn't make it, the smoke-in was a success for the people in the park. One girl said, "I thought this kind of thing could only happen in Haight-Ashbury." Sunday afternoon made it clear to everyone on the grass that they could come together in celebration and overcome New York paranoia. If they were together they could smoke in the park without fear of harassment. That is what the smoke-in demonstrated. . . .

The Feminine View

At the Be-In I circulated around the park talking to and interviewing a number of people. My smoking banana cigaret seemed to tie me in closer to the group. In one exchange on a park bench I was able to stimulate an interesting conversation with two hippie girls who gave me their view of the East Village phenomena.

Mary was 24 and most attractive in spite of her blue denim work clothes. She had piercing blue eyes and turned out to be one of the brightest girls I had yet met on the scene. She was from Ohio, had completed three years at a Midwest college, and her parents were both teachers. (I later found out she was Boo's girlfriend.) The other attractive girl, Rose, was rather round and obviously pregnant.

Our discussion covered a range of female hippie subjects and issues.

LY–Why are you here at the Banana Be-In?

M–It is supposed to be the ideal scene where everybody who smokes pot would come right out in full view and do their thing. I was really expecting a lot more people to have "grass" and very few people do. It's almost all banana. I was giving out cigaret papers for rolling. If this was California, very few people would be smoking bananas—they would be smoking pot. People in New York are more up-tight.

LY–Why are you here in New York?

M–I'm searching for something that I know I won't find at home with my family. There it's all conservative. Here there are scared people and happy people. It's a cross section of everything. There are all the races, religions, everything.

LY–Is LSD pretty important to people who are, as you say, searching?

M–It's a tool. Like people can do it without LSD. It speeds things up. It makes you aware suddenly, but a person can also become aware through meditation or just by examining themselves. It might take longer, a period of years, whereas you can do it in about eight hours on LSD. I've had about five or six LSD trips. Actually, only two really counted.

LY–Were they hard-hitting?

M–I had one that really knocked me out. I'm still trying to recover from it and that was two or three weeks ago. It was an ego-buster trip, you know. I was inside my own mind and I really saw things. It flabbergasted me. I don't think that I'll ever be the same.

LY–Can you put into words the things you saw?

M–I can't really say, because it is something so very personal—I would like to communicate it to you but it is just a feeling, an emotion. My first trip changed my world. I quit my job and I haven't worked since then. There were a few things that happened to me before my ego buster. I was more selfish and more money-minded and I was more society-minded like where I was before. But now, it is kind of a love thing, a humanity thing. It's not social and it's not financial, it's personal. LSD enlightened me to myself. It's made me more aware and understanding of why I do things, even little everyday things. It has given me insight into myself and into other people, and a lot more understanding.

There are different types of acid heads. Some people are into the Zen or Yoga thing. Some people are political acid heads. I am not political. Somebody else may be very political and they may be very involved with their rights or what's going on in Vietnam. Other people are involved in the mystical part of it, and some people take it just for kicks. No matter what their age, or what they wear, or no matter how happy they may seem, everybody is still searching. It's a matter of intensity.

LY–Why do you think the East Village is a good place to search?

M–At home, my parents thought that they knew what I wanted. Here, nobody tells me what I want. There is just me. I'm not running into as many conflicts. I think I have learned more in the last two months here than maybe I have learned in my whole life at home.

LY–Can you put it in words? What do you think you have learned?

M–I received a tremendous amount of insight, that's all I can say.

LY–Do you think you'll wind up married with the standard middle-class two-point-eight kids in suburbia?

M–I really don't know. Right now I hope not, but like if that's what I want when the time comes, then that's what I'll do. I had no really complicated sick family scene, but I just know what I was looking for wasn't at home. And, like I was getting trapped into something. If I had finished college, I would have gone into a job and I never would have known. Everything would have been all mapped out and I would have followed the maps without exploring anything on the side. I wouldn't have seen all there is to see. Maybe I never will anyway, but like I would have just walked down one path just because somebody said, well, this is the path to walk down. It would have been a robot-type thing.

LY–Is it just your personal family or is it the capital F Family, American society that seems to be hanging you up?

M–They're both entwined. I mean, like my family is middle class and they're of the big society. It's not exactly a status problem. They aren't the country-club type, but yet they have to keep up their social face. I saw that this was hindering the development of my individuality.

The other girl, Rose, was 21 years old, came from Montana, and had been on the Village scene for about a year. She was about six months pregnant. She didn't know who the father was and didn't seem to care. Her pregnancy and her hippie costume didn't seem to blend. After a preliminary discussion I asked her some direct questions about her condition.

LY–How do you feel about being pregnant?

R–Well, I'm not too happy.

LY–Well, I thought that a lot of girls on the scene don't

worry about being pregnant, or aren't you that much on the scene?

R–Oh, I'm on the scene. I know just about everybody down here and they know me. With what Mary was saying, it was different for me. I had hassles with my family. I was split up by my family. Half the time I was with my father and half the time I was with my mother. My mother and I never got along. When I was sixteen and graduated from high school, my mother said, "Well, you're on your own, now go ahead and go out on your own." And I did. There is a difference between me and other chicks around here. I was able to go out on my own because I knew what was happening. But some of these kids that are down here are like fourteen years old. These chicks, man, they can't take care of themselves. Like they end up in trouble and like they don't even know what they're into. And by that time it is too late. And like I consider myself in trouble right this moment, but like I know what I'm going to do and I know how to go about doing it. I had to quit work two months ago and I haven't had that much money or anything. And like my friends and everybody else, they have helped me. They feed me and they help me. They help me to go on and like they have really done a lot of good for me. These are friends, real friends, you know.

These are not people that I have known all of my life. Maybe I met someone a week ago. There are truer friends down here. Sometimes they are more helpful than people that I have known all of my life, like my family. This really hits me. I know that if I went home to my family right now and told them, you know, that I was in trouble, pregnant and all this right now, they would say to me . . . tough luck!

LY–What do the girls down here use for birth control?

M–I really don't know. I used pills. But some girls don't even care. Some girls, like you say, want to have a baby.

R–Yeah, there are some fourteen- and fifteen-year-olds, especially, who want babies. I don't know why. There is this one fifteen-year-old in particular . . . she wants to get pregnant. Like she doesn't care who the father is or anything else. She wants to have a child because she thinks it would be good for her. You know, not how good it will be for the kid, or anything else. She needs someone. I think a perfect substitute would be a puppy or a kitten. I sat with her for about three hours when she had a miscarriage. She was going to start all over again, to have another baby! And like I sat there for three hours trying to talk her out of it. And I tried to tell her that I don't plan to keep the baby, this baby, because right now I don't think I am a fit mother.

I'm not settled down enough to raise a child. It wouldn't be right for her. And like I was trying to tell her this 'cause I'm like in a better position to go about raising a child than she would be, and I was trying to tell her this but she wouldn't buy it.

The girls and I further discussed the issues of child raising in their world. Both agreed that "it was a mess" to raise children on the hippie scene, partly because the nomadic life implicit in the situation produced an insecure condition for raising children.

During my conversation with Mary and Rose I noticed a young man of about nineteen seated nearby listening attentively to our discussion. He was a participant in the Be-In, and was dressed in hippie garb. His main distinguishing feature, however, was a wide plastered bandage that covered half of his face.

He apparently knew the girls and joined in readily with our conversation. He angrily commented, "Why don't you tell this guy the real reason it's ridiculous to bring up kids in this hell-hole. They're liable to get killed. Look what happened to me!"

He pointed to his bandage and told me how he had been slashed by a Puerto Rican. The cut required twelve stitches.

He went into detail about the violent incident. I was surprised to learn that the Puerto Rican youth, Frank, whom I had met at Galahad's Pad was the assailant.

I talked for about an hour to the young man, whose name was Al. I later went back and re-interviewed Chuck and Frank. The East Village cultural background conditions and the case example involving Al, Frank, and several girls and boys from Galahad's Pad reflected some of the forces of violence at work on the scene.

Forces of Violence: A Case in Point

A dominant problem in the East Village was the violence that seemed to emanate in part from the oil and water mixing of the hippies with the longer-term minority-group residents of the community. The older residents reacted to the hippies in a variety of ways. Many were puzzled and hostile about the garb, the talk, and the hippies' obvious sexual freedom. One long-term resident who had grown up in the neighborhood told me, "I don't understand these creeps. They all come from wealthy homes. I've been trying to move out of here with my family for the last ten years and can't. I really want to go now. Let me tell you, one day I saw two of these hippie animals screwing in the park—right out in the open! Is this any place to bring up my kids?"

The children of minority groups often act out the frustrations and hostility felt by their parents. A vehicle of aggression, often found in slum areas, is the violent gang. Although not as predominant or as organized as in the past, the lower East Side still has its violent youth gangs. Gang violence is the action tip of the arrow often reflecting the entire neighborhood's tone of aggression. Frank's slashing of Al's face took place in the context of this community cultural complex.

The violence, as nearly as I could piece the story together, took place as follows. Along with several members of his Puerto Rican gang, Frank admittedly had been molesting some of the young hippie girls on the streets and in the hallways of the Galahad tenement. On one specific occasion Frank and several of his gang raped a hippie girl who was staying at Galahad's Pad.

Several of the young hippie boys in residence at Galahad's angrily, in violation of their avowed love ethic, threatened Frank with a beating if he repeated his attacks on their women. Frank got his boys. They came to the apartment where the hippie youths were staying, and when they were refused entrance they promptly battered the old door down. In the melee that followed, Frank slashed Al with a switch-blade knife across the cheek. Al went to the hospital and the wound required twelve stitches.

This vignette was typical of many daily conflicts of this type that occurred in the neighborhood. Some more severe attacks resulted in homicide. The hippies, violent youth gangs, frustrated and aggressive minority groups, and the police produce a caldron of emotions that has resulted in increased violence in "love communities." The East Village is typical of the complicated love-violence problem produced by the invasion of hippies into other depressed urban areas around the country.

CHAPTER EIGHT

A Village High Priest

IN THE CREVICES OF THE HIPPIE movement are many unsung heroes. Stars who are not yet as glamorous and famous as Tim Leary has become in the popular mass media or Gridley Wright in the underground press. These lesser-known hippie high priests influence the novitiates and teenyboppers enormously. Their "rap" is delivered at all hours and in all hippie locales to youths seeking "the way" that they have found.

One young man of twenty-two who represents this significant role in the hippie movement was Sonny. I first noticed him at the Banana Be-In carnival where he seemed to be an important figure in the festivities. Sonny was later introduced to me by my hippie guide Chuck as "a truly beautiful religious cat." After a brief discussion with him, I decided it would be important for me to get his "rap."

Sonny grew up in a wealthy eastern suburban town. His father was a $50,000-a-year executive. "My father is a proper super-straight cat who belongs to the right country club, drinks his share of the liquor on Saturday night, and is very taciturn, particularly when it comes to talking with his wife." His mother was "a standard hysterically square broad who pampered me to death." (Sonny, I later found out, prior to turning on to LSD and his hippie way of life, had attempted suicide around twenty times.)

Sonny seemed older than his twenty-two years, and was handsome by classic Hollywood standards in the image of Marlon Brando. He had a brilliant smile that he flashed on me many times during our brief but intense encounter. He had long black hair, wore a walrus mustache, and was properly festooned with beads, bells, and rough leather boots.

I interviewed Sonny in the Village pad of one of his disciples. He was enormously turned-on by some "great pot" he had recently smoked. Sonny's "rap" was for me a remarkably good summary of the hip philosophical sounds I had heard in many corners of the East Village. Although some of what he says is a "repeat," the totality of his dialogue is a coherent statement of the hip life style and viewpoint in the East Village and other urban centers of the hippie world.

S–I was a super-straight young man from respectable parents in a middle-class Roman Catholic home. We, of course, belonged to the country club. My eyes were on the commercial stars of America. I had a nice little sports car—the whole scene. Well, for a good period of time, I thought I'd be a marine biologist and I always had an interest in writing. It was kind of a toss-up between the two. I was going to be something very earth-shattering, very noble, very respected.

LY–What kind of hangups did you have? What things bugged you?

S–Oh, I had the typical hangups caused by psycho-repression and everything that every young person in America has—religious hangups, family hangups. I guess it would be easier to list the hangups I didn't have. I had the whole gamut of frustrations and indecisions that most young people in this country face. Most young people go through a period of indecision, doubt, rebellion, etc., and then figure, "Okay, fuck it. I'll accept everything."

LY–Did you ever get tangled up with any psychiatry?

S–Oh yeah, I had an out-of-sight psychiatrist! After the

second time I quit college. My psychiatrist was probably the most neurotic man I ever met in my life. If you can picture a psychiatrist's office with a cross and crossed American flags underneath it, you get some idea of this man. To me he seemed very sick. I was fine when I came in, but he convinced me that I was out of my mind. I guess at the time I was going through a rather traumatic period where I still had the kind of held-over guilt feelings that are fostered from having a rather dogmatic world view pushed upon you. I still had emotional ties to that world view that had been drummed into me ever since I could begin to understand and comprehend. There was a very real conflict going on between, you know, my mind, my conscious mind and my subconscious mind . . . if you want to call it something like that. I'd get extremely uptight. I could see nothing but the hostility and anger that the people I cared for, my parents, were experiencing.

I had a very dark view of the world. I had already dropped out of college. My principal interest at that time had been philosophy and I traced Western philosophy to the point where I had absolutely smashed any positive view of the religious thing that I could have. I became wrapped up in despair and I suppose it became a kind of despair I liked. It became sort of an ever-present thing. It got to be too much and, you know, I slashed my arms and wrists. (I noticed around twenty slash-mark scars on his arms.)

LY–How many times did you try suicide?

S–Oh, I have absolutely no idea. I had the main hassle of our time. My refusal to accept the life that my parents picked for me. Most parents within the society are doing something they don't really want to do. You know, there's always some dream that they always wanted, yet they can't do it. And they're caught up in a very materialized sort of game structure. And they excuse this or they rationalize that by saying, "Well, we're going through this so our children can have a better life." That's the excuse that every parent uses, you know, when he isn't leading the type of life that he'd like. And so, when a child grows up and decides that he doesn't want what they've had in their mind for him for all these years, they kind of forget that perhaps he has the right to decide his own form of life. And so you get into a real conflict with them and yourself at that point.

The whole society's based on a very egocentric form of game structure. All the games within the society are ego games. Of prime importance within this society is the self-image and the image presented to others. It just becomes a very paramount thing in everybody's life. It's influenced by movies. People try and be a movie star like John Wayne or somebody like that. They stroll down the street looking tough. They grab onto certain concepts of masculinity and femininity which have nothing to do with what's masculine at all . . . it's just a facade. This allows the self, or ego, to dominate feelings and true expressions. So you become not really yourself, but just kind of a shallow mirror image of some originally false idea. The games would break down if the people became aware that they are games. . . .

Here's how I came around to this way of thought. When I was young, I was kind of a mind worshiper. You know, I was a very young, snotty intellectual and I went through that whole academic rap game. An intellectual just reads for the sake of later talking to others and impressing them. But eventually, if you read enough, it begins to sink in. So when I got to college, I went into philosophy. It completely disappointed me. Western philosophy has broken down. The questions that it . . . it originally tried to answer . . . metaphysics, ontology, etc. . . . had broken down to the point where now it was just an intellectual semantic word game.

I found the educational system ridiculous. I'll tell you how ridiculous the educational system is. Everybody there is there only for a degree. For example, whenever I need money badly all I have to do is go to a college town and let it be known that I write term papers and I can make around $150 a week. That, I think, is comment enough on the attitude of most students. The curriculum and the courses themselves—they're just absurd. I think it's a waste of time for anybody who wants to learn anything to go to college, really.

LY–When did you have your first LSD experience?

S–I guess it was about a year and a half ago.

LY–What did it do for you?

S–When I first began to take acid, I wasn't really ready. I was still in a kind of depressed, masochistic stage and it intensified that quite a bit. But eventually there came a period where I began to understand what acid was about and began to use it properly. The first thing it should be used for is to go through your own mind. To look at yourself from outside of yourself to see what kind of things are working in you that are fucking you up, that are making you a manic-depressive, or whatever form your insanity takes.

LY–Did you find anything specific you could put your finger on or was it a general reaction when you began to explore your own, I guess, inner space?

S–Well, I think the most specific thing I thought was that I'd been blind all my life to what is beautiful. You're surrounded so much in this society with what is ugly that it becomes almost the only aesthetic value you can judge. You can see the ugly. You can always see the ugly. If you want to you can get upset by it. People aren't raised to be willing to see the beautiful and I began to see the beautiful. I began to know things such as good karma. I began to be able to sit in the woods and feel a part of it . . . feel a part of nature . . . feel the oneness that is possible. I began to understand what love and beauty are all about.

LY–In your opinion how did the hippie movement start?

S–The hippie movement, if you want to call it that, is a natural outgrowth of the 50's beatnik movement plus the important extra ingredient—acid.

Beat people like Kerouac, Miller, Gregory Corso, Allen

Ginsburg are still with us. These are people who have become dissatisfied with American society and the American way of life. At that point, they were beginning to see the ridiculousness of it. That's pretty much all they were seeing. They were looking at the negative side of society and they weren't reacting really by trying to change anything positive. They were associated, of course, with the left. The beatnik movement of the 50's was basically just a commentary movement. A group of people expressing themselves principally through the arts. They said, "This is ridiculous, fuck it; we want no part of it."

Their rallying cry, if they had any, was the sexual revolution. Probably their best spokesman was Henry Miller. Their movement, if you want to judge it by the sexual revolution, was fairly successful—at least in this country. There's been a very definite change in sexual mores, particularly among young people.

That period is pretty much passed now. The junction point between what you might call the hippie world and the beatnik world of the previous generation was the introduction of LSD and other psychedelic drugs. Probably people became aware of it at first through Huxley's essays. LSD, mescaline, grass, have been on the scene almost forever but it's spreading now. And I would say that if the hippie movement has a rallying cry it would have to be the psychedelic-drug revolution.

Instead of people saying everything is shit and walking around with their eyes to the ground, kicking stones, mumbling curses under their breath, and adopting a very superior attitude, like "We know where it's at and nobody else does, and you people are too far gone to even approach it," you have, well, things like we just saw in Tompkins Square Park—people with flowers on . . . you know, running around ringing bells. They're kind of happy.

It's been going on in small groups since the time of . . . Christ. It's nothing, I think, but people becoming aware of their humanness. People dropping off all the hangups and the frustrations that society has foisted upon them. Society exists, I think, almost as a third thing—as an entity in itself. For its own self-preservation and perpetuation it has to install certain attitudes within the people who are in it. These attitudes may be fine for maintaining *that* form of society and keeping *that* form of society alive and functioning. But it has a very real tendency to fuck up the personalities and the minds of the people within it.

The hippies or the flower people or whatever you want to call 'em are nothing but people who've dropped these hangups. People who can behave as children when they want to, unashamedly. And I don't think there is any human being alive who wouldn't want to just run and skip in the streets like a kid. Swing from light posts, climb trees. People who aren't afraid of loving each other. People who aren't suspicious.

Friendship no longer becomes a thing of dominance, you know, where one friend dominates the other or where you're always suspicious that maybe someone's out to get you or knife you in the back. It's . . . it's just open. It's dropping all the false trappings of society.

If you need money or anything, you ask somebody for it. If you want to, people turn you on free. I went to three different places last night. Every place I went, I got stoned. I had some grass this morning so I found some people in the park and came up here and got nicely stoned. . . .

The concept now is to try and get away from trading and bartering. I kind of feel that everybody has one thing which they like to do. Sometimes more than one thing. One function that makes them happy. And to a lot of people that are here in the Village the only reason that they got the courage to come here is because that thing is in the arts. If you're serious about art, you can't really exist in this society because there's just no way to live. This society isn't geared for serious poets, artists, painters.

The people here have their thing. But there are also other people. For example, people down on Wall Street—maybe they would really dig being farmers. Nothing would make them more happy than to till the land, till the soil. To other people, they have a thing like they keep building things. All the frustrated little fix-it shops out in suburbia. Those people would really be happy if they could make something beautiful. And although it isn't very practical in this society now, or in the very near future, it's plausible to envision a society where everybody could just go out and "do their thing." The only way that that could work, each one doing his own thing, is if you do away with the whole concept of pay.

These ideas are working now. It's working down here and it's working in the communities and tribes out in the country. When you do your thing. If you dig farming, you give the food away, except for what you need to eat. If you're making things—chairs, tables, or anything like that—you give them away to those who need it. And if you need help on something, you just ask somebody, "Hey, I'm doing this today," and so they come and help you. It's sort of a total sharing.

I don't think it's a socialistic idea at all. I think it's more a humanist idea. And it will work 'cause it works down here. If you're hungry now, I'd tell you where to go where people have food. You just walk in the door and they'd give you a plate of food. If you wanted to get stoned now, I could tell you where to go.

LY–What you're talking about now has only really come about in the last six months or a year.

S–I'd say last year. This whole thing, we'll call it a movement, has grown so much in the last year it's unbelievable.

I've been traveling through college towns. The academic atmosphere is nice to visit every once in a while. The number of college students who are turning on to dope, love, and beauty is unbelievable! I can see it in the schools. The school I went to a year ago and returned to again last year has changed. It was textbooks before, now it's flowers and love.

LY–Do you think it's a real love?

S–Oh, well, speaking on a general basis is ridiculous. I can only take you out and show you people that I know. I undoubtedly have sort of surrounded myself with friends that have the same sort of ideas and feelings that I do.

LY–What is it that you see? How do you think square middle-class Mr. Jones is going to react to the hip movement?

S–It's not only Mr. Jones. Puerto Rican Mr. Gonzales is carrying a knife. I think that his reaction to it right now is one of basic hostility and anger. It stems a great deal from envy. I think a great deal of the hostility is because they're seeing people who are happy doing things that they've been told all their life will never make them happy. People in this society have been told you have to work eight hours a day or you won't eat. And there are people down here who are just happy in doing their thing. People who are not working for anybody in the Establishment are staying alive and they're eating.

They've been told that promiscuous sex is bad, so they have filled themselves with sexual frustration. They have all kinds of hangups and probably the most warped sexual fantasies that you could imagine. I know from some of the chicks down here who get weird propositions from straight cats all the time.

LY–What do they come on with?

S–That whole thing is very negative and it's not really worth going into.

LY–You mean they're perverse sexual propositions?

S–Sure, perverse propositions. Their attitude of sex is basically a very sick one. Sex in this country is such a fantastically important thing. It's put on an unattainable pedestal and it has so many ties. It's a confused thing. It's almost designed to bring guilt. Most people don't enjoy it. They don't know what they're doing. They can't really have sex and be a part of it. Sex is a very human thing and it should be a very natural thing and a very beautiful thing which, for the most part in this society, it is not.

I don't mean sex in the sense of going out and getting laid—or going down to a bar, getting drunk, and then driving some chick out in your Chevrolet and, you know, screwing her in the back seat. Sex is a very beautiful thing, but in this society it isn't.

LY–Is it beautiful in hippie society?

S–For the most part, it is. It's free. It's natural. Nobody makes a big deal of it. It's not a big deal. It isn't the big, you know, all-important question. If a group of hippie males get together they really don't talk about some broad's bust size or who got laid last night. You know what locker-room conversation is like. I don't know whether you've ever played football and that, but the all-important questions are drinking and sex.

I'd like to go back to one question. You said, "What do you think the reaction of Mr. Jones will be?" And I think that's completely dependent on how the hippie attitude or the hippie movement, if you want to call it that, is expressed in the arts. It hasn't been expressed well, yet. The only way that people are going to understand what's happening is if they can understand the people who are a part of this. What they see now are bearded freaks.

They assume that all the bearded freaks take drugs. They don't differentiate between LSD, grass, cocaine, or cough medicine. They put them all in the same category and then imagine that we're all out to beat them, steal their color TV sets, and rape their daughters. So you know they're antagonistic.

A large number of people in the hippie movement are in the arts. Most of them are very bad, but most artists of any period are very bad. You only get a few very good ones. If artistically these ideas that are happening now, if the feelings that people are beginning to get now can be expressed, and expressed in such a way that not only other hippies will understand it but the straight people will understand it too, then perhaps there can be a meeting of minds. Perhaps if the harsh edge of hostility toward hippies by Mr. Jones was taken away, then when a hip person went through Ohio these people could see more than bearded freaks. If they can see people who are happy then the power of the movement is expressed to them.

The power of the movement is through artistic expression and through just being. That's what the Be-In concept is. The whole idea of a Be-In is just to have a whole bunch of hippies, or people who feel like this, in a group—happy and doing their thing. When straight people go by and see somebody else happy when they themselves aren't, maybe they'll begin to question why they aren't. I've expressed these feelings in a poem. Would you like to hear the poem?

I, of course, wanted to hear the poem. Sonny went into another room and came back with the following poem neatly typed out. He gave it a magnificent reading.

The Children of the Flowers
a parable of parts

The Children of the flowers
burst from their winter caves
gathering in fields of spring
to lift their collective mind
                    in song.
They run—
          smiling color
                    through the trees:
dancing down dirt warmed
roads.
Toes curling the warmth of
                              earth
swirling dust devils
          and
shimmering waves of heat
past fields of magic mushrooms.
Their world
    the land of elves and hobbits

the sparkle colored
being
of aware.
Their smell
the odor of fresh earth,
spring rains
and roan goats skipping
through dew-covered fields.
They come
an army of joy
viewing new worlds
through the open doors of perception.

II

Entering the town
fences vanish
at the touch of flowered seed.
Laughing down yesterday's somber
streets
to the splash of
smiling bodies
churning, swirling,
in the shimmering crystal water
dissolved in village
green.
Their thoughts flee unseen
down dimlit alleys
building barricades of love
to bar the passage of blind hostility;
the time of flowers is at hand
the tribes of coral-colored gypsies
have descended
from the hills
to blot the games with billboards
of awareness.

III

Playing
the mad music of alive
on violins of cosmic energy

they
run through streets
turning pushcarts into apples
and mending holes in old men's shirts.
The merchants
standing in their doors
scream their indignation
with
the bellow panting of bald cigars.
Faces red
with neck veins bulging
they stamp their feet in
hollow fury
at the impertinence of love
between nine and five.
"What is the meaning
(of all this)"
one mumbles around the chomped-down end of a
fine Havana
ten dollar bill.
The children of the flowers
laugh
and dance through the plastic
rain forest
along one wall.
They go
from shop to shop
spreading good Karma.
The merchants
close their shops
with strings of summer flowers
feet dancing unaided
to the sounds
of the mad calliope-player.

IV

Who are
the Children of the Flowers?
They gather in small tribes
among the cliffs—
children of the chemical goddess.
I
the ego
is dead

killed during its last hysterical
ravings
to become we.
Words are nothing
lost
amidst sunlit fields of
empty water towers.
It is whispered among the trees
and through the
swirling ocean mist
that the time of flowers
is at hand.
Rocks upon the hillside
are
scattered of their own volition;
fish hawks glide among
the cliffs
searching for the memory
of a dying youth.
The tide is sweeping inland
the ancient sea walls crumble
before the cleansing sea.
We
are the Children of the flowers—
the Children of the flowers
are
now.

I was enormously impressed with the poem and said so. Sonny was happy to give it to me for publication. We took a few-minutes break during which he rolled up and lit a "joint." We then resumed our discussion.

LY–To go back to the community reaction thing—why do you think middle-class people are so hostile toward hippies?

S–Mr. Jones is hostile in large part because he sees joy and happiness where joy and happiness shouldn't be. He isn't so much worried about it for himself, but he's worried about it for his sons and daughters. Because Mr. Jones is basically not a happy person. Mr. Jones comes home at night, he's tired—he has a beer, he watches TV, and goes to bed. He gets up the next morning and goes through the same thing. Mr. Jones is caught up in a very depressing sort of life and he knows that his children would say that he is not basically a happy man. Mr. Jones drinks too much. He gets pissed off a lot. He grumbles and complains a lot.

And then he sees these people out there having fun. Mr. Jones doesn't believe, because he's very skeptical, that they're really happy. But he's afraid that his sons and daughters will see "the flower children" and believe that they really are happy. Perhaps his children do not want to grow up and be grumbling and mumbling like Mr. Jones. They may want to go out dancing in the streets and do what they want to do.

Right here on the East Side, if you want to speak about a very local matter, we're living in what basically is a ghetto. Predominantly Negro, Ukrainian, Puerto Rican, and hippie. Next to the hippies, the Puerto Ricans are the latest arrivals, so they're the poorest. And the ones with the most frustrations to take out on someone. They're pretty well boxed in and they don't have too much of a chance.

The hippies have been condemned by society, particularly since the Tompkins Square incident. That kind of showed the Puerto Ricans down here that the Establishment police say it's all right to hit a hippie. The hippies are bad. It's giving them a scapegoat. They can hit without getting hit back. There are no gangs of hippies walking the streets with switchblades who are going to, you know, get revenge. And now that they've seen that the police can beat hippies, they've found out that the law probably won't get after them for beating up a hippie or two—or cutting them. That's how you get this natural violent reaction.

LY–Where do you see the movement heading?

S–I see a lot of people coming to the rather obvious conclusion that cities are an unnatural place to live. Cities breed hostility. Cities as a human environment are architecturally negative. I think a lot of hip people are coming to the conclusion that the cities, for them at least, are a very unnatural way to live. And people who have the kind of ideas I've been telling you about have decided to get out into small tribes, find an open area of open land or woods somewhere, do their thing, and live in the country.

My tour of the East Village had tuned me in to various significant sights, sounds, and problems of the movement in urban areas. I was impressed with the eloquence of some of the "love-seekers" and frankly dismayed with the chaos, poverty, and violence that dominated much of the scene. There was little stability or permanence. The city "tribes" seemed to be quasi and feeble efforts at community.

There were no active, even slightly organized efforts toward communities of the type I had heard existed, for example, in San Francisco's Haight-Ashbury district. The country hippie scene in the East was also apparently very underdeveloped.

In some respects, the New York hippie scene appeared to be a loosely organized camp or staging-area for the more evolved West Coast scene. All hippie eyes seemed to be turned West toward the meccas of Haight, Golden Gate Park, L.A., and the Nirvana of California's highly touted hippie rural communities. I planned to visit them on my return to California and looked forward with great anticipation to my trip through these greener pastures of the hippie world.

CHAPTER NINE

Holiday Lodge

THE SURGE TOWARD THE COUNTRY hippie life of communities and away from the cities was rampant in New York and other big cities. As Sonny put it, "Cities have too many sharp edges."

Two California hippie communities I had heard a great deal about all over the country were Holiday Lodge in the city of Ben Lomand, a community just north of Santa Cruz, California, and Morningstar, a community about 70 miles north of San Francisco. Both were on my itinerary, combined with a sojourn in the capital city of the hip world—Haight-Ashbury.

The trips were planned with Gridley. When I returned from my New York trip, we had many lengthy and valuable discussions. We were now really "partners." It was clear to both of us that he was my primary consultant and guide. Our association was for the most part direct and "out-front." There was, however, a touch of conflict between us because of my negative views on drug use. Most of the time I was able to keep my feelings below the surface of expression. In a subtle way, however, Gridley and his gang were trying to get me to use drugs—"so you'll see where it's really at."

The only concessions I had made was that by this time I was not "paranoid" about being around "my partners" when they used pot and acid. For some reason I was no longer especially nervous about their drug scene. The people I was now communicating with daily—particularly Gridley and the group—were "stoned" most of the time. I could no longer detect whether they were high or not because drugs were such a "normal" part of their condition. This pattern of drug and personality fusion was especially true of Gridley. Acid and pot were such integral parts of his life that he couldn't discern any differences in his feeling state. "I really don't know anymore whether there is a separation between the acid and me. I know I feel good most of the time now."

I felt that at some point within the context of my research, in spite of my anti-drug position, it was necessary for me to try some marijuana to more clearly understand this widespread aspect of the hippie scene. One day while in the company of the group I made an abrupt decision to turn-on to the "joint" being passed around. We were in an abandoned house that was rented by a hippie friend. It served as a temporary headquarters for the now floating Strawberry Fields. About five people in the circle were talking and passing around the marijuana cigaret. Instead of blurting out my usual "no thanks," I took a puff on the "joint."

It was acrid, strong, and more distasteful than a regular cigaret. My main hangup was the fact that I did not smoke ordinary cigarets and consequently did not know how to inhale. One member of the group began to draw the marijuana smoke up through a cardboard cylinder that he had made especially for this purpose. I had about five or six pulls on this cylinder of marijuana smoke.

It seemed to produce a mild high. My time-span concept was affected. I began a story about something and stopped somewhere in the middle of it. About fifteen minutes later someone said, "Hey, man, you didn't finish that story." I remarked that this was the first time in twenty years that that had happened. Everyone laughed.

The other scene I remembered vividly during that afternoon was a wild dance to a Ravi Shankar sitar record performed by 17-year-old Wanda. All she was wearing were flowing flowery colored silk pants. Her topless dance and the whole scene was, I had to admit, rather provocative.

On my way home I questioned myself about sinking into the malaise and excesses of the hippie scene. Of course, I honestly believed that my brand of research involved true participation-observation and that this was the only valid way to operate. Yet the requirement of tuning-in and the seductiveness of a series of situations was over-involving me in behavior inimical to my own values and life style. The overriding consideration, I decided, was that if I was going to research the scene in a valid way I had to join in on much of the action.

The next day, Saturday, Gridley and I took off in a rented station wagon for points north. Our research plan was to include trips to the hippie communities of Ben Lomand, Morningstar, and Haight-Ashbury.

On our way to pick up two girls in Gridley's group, Wanda and Ginger, Gridley stopped on the Pacific Coast Highway at a friend's house. He apparently purchased a bag of grass. When he returned to the car he rolled and lit one, took a few puffs, and offered me a drag. I told him that the one joint I had puffed at was sufficient for my research and that I really had no interest in smoking pot again. This seemed to disturb him, although he didn't say anything at the time.

The girls had been staying at Ginger's family's home. They were silly and giggly when we picked them up. According to Ginger, "Man, we just blew some beautiful, strong pot." We all piled into the station wagon with sleeping bags and other camping gear and headed north.

We arrived at Big Sur that night around 11 p.m. The Gorda hippie community had, according to a friend of Gridley's that we met, been demolished by the police. It was desolate and fenced off near the road. We later learned that the people who lived there had simply spread out farther into the hills.

We stopped at Hot Springs in Big Sur—the home of Esalen, a hotel complex that was one of the several philosophical weekend lecture centers that had sprung up in California. It was a weekend affair for many real and pseudo intellectuals who sought to participate in seminars with such psychological luminaries as Fritz Perls, George Bach, and Abraham Maslow. Interestingly, the management of the bars, kitchens, and other odd jobs was handled by hippies. Gridley knew most of these people.

We stopped at the hotel for coffee and learned from a friend of Gridley that there was supposed to be a hippie wedding party that night somewhere in Gorda—in the hills. We all got back into the station wagon and went on a search for the wedding. We scoured the winding coast highway roads within a radius of 25 miles and did not find the party. (We later heard more about the wedding from other hippies at Ben Lomand and elsewhere. I never met a person who had actually attended the wedding and I concluded that it was a rumored event like many other "wild" non-happenings I heard about in my hippie travels.)

Around one a.m. we all decided to camp out in our sleeping bags by the side of the road. It was a beautiful, cool, and starry evening. The sound of the mountains and pounding surf were magnificent. In spite of this beauty my "civilization" hangups made the possibility of sleeping out on the ground not particularly appealing.

I decided to unroll my new, unused sleeping bag in the back of the station wagon. Gridley and Wanda stretched out in their bags on the ground, apparently made love, and went to sleep.

Ginger joined me in the station wagon. My middle-class square up-tightness came over me. In over four years of a happy marriage, I had not strayed once into unfaithfulness. Yet here I was in the middle of the night in a remarkably romantic setting with a rather attractive hippie girl, who was blatantly nude. Was the hippie philosophy of a sexual happening true, or were the usual middle-class values in operation? Was I a researcher or an actor on the scene?

Just the thought of moving into the situation produced enormous guilt and anger with myself. My partner apparently felt none of these feelings. It seemed that she would happily roll over and participate in a sex scene or just as readily roll over and go to sleep. I got up and took a walk.

If it can be placed in a research perspective, this one fragile experience that almost happened, combined with many other observations and discussions, convinced me that sex in hippieland was as described. It involved no possessiveness, special expectations, or the necessary romance that is associated with middle-class sexual behavior. It also became abundantly clear to me that my sincere research role was producing more personal involvement than I wanted. For me, "acting out" in the hippie culture was not resonant with my basic personality and value system.

Later during the trip I saw many other people casually involved in rather wide-open sexual scenes. The situation I was in and these other scenes validated the notion that sex in hippieland society was a free and rather uncomplicated expression if one was properly tuned-in to the values of the "new community."

Holiday Lodge—Ben Lomand

The following afternoon we arrived at the Ben Lomand hippie community. It was interchangeably called Holiday Lodge (the name of the motel that was originally on the grounds) or Ben Lomand, which was the name of the city in which the commune was located. It sprawled over about twenty rather rugged acres of uneven and desolate terrain. The various run-down buildings on the property were formerly part of the motel complex. The property was rented to the hippie community by a friendly landlord who apparently believed in what the people were trying to accomplish.

There were approximately forty people who lived there regularly. On weekends the population would sometimes rise to one or two hundred. People who stayed overnight had to be accepted guests of a regular resident.

Essentially, the community was organized for people to

"do their own thing." There were cliques of people of both sexes living together in the different cottages. Some were actually legally married families with children. One group was a six-piece rock band.

Each clique seemed rather separate from the total. In fact, the lack of togetherness was one of the things most deplored by the overall group. The total community was not especially friendly to visitors but somehow our group, because of Gridley's reputation, was positively accepted.

We all went our separate ways to do "our thing." Gridley became involved in a discussion with a rather beautiful girl named Michelle. She had formerly been a fairly successful Hollywood starlet who found "the games and the plastic society complete bullshit." After several extensive acid trips, she went "into the woods of Big Sur alone sometimes for weeks." She had found a temporary resting place at Ben Lomand.

The girls, Wanda and Ginger, were quickly attracted to the swimming facility at Holiday. There was a beautiful waterfall and creek that ran through the property. The swimmers were all nude and abandoned themselves to the natural environment.

I began to probe people I met about the organization of the commune. At first I talked to a frail girl named Cora. She had apparently been living there about two months and liked it. She described other communities she had lived in that practiced Zen and other cultural emphases. By comparison she found this one "the most satisfying."

Fully aware of the stigma of the leadership concept, I began to probe Cora about the leadership at Holiday. The "emotional center" of the community, she told me, was located in a young man I will call Gary and his wife Sue.

I was taken to see Gary. We tuned-in to each other rather rapidly. He was a slim young man, 28 years old, and about 5′ 9″. He told me that his long hair was especially kept that way "to get people's attention. Then I can rap with them."

He told me that prior to his starting Ben Lomand he had

had a complete psychotic break. I later affirmed through talking to the director of an unusual mental hospital community in the area that "when Gary was brought in he was totally out of it. He sat in a catatonic fetal position for many months." Apparently LSD and Holiday Lodge were responsible for Gary's salvation.

Gary gave me an extensive rundown of the social conditions and life experience that brought him to Holiday Lodge.

G–A group of us who have been together for over two years started the commune. We first gathered together because we were all interested in the same things. We were all interested in our spiritual growth. First it was just a couple of us, then it kept building up. The first year we were together, we lived in bachelor apartments in the city of Ben Lomand.

I don't think we formed because we were dissatisfied with society. I think that man, all human existence, is on a path—a spiritual process of breaking down limitations and becoming perfection. And our goal is toward a higher consciousness. I grew up with certain ideas and certain ideals. They were good because they were the only ones I knew. I was raised with them. I had to believe in them. You have to believe in something.

I grew up and got to the point where I was making $300 a week, had a new car, and was married. I managed bars and hotels in Hollywood, Hawaii, Carmel, Sausalito. I even thought I was going into real estate. I was going to get my real-estate license just to get even more money. But there was something missing. I could see that I was getting farther away from something. Rather than fulfilling myself I was becoming more empty. And then I got a divorce. I finally said, "Well, it wasn't worth it." Nothing was worth it. I went on kind of a destruction thing: "Well, if this is all life has to offer me, well, screw this. I'm gonna go out swinging." So man, I started taking all kinds of speed pills and then I started smoking grass and taking acid. I went on a total "trying-to-blow-my-mind thing." I was taking acid and I began to recognize a new self; I didn't even really understand it. I found that I was great. I recognized that if I centered myself into being, I could be Einstein or anything I wanted.

I was still trying to break away from my old role. Eventually I went down to Big Sur. I lived in the woods, in the stumps of trees. I really blew my mind. By blowing my mind I mean I had a total breakdown—a breakdown to where I even lost the awareness of this earth even existing. I broke myself down to one light—to my soul. And it was from that point that I chose to put myself back together piece by piece. And each piece that I put back together would be a piece that I liked and wanted. And so . . .

LY–Was all this through LSD?

G–It was definitely through LSD that I did this. It might have eventually come anyway. LSD just made it happen that much quicker. I was pushing for a breakdown because I was looking for a whole new identity.

Other people here were in the same bag. My brother-in-law was a junior in college, majoring in physics. The same thing happened to him. There's another kid here; he's got a mechanical engineering degree. There's another kid that was living with us a while back who was a junior at Stanford, majoring in music. And many more.

Well, I was lucky—I found a place where there was a woman that knew where I was at with myself. It was up at Bridge Mountain, a mental health community. She helped me put myself back together. And so, everything that I'm putting out here is partially what I learned from her—running this kind of a foundation. I was totally psychotic when I got there.

Let me explain where I was when I came to Bridge Mountain. I was at a place in myself where every possible fantasy that exists in the world was my reality, except earth. Earth was the only thing that I didn't want to look at. I recognized that all the other worlds were as real as this one. And so I couldn't give this one any more power than I could give them. And I was afraid to give this experience—earth experience—any power. You can see the insanity?

I was at a point where I walked around for several weeks in the woods of Big Sur thinking that I was dead. When people would come up to me and tell me that I was all right, I thought I was creating them just to convince myself that I was still alive. I would ask somebody if they knew what I was talking about, you know. I was talking to all these other worlds that nobody knew. The simplest way I can describe it would be like in the Bible where it says that God created us in his image. Only that our souls are creators, I was creating the pictures I wanted.

It's like this: I realized that my soul was nothing but a creator making pictures. Now, the picture for me is earth sharing its realities and its experiences. And I believe that the love things that we're all sharing is what we believe to be real together. But yet this is where my whole life comes in now. I devote it to making people have better pictures, or make their pictures more beautiful. I believe that if we all find out that we have this in common, then we can create beautiful pictures for each other.

LSD has given me two of the most crucial things in my life. One of them is I recognized that the spirit lives on forever. Once you realize that your soul lives on forever, you can't really have that much that you could want because you've got forever to have it. And so, this releases a lot of tension.

Also, like Einstein's theory of relativity, we know that this chair is energy. We know that our bodies are energy. And we know that the air between us is energy. But coming to a state of consciousness where you can see it in a relationship, well, I believe this is where Christ walked from. He was in such a relationship with relativity that he could look at the energy and raise or lower the vibrations in it. He could walk on water, or, in the picture world I was talking about, he could manifest pictures he was holding in his soul. He could heal people from just the perfect picture that he had of them.

When I was down in Big Sur, I saw some amazing things. I saw some people who were very much in harmony with energy. By that I mean that they would do things like run down cliffs falling end over end and get up at the bottom without having a scratch. It was only because they were that much in harmony with everything. They were flowing with everything. One of the first frightening things that I really recognized when I was messing around with LSD was—I don't even like to mention it—but it did straighten me out. It put me into where I didn't really screw with it anymore after that. I disintegrated a couple of moths, you know, just *psssznt*. [He waved his arm like he was casting a spell.]

LY–Would you elaborate a little on that experience?

G–Well, like everybody trips out on acid trying to blow each other's minds. I was showing this kid and said, "Well, you think that's cool, watch this," and *psssznt*. I really disintegrated these moths and it blew his mind and put everybody on a bummer.

LY–Were other people there? Where did this happen?

G–Down in Monterey.

LY–That's wild. You actually saw the thing happen?

G–Yeah. It blew my mind, too. I mean I was just like I was just feeling, "Wow, man, it feels great! I can do anything!" I was on a real power thing—ego-power thing.

LY–You had used some acid at that time?

G–I was on acid then.

LY–How many trips would you say you've had?

G–I've only taken about 10 acid trips.

LY–Is that right? That's unusual. Most people on the scene take many more.

G–Yeah, this is why people are screwing up. Each acid trip you take, man, gives so much to you—you've gotta come back and work it out. It's just laid out, man, and you've got about 8 months work ahead of you.

LY–To put it together?

G–To read, to meditate. Yeah, to put it together. Right. If you keep taking acid you just keep piling so much homework on you that it's all wasted—it's no earthly good.

SUE [Gary's wife]–When you go back to the acid all the time for the experience, instead of trying to work it out, it's like you make a whole central point of your life out of acid.

G–Yeah. Right. You're giving acid more power than your soul. You're setting acid on a shrine. You're not setting your own soul on a shrine.

LY–In other words, in a way, you're talking about acid—properly—as a vehicle rather than an essence?

G–Remember one thing clearly. Even this place here, this community, is only a vehicle. The first six months I came down from those mountains, my new wife Sue and I had to learn a whole new trust thing. For example, we wouldn't take any money. Like we'd go out and hoe weeds, not for money, but just to be doing it—just to prove this point that life will provide. What you put into life you get out of it. Of course, we had times when we doubted this and we went hungry. But we kept our picture in a positive light.

S–As long as we believed it, it worked.

G–It worked. This was a very trying time for us because we had times when we had doubts.

LY–How long have you been married to Sue? This is your second wife?

G–Right. Sue and I have been married about a year.

LY–So you met her about the time you came down from the mountain?

G–Yeah, we've been together just a little longer than that. So this was the first thing we learned—this whole new trust and believing in life.

It was beautiful because like the first couple of months

we were there we were like smiling at people all the time. Like a lot of them would turn their heads, but we just kept smiling at them and gradually they were too embarrassed not to smile back. This is why I choose to wear long hair and stuff because more people look at me than if I had short hair. So it gives me more of a chance to smile at people.

I believe that part of what originally made me go insane was recognizing that every living soul is right. Every man on the whole earth has been right and this was hard for me to accept. I've done so much judging on people and this and that. So, I had to say, "Well, I forgive myself because I didn't know any better."

People are always hitting themselves. It's like the whole mind thing. They're trying to kill that ego. They're trying to destroy that thing that makes them do that, man. And everybody does it. It's the only way they know how to love because they've got themselves so limited that they have to explode.

LY–How would you describe the concept of what's happening here at Holiday Lodge? What are you attempting to do?

G–We're not going for any end product. This is just an experience. This is why we won't even officially name the place 'cause it doesn't matter. We choose to come here and to live together and to learn together. And here's what we have learned. Some people are strong in being aware. Like a lot of people come down here and they think they're just gonna lay around and eat and get high and that's where it's at. I love them too much to support the laziness in them. I know that functioning, loving to work and loving each other is much greater where it's really at.

LY–You're not going to reinforce their symptom, in a sense?

G–I can't support people falling victim to different things like that. You know, victim to—like, "Here I am, I'm turned on, man. I just lay here and let life happen." No, it's much greater than that. It's love to work and it's love to be functioning. We haven't had to kick one person out yet. This is the most astonishing thing. We're so strong in our belief that people remove themselves if they're not ready to go with it yet. One of the things we've been doing here is rotating responsibility among the houses. Each person for one day is responsible for running the whole place. We try to give him a stronger sense of responsibility. We hope they learn to assume the total responsibility every day.

LY–How would you define leadership here from your viewpoint?

G–I'd say about a quarter of the people here are very strong. We all know that leadership exists in everybody. We don't pick a leader here because people would say, "Oh, he's the leader, he'll take care of it." It gives them an excuse not to be strong themselves.

We don't put signs up about rules and this and that, because that's like putting a sign up to not do what you have to do. And so this is the thing that we keep laying down every time somebody comes up with like, "Well, here, I don't want to be responsible." We go "NO," and we lay it right back on them. This is part of what the whole school is. The experience here at Holiday is that we're building strong people by laying responsibility back on them to make them strong and aware people.

LY–Well, what if they give you kind of a big hassle about it?

G–Well, usually when you're dealing honestly and speaking the truth straight to people, you don't get that many bad reactions.

LY–What is the sex life like of people in this situation?

G–I'm married. I'm very happy with my wife. In our relationship we belong to life and we just choose to travel together through this experience. If she chooses to go off and travel with someone else, or something, it's not for me to doubt because she must feel that there's a greater need for learning something there. We haven't been confronted with this. We have no jealousy. We have no doubt in each other and we've never had another person since we've been together. We haven't had to. It's just that we enjoy being together. We enjoy traveling together because we're learning things together.

With some others it's just like the pendulum—they came from an extreme of sexual up-tightness and they're going through the other extreme. I believe that if they balance it out, they'd come back basically to what I said. I have a strong love for everybody but yet I still do choose to travel with my own wife. I don't need anybody else. You can't build security in each other. Or you can't say, "Here. I love you. Here's my soul, be responsible for it," you know. I came up with a phrase about a week ago and it goes like this. "I will never fall in love again because I can only be love." How can you fall into something that you are in total? I won't give my soul away. Falling in love does imply kind of a slavish attitude, doesn't it? It's like falling victim. It's like falling into a pool you can't get out of again. My wife and I work a whole day to turn ourselves on to that day. Like making ourselves happy so that when we come together at night, we can share this feeling of love.

Gary, his wife Sue, and I went on a tour of the community. It was Sunday and there were many visitors, including the landlord. He was an elderly man who seemed to enjoy the use of his property by the people who were "searching."

Down by the beautiful stream, around ten people—men and women—were happily swimming in the nude. Among them were Ginger and Wanda. Most of the people seemed natural and comfortable with their nudity.

We stayed overnight to attend the community meeting scheduled for the following day. The next morning after breakfast, all of the members of the community gathered on the lawn for the meeting that was led by Gary. The session was much like the one I had attended in Big Sur. At first many gripes were aired and discussed.

At one point a critical conflict emerged around the use of

the commune's main house. The rock band that lived in the commune encountered a large number of people who wanted to have a meditation room in the main house. The main house was also the locale where the band practiced.

Marty, the leader of the rock group, pouted. "Well, if you wanta have a meditation room, go have a ball. I'll take the musical equipment out . . ."

G–Don't fall victim to it, Marty.

M–I'm not fallin' victim to it; I'm telling you, I don't wanta hassle it. Because I can groove anyhow and I don't want to come down to your bullshit. I hope you find it through that meditation and you better, 'cause I'm movin' my music out for you to do it.

G–People don't want to meditate twenty-four hours a day and they don't want to play music twenty-four hours a day. There's that many hours in a day, so why can't we have both there?

M–That's what I say—why can't there be both? Make room for both.

Gary successfully mediated the meditation-music encounter by arranging a schedule for each faction to use the facility at different times. The group then discussed cleaning responsibilities, the "people who did nothing," and the difficulty of collecting the rent that was supposed to come more freely and easily from each individual "camper."

The arguments over various details did seem to clear the air. But I was rather surprised to find that this celestial community was managed somewhat like a coed boy scout camp. The issues discussed seemed rather trivial compared to the "spiritual trip" Gary had taken me on in our lengthy discussion.

After warmly saying our good-byes to Gary and the other friends we had made at Holiday later that afternoon, we got in our car and headed for Morningstar.

Ginger got into the car topless. After a while I felt sufficiently uncomfortable to ask her to put on her blouse since we were now heading through some small towns. Ginger resisted and said she felt more natural that way. Finally a group decision prevailed and she put on a blouse. The incident provoked a discussion in the car which was of some relevance to the scene and how I felt at the time. (I tape-recorded parts of our encounter.) Mainly, I queried Ginger about her "trip" —which I felt to be somewhat phony, like some others I had seen in my travels.

LY–What are you really up to, Ginger? I'm impressed with Gridley's trip, with Michelle's trip, with Gary's trip, with a whole variety of other people I've talked to in New York and elsewhere. But your behavior is kind of phony. This is part of my response to you. You haven't said or done anything that would lead me to believe that you're doing anything more than fooling around with some kind of adolescent drug reverie. I feel you're a pretty plastic person, kind of a "put on."

GRIDLEY–I get the same feeling. I don't use the same words that Lew uses. To me the term "put on" implies a kind of a knowledge about what you're doing. I feel that a lot of people like you who are taking acid for the first time get blasted open to something new. When you're under acid you feel a certain way about it and then when you come down to a kind of reality you hang on to the memory, maybe too long.

LY–When I see you in the nude, I see kind of a middle-class broad who's taken her clothes off and is watching the way men react. You're simply showing off, or something like that, like a big kid.

GRIDLEY–Yeah, I feel that too, and I see that you do a lot of things to cause a reaction.

LY–Would you cop [admit] to that?

GINGER–Not to what you said, Lew. I don't feel that at all. But what Gridley says. Sometimes I do do things to watch people's reaction.

LY–The first couple of times I think you kind of went into a number for shock value or for demonstration.

GINGER–When was this?

LY–Oh, you know, back a few months ago when I first came up to Gridley's place. For example, Gary said to me, "I wear long hair and this cap because when I go somewhere people react." And he said, "I want to click with people so they look at me and I can smile back at them." That's great and I can see the point of it. For example, in part Gridley dresses the way he does for that purpose. You role-play rebellion.

GINGER–No matter what you two say, I feel I'm being myself and I feel comfortable with it. Like I've unraveled enough shit about myself through acid that I can know that this is really the way I'm feeling and I'm not covering it up by a ton of nonsense.

LY–While we're on this little tour of our feelings about each other, I'm certainly vulnerable. Does anybody have any arguments with me?

GRIDLEY–Only one thing that I've had kind of a discordant thing with you since it happened. When you said—someone passed you a joint and you said that they didn't need to pass it to you. That if you wanted any you would ask for it. I thought that was kind of amusing. I mean, like you know, you offer me chocolate milk or you offer me sandwiches or you offer me conversation the same way that other people would offer you a joint. And to say, "don't offer it to me unless I ask for it" is to limit their side of things. If someone wants to they should feel free to be able to offer pot to you and you should feel free to say "No" without being defensive about it.

LY–I see your point.

I wasn't completely honest with Gridley. I didn't want to smoke any pot for several reasons. First, it was illegal, and secondly, I didn't like even the one little marijuana experience I had. In general, I had no inclination to get high again. I enjoy the reality of life without drugs and I probably missed an opportune moment to "blow" Gridley's mind with that position. Our little talk, however, did clear the air among our group.

None of us had been especially overwhelmed by the Holiday commune. However, we drove on to Morningstar with great anticipation. According to all we had heard, and some I had read, it was supposed to be a truly ideal and beautiful hippie community.

CHAPTER TEN

The Morningstar Bummer

MORNINGSTAR IS LOCATED outside of the small city of Sebastopol, about 70 miles north of San Francisco. It was founded by Lew Gottlieb, 43, a former member of the Limelighters musical group. Gottlieb founded Morningstar on the hippie principle that if people are given an opportunity to freely "do their thing" they will be happy and productive. His basic assumption was a usual one dominant in the hippie world that if people are given total freedom, leadership and planning will emerge from the group in a spontaneous fashion.

I had heard positive reports from many hippies who had been to Morningstar. It had also received a favorable mention in the *Time* magazine (July 7, 1967) issue on hippies:

> An hour's drive north of San Francisco, in apple-growing country near Sebastopol along the Russian River, some 30 to 50 country hippies live on a 31-acre ranch called Morning Star. . . . The ranch is owned by Lew Gottlieb, 43, former arranger, composer, and bassist for the folk-singing Limelighters, who has his hippie followers hard at work—rarest of all hippie trips—growing vegetables for the San Francisco Diggers.
>
> Most Morning Star colonists avoid acid. "I'd rather have beautiful children than beautiful visions," says a

> tanned clear-eyed hippie girl named Joan. That hippies can actually work becomes evident on a tour of the commune's vegetable gardens. Cabbages and turnips, lettuce and onions march in glossy green rows, neatly mulched with redwood sawdust. Hippie girls lounge in the buffalo grass, sewing colorful dresses or studying Navajo sand painting, clad in nothing but beads, bells, and feather headdresses. (Not everyone is a nudist—only when they feel like it.) A shaggy sheepdog named Grass plays with the hippie children, among them a straw-thatched 17-month-old boy named Adam Siddhartha.
>
> The new-found trip of work and responsibility reflected in the Morning Star experiment is perhaps the most hopeful development in the hippie philosophy to date. . . .*

When we drove into the parking lot in the center of the commune, for no reason that I could at first identify I had a sharp feeling of fear. People of various ages, in standard hippie costumes, were sprawled all over the grounds. Their facial expressions varied from grimness to sickliness to pure hostility. No one greeted us with anything resembling friendliness.

I chatted briefly near our car with a fellow from New York City, who quickly told me about his drug-addict background, his time in prison, and his new-found self-administered LSD rehabilitation program. Most of the people seemed to be wandering around aimlessly.

A nude girl went running down the road flopping in all directions. Some of the young men chided her about her "sloppy figure." She snarled back that she was just doing "her thing" and they could "go fuck" themselves.

I planted myself in the center of the commune near a rock square that had once been a water well and chatted with some of the people sprawled on the ground. One attractive girl about eighteen, clad in a micro-mini shift, told me about the greeting she had received at Morningstar.

GIRL–I got raped here when I first arrived by two spade [Negro] guys.

*Courtesy TIME, The Weekly Newsmagazine; copyright Time Inc. 1967.

LY–Didn't anybody help you?

GIRL–Yeah, they helped me. They took me to the hospital. I got some shots and stuff like that at the free clinic in San Francisco. That's all.

LY–You mean two guys balled you, one after another, and no one stopped them?

GIRL–No, one didn't get me because I put up too much of a fight.

LY–Are the guys still here?

GIRL–. . . I guess they were leaving the farm or something and they didn't have no intention of ever coming back—it was my first hour here.

LY–Nobody would call the police on them?

GIRL–I didn't. I'm not going to, either.

A young man about nineteen entered the conversation. His name was Pete.

P–There's like not too much of that—calling of the cops.

LY–Will people join in and protect someone who is being attacked?

GIRL–Yes, I think so.

P–Well, like they'll try to but most of them won't get into any violent thing. Like there's some people that live here that are violent and like they sort of get pissed off because a lot of people here won't get into violence, you know? They see themselves as protectors. But I don't believe you can fight violence with violence. If you just show somebody that you love them and that you're gonna be their friends, there's no need to, like you know, fight.

LY–Well, if a guy's coming at you with a knife there's no time to . . .

P–Right. If somebody came at me with a knife I would have to defend myself. But I wouldn't defend myself to the point of hurting the other guy. I would just try my best to do my thing under the circumstances without getting violent myself.

About that time I saw a student of mine, Rick, who was taking his own trip and at the same time had agreed to assist me with the research. He had been at Morningstar for several days. Rick was about twenty and very idealistic about the movement. He had dropped out of Valley State College in his senior year and joined the movement. He was a rather loving, humble, and intelligent person.

We talked a while and he confirmed the feelings I had of "bad vibrations" and violence at the love camp. "Last night we had a community meeting about potential violence. . . . There's a spade cat here named Mystery who threatens everyone with assault. He, along with about ten or fifteen other Negroes from Fillmore [the Negro ghetto in San Francisco], literally believe the Diggers' invitation posted in their Black Free Store and decided to come to Morningstar. They have no concept at all or belief in the hippie philosophy. They're all up here drinking wine and messing around. Last night all hell almost broke loose. There are some real bigoted hippies here who actually use expressions like 'The niggers should be put back into slavery'!" This apparently amazed Rick.

As we were talking I heard what I thought were gunshots. I didn't believe my ears—until Rick confirmed for me that it was in fact gunfire! Apparently some demi-hippies visiting Morningstar were having target practice.

Rick told me about a big house on the property that was dominated by the Negro group he had described. I decided to walk up and investigate.

The sight was bizarre. There were some young white teenage hippies, boys and girls, milling around. A "soul" jazz record was blaring. Several Negroes were dancing, obviously very drunk. A hefty Negro man, who I later determined was Mystery, leered at me. "Who the fuck are you?"

I introduced myself for some unusual reason as Dr. Yablonsky instead of Lew. He yelled out to the entire group, "The Doctor's here, anyone sick?" He apparently assumed I was some kind of volunteer medical doctor. I then told him as clearly as I could that I was a sociologist writing a book

"What the fuck do you have in that briefcase?" I told him about the tape recorder. He checked it out and was convinced I was a cop. He took some more swigs out of his wine bottle and became more belligerent. I gracefully moved out of a scene that from past experience I knew had all the potential of erupting into violence.

I felt (possibly in my paranoia) that the only safe place for me was back in the "Village Square." When I got back to it, I noted that Gridley, Wanda, and Rick had drifted off into other areas of the commune. Pete was still seated there and he began to tell me about his trip and his life and times at Morningstar.

P–The other day I was thinking that maybe I could do more for "the movement," if you want to call it that. You know, like help people—make money somehow—feed people—help clothe people. The whole scene is to live as brothers—in love.

LY–What was the place like when you got here? I'd be interested, for example, if you'd rap a little about that and any changes you've seen take place here.

P–Most changes are within the people themselves. There's a big influx of people coming in and out all the time. And there's only like about thirty people who really live here. Even though sometimes on weekends they feed two hundred people.

LY–Where does the money come from?

P–Well, the money comes from a lot of people who donate food. They grow food here, too, and they take some food like vegetables every Tuesday into San Francisco. They take it to the Diggers' Store in San Francisco and we get grain and bread sometimes in exchange. Another way money is made here—and I don't dig it—is by panhandling or begging. It's done in the parking lot. Like in Morningstar when a tourist comes, or someone who looks like a tourist, the first thing they do is ask, "Do you have any cigarets?" It's done maliciously at times. If a visitor has a nice car, everybody runs up for money. Like they'll say, "Do you have any loose change?" The spades hit people up for money, too, so they can buy wine.

LY–People actually beg for money?

P–Oh, yeah. Some people say, "I have to go make some money tonight for wine; I'll go panhandle in the parking lot." That's an attitude that strikes me wrong.

LY–How's this place organized? For example, how do you maintain cleanliness?

P–Well, the thing is you're supposed to clean up yourself. Nobody tells you to do it, but for your own health and comfort you know you should do it. And that's supposedly where it's at.

LY–Does it work?

P–No.

LY–Why not?

P–It works to a certain extent, but you know, things get dirty. Because there are so many people here and so many people coming in and out. Things just pile up. Animals are left here by people. They come in and they leave their pet dogs and cats. They figure it'll be better off here than with them. A lot of people come in for a day or two days and then split.

LY–How do you think the kids are being raised here—in your honest opinion?

P–The kids? There aren't too many kids, but I guess that they could be raised better.

GIRL–They could be watched better. They live okay, but they should be watched.

LY–They kind of roam around from what I can see—rather bored. What's the leadership like? I know that isn't the right word, but . . .

P–The leadership is Lew. He owns the place. He doesn't want to be known as "The Man" as he puts it—the cop, the Gestapo. If there has to be a decision made, people sort of go to him—you know, when they can't figure it out themselves.

LY–How do people feel about Lew?

P–Everybody loves him. Even the people here that are rowdy and like to fight and cause trouble love him. When Lew comes around they sort of calm down and respect him.

LY–What about fights? Are there many fights?

P–Well, nobody really fights, but like sometimes some servicemen come up and they don't dig the whole thing. They seem to believe that we're their enemy or something. And there has been trouble with cars being wrecked in the parking lot and a few shots being fired from the woods. And like my house that I live in was torn down completely, you know. People just went in there and tore it all down.

LY–Who did that?

P–Well, some servicemen.

LY–Why do you think they're so hostile?

P–I don't know. I guess once you've been in the service and like you've been in Vietnam and seen your buddies dying and all that it sort of does something to you. And like there are ex-servicemen that live on the farm around here. That's how they explained it to me. Like, to put it bluntly, you're really fucked-up after you get out for a while and like sort of hostile toward everybody and especially to somebody much different than you are—like hippies. So they think that we're so different. I don't believe there is such a big difference. I think maybe a lot of them would even dig doing it—like being this way in a community.

The point of this place is to live and be brothers and to share—commune, to share as brothers and to live happily in peace. You know what I mean? Like not to have to worry and be paranoid. You know what paranoia is? Well, there's certain fears like to walk down a street and to be afraid that you might be jumped or something in a bad neighborhood. Like it's nice to walk down a street and everybody coming your way says hello, you know, and be friendly, and you have a good feeling.

I've experienced that many times in San Francisco. Like

I would go out for a whole day, just meet fifty or sixty people, and just talk to them for five minutes or an hour and eat with them and get loaded with them and just have a really groovy, groovy time. And at the end of a day you have this feeling inside you, this love feeling that just can't be expressed. And like to me, once you experience that, like there's no room for any kind of hatred. Like people are people and they have moods and sometimes they do things that they don't want to do. You know, I'd like to be all good, but I can't—you know what I mean?

LY–What's bad with you?

P–Well, like I've said, everybody has their moods and things like that. It's hard for everybody to be kind to each other. It's like giving a lot, if you know what I mean. You don't have to give material things—food and clothing, which does help, but just like friendship on the streets to everybody.

LY–Do you feel that love is happening here at Morningstar?

P–Well, it's trying to. That's what it's here for. Like that's the purpose and there's a lot of love—but there's a lot of unlove, too.

LY–What fouls it up? Why is there unlove?

P–Well, fear mostly.

LY–Fear of what?

P–Well, there's—like what's happening now with these people in the big house. They're mostly colored people. But like it has nothing to do with race really. A lot of people are afraid of them. They get drunk and girls come by and they try to grab them. One girl got punched in the mouth the other day and she left the farm. This chick over here was raped and you know, that's were fear comes from.

As we were talking I felt compelled to switch off my tape recorder and attend to a little blonde child about four, who was wandering aimlessly about and crying. It wore a long green velvet gown that was filthy. The pathetic baby had one shoe on and one shoe missing. No one seemed to pay any attention to it. It appeared abandoned.

I went over and picked the baby up and hugged it. I became aware that the child smelled badly from urine and feces. I hugged it again. The little baby and I looked into each other's eyes and I'll never forget the child's simple words, "I'm lonely."

I asked someone about the child's parents and received a matter-of-fact reply that the baby's mother was "out in the woods freaked-out on acid."

I resumed my conversation with the young man as the baby stumbled up the hill. I told him:

LY–That thing got to me. This little kid is wandering around aimlessly. It is all wet and dirty. You know what that kid said to me, "I'm lonely." These kids are really not taken care of, are they?

P–A kid got run over yesterday. His mother had taken acid and she had left him with someone—she didn't know who. He was run over by a car, a dog bit him, and he was taken to the hospital. He's back today and fortunately, he's still alive.

LY–How did it affect people? Didn't anybody care?

P–Most people don't know about it.

LY–What? Most people don't know about it? Weren't there a lot of people upset or concerned?

P–I had a few friends who were near the baby. They took care of getting the baby to the hospital. And they were upset. In the rest of the community no one said anything about it.

Gridley returned about this time. I told him about my experiences and said that I had seen enough. I was completely turned-off by the anarchy, human desolation, and chaos I found at Morningstar.

I also related my fear of being there when night fell. I was pleased to learn that Gridley shared my feelings. He too was ready to leave. I told Gridley the story about the four-year-old child. He told me about a similar experience of his:

G–Man, when I went walkin' up to this house, here's this baby cryin', man, that's been left alone all day in filth. It hasn't been fed and it can't get any milk out of the bottle 'cause the nipple's fucked up. The baby hands me the bottle like, "Here, fix it." I tried and I gave it back to it. It wasn't fixed and it sucked on it for a while. And it gave it back to me again. I finally fixed it, man, and it was so cool. As soon as the baby knew that there was someone who was listenin' to it, it didn't cry or anything. But the people had just gone off and left it. You know, he's got his bottle and his paper bag, now he can have fun.

There are other problems here. I can tell you what goes on here without even being here a long time. Just walk into that kitchen and see the unbelievable filth. It was never this bad at our place. Food is holy, man. And what you put into your body is holy. And where you cook and prepare your food is as holy as any other place you go. And yet there was nothing there. There's no awareness here.

What has happened here is that Gottlieb has this place and is no doubt doing what I did at Strawberry. He's just letting people do whatever they want to do. There are no rules and no regulations. Maybe he thinks that this is the way he can abdicate the responsibility he assumed when he opened the place. His opening this place and saying "here it is" assumes that he knows what freedom's all about. It is a heavy undertaking to open up an atmosphere for freedom for people.

You see, I felt that way for a while at my community. I was the leader. They just made me be that. So what I did was I'd rant and rave and scream and yell and stomp and curse and shout and bad-rap people. I'd try to get them to think about and review why they were there and what was happening. Things'd be cool for a while. But like Gottlieb I never told anyone they had to leave—I would say, "I want you to leave, you motherfucker, I wish your ass was outta here. You're a drag. You're a bring-down to me and to yourself and to everybody around here." But that's cool and if he leaves for that reason, he should leave because he's not behind it enough to stay.

Gottlieb, we found out, was in L.A. But apparently the chaotic violent scene we were viewing was the normal condition at Morningstar. I repeated to Gridley and Rick that I definitely didn't want to stay until dark. As a kind of authority figure, I felt the fear that with all of the chaos at dark, someone might take a notion to take me on. Gridley and I gathered together Wanda and Rick, who were going to leave with us.

I felt a sense of great relief as we pulled out onto the main road on our way from Morningstar. At least Ben Lomand and Gorda, despite certain problems and negative conditions, were not as violent as Morningstar. Gridley, Wanda, Rick, and I began to discuss the Morningstar scene in the car. Rick was visibly upset about having to relate the negative views he had gathered during the time he was at Morningstar. He was, for personal reasons, trying to maintain an idealistic view of the total hippie scene.

LY–Let's put this situation in perspective. I've experienced many beautiful happenings, people, and ideas on the scene. So, speaking for myself, I'm not discouraged. But I think, for an honest book or report, we should not ignore negatives. Let's discuss these factors of Morningstar.

R–When you first come to Morningstar, it's cold. And you don't know anybody and nobody looks at you and nobody cares. They don't care who you are or where you are or tell you anything. The whole place has a very mobile population. It moves very quickly. There's only about six people who live there whom I'd consider to be really part of the community. They live on the outskirts. They have children. The children are fed early in the morning when they get up. I've seen the mothers feeding their children. The children are not usually in the center of the commune, but they're there. You seldom see them, just like their parents.

LY–What were your dominant feelings during your four-day stay? Did you feel fear, or love . . . ?

R–I never felt fear. I didn't feel much love except with a few individuals. The rest of the time it was just sort of indifference—just indifference—"I couldn't care less"—people sizing everybody up. Every time I tried to get near anyone I felt they slapped my face.

LY–In what way did you get your face slapped? Give me an example.

R–Oh, you're talking to somebody and they start talking about "slavery and those goddam niggers." And given my views on prejudices, it's very painful to me to find a hip person that's prejudiced.

One cat had a long black beard, beautiful beads, leatherwork all over him, and he was the cat that was blowing slavery. He said, "We should send the niggers back to Africa 'cause they're obviously meant to be slaves." He just knew nothing about love or people.

LY–Rick, what was the problem up at the big house?

R–I was told that there was a hassle when the people around the center house got together and decided that they didn't want people who drank wine and got drunk or were hostile around the place. They had a meeting to determine what they were going to do about it.

LY–Who are the people who drank wine and were hostile?

R–Mostly spades. Mostly spade cats from Fillmore—San Francisco.

LY–What are they doing up there in that house anyway—besides drinking wine and threatening people?

R–I don't know. There's a lot of freedom here. In the Black Diggers' store there's a sign stating "Diggers' Farm" with directions to Morningstar. Apparently some black people just came out to see what it was. They came and stayed. This spade cat they call Mystery has taken over that big house. What he does is when he doesn't like what somebody's doing he just tells 'em to get out, "you'll get out—now!"—and they leave, "yes sir!" type thing. He has total rule and people tremble in front of him. He's very dark and he has these beautiful eyes—people see him when he looks straight into their eyes. They get shaken up, terribly shaken up, and he can do anything.

Lew Gottlieb has never interfered with Mystery's total rule. His word is law—literally, it is the law. There are some turned-on people around the edges of Morningstar that stay away from the entire scene. They just come here for food. And they're doing their own things on the outside—very beautiful people.

The people in the center of this place where people think the action's going on blow my mind. Like I said, there are hippies here who are full-blown bigots! People who talk about killing cops, and there are people here who talk about putting the Negroes into slavery.

G–There are psychopathic people here. There is no leadership. The place is going to blow up, man, unless something is done now. And if it blows up, it's gonna fuck it up for our people, man, in a lot of places. It is Gottlieb's fucking responsibility to get back there now and clean house now.

R–Last night people in the center of the community, the ones who run the place, decided that they wanted to have a community meeting about people who drank wine. They're hostile, they're noisy, and they're not going anyplace. I don't see the other people growing either. But, okay, they do cook the food. They do a lot more work than the people who say they're growing. They're more down to earth. They can do menial things and they help keep the place running.

Anyway, they had this meeting and they were discussing whether they were going to throw the people who were drinking wine out. And it went out like, "You know, they're drunkards, and drunkards are like this." And then the people from the upper house came, the Negroes, and they heard what was happening and they started hassling the community. As soon as they started hassling, everybody fell apart and backed off from them. They were still in charge with their threats of violence.

They said that people who trip out on acid jump off trees, become monkeys, blow their minds, and are all screwed up. After the spades threatened violence the entire meeting fell apart. Everybody I spoke to said they were very frightened of all the spades. They mentioned the fuck-ups by name and every person they named was a spade. They didn't like wine-drinking people around 'cause they weren't going anyplace. I sort of feel they were using the spades as a scapegoat. They blame the spades who drink wine for all the ills of the community.

LY–It's somewhat like it is in the larger society.

R–That's right. That's why I say it's scapegoating.

G–Well, what is lacking is that they got together and nobody did anything. They talked about how bad it is but no one was able to overcome their own sociological neuroses about black people. No one was able to look a black man in the eye and say, "Listen, you black motherfucker, get your fuckin' ass outta here, man. We're not playing Charley's game here and if you want to play Charley's game with your bad-rappin' and shit just go play it somewhere else!"

R–You know, I got nothing but good vibrations from the black people there.

G–Well, I didn't man. One cat was gonna beat me up—kinda short, kinda fat, with one eye. One eye that wandered off and he was standing at the door and I went to him and I touched his arm like this and he jumped back and wanted to throw a punch at me. A complete violence game, man, I've seen it a thousand times in detention—in jails.

I said to him, "Are you afraid of me, brother?" He mumbled and didn't answer my question, and I said again, "Did you think I was going to hurt you?" and he carried on again.

LY–I had this experience. I went up there to the big house and I had my black briefcase with me. Somebody said,

"Are you the doctor?" And I thought maybe someone had mentioned that I was the doctor writing a book. Some of the people there thought I was a medical doctor. And then this guy shoved some wine in my face. I said, "I don't drink wine, no thanks." This kind of got him pissed off. I've been there and it's like "Oh, you hate niggers, eh? You son-of-a-bitch."

Then he said, "Let me see what's in the bag." I could have said, "The hell with you, none of your business." I decided to open up the bag and show it to him. He looked at it like it was property that he might be able to pawn. His reaction certainly wasn't what I expected to find in a hippie love community.

G–There's no such thing as Utopia. There's no such thing as perfection—in you or in society, man. You know that. Every other movement has always had to be so pure and wanted to make out, man, like it was perfect or groovy. That it was all love—flowers and flower children. Bullshit! Remember, no one ever said the trip was an easy one!

Hippie Communes: An Emotional Assessment

A return to the land and a natural environment by the hip people "turned-on" to nature is an admirable and adventuresome goal. However, the quick switch for city dwellers to this new way of life seems beset with complicated problems.

The central one is the hip view of leadership. No one seems to want any heavy authority telling them what to do. In fact, part of the reason for them being on the scene is to escape structures of government and leaders. Yet the avoidance of this natural law of human organization related to the need for a leader defeats the possibility of a successful community.

Since The Beginning, according to all recorded history, a select few in any tribe have assumed power and decision-making function. The ignorance of this by potential hippie "leaders" and "followers" has produced chaos and mass confusion in the communes that I have seen.

Non-compassionate, physically strong people fill the leadership vacuum and take over when there is anarchy. The hippie assumption that when "everyone does their thing" order will prevail doesn't seem to work. The inevitable psychopaths in the group, who have a thin veneer of "love" on the surface, begin to take advantage and push people around, including the natural, real spiritual leaders in the group.

Another devastating problem seems to be the socialization of children. With all the "cleanups" and rationalizations about their being in a more natural environment, children grow up better in defined social orders rather than in the hippie conditions of anarchy and chaos. Children hunger for boundaries to give meaning and style to their lives.

Parents in the hippie community are admittedly engaged in an intense search for identity and religious experience. This totally time-consuming effort that characterizes the hip community places children, in many cases, in an abandoned position. People freaked-out, or even mildly loaded on drugs, are not in my judgment sufficiently stable to teach children what they need to know about life. They are much too egocentric and self-involved.

An even more reprehensible practice is the giving of drugs like LSD and pot to unformed bodies and brains. This is a prevalent practice in the hip community. Pushing drugs into children, it seems to me, is done more to rationalize the doubts of the parents' *own* drug use than for the stated noble reason of "turning-on" children to a beautiful experience. Children need ego development, not ego reduction or destruction.

Children in the communes tend to be viewed as playthings—toys for the adults to enjoy while they are engaged in mind-bending or mind-expanding pursuits. They are adored and adorned with affection and trinkets; however, in the communities I observed, they are not cared for with the basic necessities of food, clothes, and adequate health facilities.

The health problem is another basic difficulty in the hip

communal experiments. People tend to defecate and urinate rather freely in their natural environment. Pet animals wander around often in a neglected filthy condition throughout the community. Food cooking and kitchen facilities are generally unsanitary. The resulting diseases of hepatitis and dysentery are natural consequences of this way of life.

The diet in most situations I have seen seems to be rather unhealthy. In their show of "back to nature," brown rice and other natural foods are eaten—but the dietetic balance is generally uneven.

The avowed goal is a society with minimum rules and restrictions. This seems to lead to license. Some people work hard and others do absolutely nothing but "their thing"—which may in this context legitimately involve 24-hour-a-day meditation. People raised most of their lives in a work-oriented culture are bound to have negative feelings on a deeper level about their self-indulgence or total indolence. This seems, in some cases I have observed, to intensify drug consumption.

A hypocritical dimension of the hippie community scene is the aggrandized rejection of materialism and the toys of American society that exists alongside of a predatory usage of food, clothes, and tools produced by middle-class America. It seems to me that if the hippie rural communities were to be totally sincere, they would begin from complete scratch on a bare piece of land and create everything they need (tools, food, clothes, etc.) from the natural environment. Or they should admit in a more honest fashion the use in communes of such staples as canned soup, vegetables, radios, hi-fis, and cars.

Aside from these criticisms related to certain hypocrisies and the ignorance of fundamental human organization, there is certainly some merit in these experiments. More of the people involved, especially the leaders, should take a clearer look at some obvious realities. They are not starting anew—they have physical and emotional sets for work, leadership, certain foods, and patterns of human interaction that have not (as yet) been wiped out or obliterated by acid and pot. Being the twentieth-century men and women that they inescapably are, they have fears, frustration, and in some cases violence under the surface of the natural mask of total freedom they attempt to wear on the surface.

An honest confrontation and acceptance of the social imprints that exist in their individual and group minds would enlarge the meaning, scope, and value of their experiments with a new community. Man has learned some things over thousands of years about solving health problems, raising children effectively, the processing of foods, and the proper use of machines. Why shouldn't the hippie communities benefit from the knowledge which is around them and in their guts and minds? Perhaps with less hypocrisy about *totally* dropping out and starting brand new, these experiments in tribal and communal living would flourish and prove of greater spiritual value to *all* of the people who are trying to love each other in a natural environment.

CHAPTER ELEVEN

Haight Is Love

"Haight-Ashbury is the largest undergraduate college in the psychedelic movement. Our successful graduate rate is higher than the Harvard Medical School."
Tim Leary

WHEN OUR WEARY TROUPE landed at the foot of Haight Street near Golden Gate Park, Gridley let out a howl of delight. "Wow! Dig all of the beautiful freaks." There was an electricity in the air. People *were* in motion. It was a phantasmagoria of bells, beads, Indian headbands, robes, flutes, and bizarre musical instruments of every description.

Hippies dressed in the wildest, most colorful, and unique clothes I had ever seen were standing on corners. Others were slowly walking, almost in a processional, up and down the fifteen blocks of Haight, the main street of the Haight-Ashbury district.

There were friendly, smiling panhandlers who weren't very aggressive about getting the loose change they requested from every hip or square passer-by. One bright young man facetiously entreated you to "take a hippie to lunch." On almost every street corner young hippies hawked underground newspapers like *Maverick*, the *San Francisco Oracle*, and the *Haight-Ashbury Gazette* to passing cars—generally full of gawking tourists.

Not everybody was on "the take." At several points loving entrepreneurs in hippie dress were freely passing out bread or cookies, and one young man was distributing peanut-butter sandwiches. This was a small distribution of food compared to the large pots and cans full of food distributed freely by the Diggers (a hip benevolent organization) daily in different locations of Haight.

Tourists in straight clothes were everywhere, slyly smiling at times and apparently more excited by the action than they would openly show. From a hip viewpoint, they too were "digging the scene."

The tourist invasion was informal at this time; however, in the early days of Haight's evolution, the Gray Line Company ran a tour in San Francisco called in their brochure "The only foreign tour within the continental limits of the United States." The guide's canned speech for the tourists as the bus glided through the area was a classic:

> We are now entering the largest hippie colony in the world and the very heart and fountainhead of the hippie subculture. We are now passing through the 'Bearded Curtain' and will journey down Haight Street, the very nerve center of a city within a city. . . . Marijuana, of course, is a household staple here, enjoyed by the natives to stimulate their senses. . . . Among the favorite pastimes of the hippies, besides taking drugs, are parading and demonstrating; seminars and group discussions about what's wrong with the status quo; malingering; plus the ever-present preoccupation with the soul, reality, and self-expression, such as strumming guitars, piping flutes, and banging on bongos.

The everyday residents of San Francisco have mixed feelings about Haight, or as a popular poster aptly identifies the culture complex: "Haight is Love." Generally a liberal city with its origins in the Gold Rush days, the city welcomes all. After all, it was the home of the International colony and the original topless craze. Despite this there appears an underground and sometimes vocal wish that the hippies would go away. The possibility of this happening in the near future is improbable in spite of a fair amount of police and other harassment.

There are several distinct yet interrelated scenes to be found in the Haight-Ashbury culture-complex. (1) The first is the open picture on the streets of Haight and the love-in patterns in the surrounding parks. These are the most apparent manifestations of the Haight hippie arena. (2) The second significant scene comprises the living arrangements: the tribes, communes, extended families, and pads that honeycomb the area. Within a radius of about a mile of the geographic center of the new community at Haight and Clayton, there are literally thousands of hippie pads or apartments. Most of these have a core live-in group of perhaps five to eight people. The remainder of sometimes up to twenty-five people are transients, who in the parlance have used the apartment as a "crash-pad." Hippies are hospitable and the "crash-pad" concept is an important part of their way of life. (3) Another significant situation is the community effort to develop a sense of identity and group affiliation. Here many of the high priests and philosophers of Haight, in cooperation with some straight professional people, have assumed the responsibility for developing cohesion, a sense of identification, and solving the social, emotional, health, and poverty problems of the emerging "new community."

The Street Scene and the Park

As indicated, the most apparent on-the-surface scenes are the sights and sounds of the street. Also, on any given day the adjacent park is clearly a hippie haven—almost entirely dominated by the hip residents of the new community. One large area in Golden Gate Park that is affectionately called "Hippie Hill" is the scene of a continuing love-in.

Love-ins in the park are a hippie tribal rite that includes certain basic ingredients. There are always several rather frenetic bongo beaters. Some play from four to eight continuous hours. The drums, combined with clanging tambourines, inevitably produce a young girl who begins to sway and undulate with the music. Often a shirtless male will appear and after much teasing the couple appears to simulate fornication.

Another essential pattern at modified week-day gatherings and full-blown large sessions is the smoking of pot and increasingly the "dropping" of acid. Marijuana and acid are used by many members of the festival at all love-ins.

There are levels of so-called paranoia about openly smoking pot. People in New York are much more "up-tight" than they are in San Francisco. In a Golden Gate Park love-in, pot may be smoked without fear of arrest right within the identification range of a uniformed or plainclothes narcotics officer. Part of every love-in that I have ever attended was the incense sticks and wafts of acrid marijuana smoke. People on the scene seem to be increasingly less "paranoid" and the use of drugs is quite open.

There are standard love-ins and special ones. An unusual "love-in," but one representative of a "special," took place when I was researching Haight. It was the Funeral of Chocolate George. Chocolate was a Hell's Angel who was, according to one resident, "known and loved" by the community. A tearful hippie called the Teddy Bear (no doubt because of his enormously hairy chest that was usually openly exposed) had just returned from the "funeral ceremony" in the park. He told me "what a beautiful cat Chocolate was."

"You know, man, Chocolate was struck down in the prime of his life. He was riding his hog [motorcycle] up there on Haight Street and got run down by some motherfuckin' tourist in a car. Like the whole hip community is smashed behind this thing.

"Like I'm stoned out of my mind on acid right now—but let me tell you, Chocolate was a truly beautiful cat. Man. We had a righteous funeral celebration, baby. Everybody got stoned and had a ball. But that's the way Chocolate would have wanted it. Dig?"

The formal ceremony in a funeral parlor was attended exclusively by Hell's Angels. However, the larger scene, a quasi-love-in funeral, took place in Golden Gate Park. The "funeral" was attended by two to three thousand hippies and several hundred Angels.

The Hell's Angels were in the center of the large group and separated themselves from the general run of the hippies. They were the elite people at the event.

The ceremony began around 1:00 p.m. with the consumption of large amounts of beer and wine. Before long a large percentage of the group began to smoke pot and drop acid. Mixed in with the Hell's Angels group were some of the more distinguished and widely known hip citizens of Haight. The core group comprised of Angels and hip people received most of the pot, acid, beer, and wine—although those milling around the periphery were participating heavily in every way. The use of drugs was so wide open that it was announced over the loud-speaker that people could go to a particular location to get free dope.

Big Brother and the Holding Company, one of the best psychedelic bands in the area, played exciting music. The number that especially triggered the funeral crowd was the band's hit record, "Bye Bye, Baby, Bye Bye."

Each chorus of music, each joint smoked, and each LSD tab dropped produced a wilder and more emotional level of happening. The love-in funeral was loud, boisterous, and fun for all. But as Teddy Bear and several Hell's Angels later told me, "Chocolate George would have liked it that way."

A break of violence at one point destroyed the love tone of the "funeral." The Angels would bark orders to some of the hippies. "Get me six cans of beer and get it in a hurry." The hippies would jump. Apparently at one point a Hell's Angel gave an order that was not filled. They chased the unfortunate person (a Negro hippie) through the crowd. The crowd fearfully parted and the several Angels who caught up with the fellow began to stomp him with their boots. Blood spurted. As one hippie close to the event told me, "his face was cut open." After he had been "wasted," the Angels returned to their ceremony.

Some of the Hell's Angels were an accepted part of the Haight-Ashbury street scene. Most of the time I was on the street, I saw Angels hanging out in front of restaurants with their immaculate bikes or "hogs" sitting on the street. Some Angels acted as if they loved and were protectors of the hippies. The love, however, would often erratically change to violence.

The hippies accepted the Hell's Angels, who, after all, were only "doing their thing." Their "thing" was, as nearly as I could observe, mainly getting stoned and "breaking loose" at almost any time into blitzkrieg violence. When the Hell's Angels went on a violent rampage, they didn't fool around—blood always flowed after their fists and boots stomped someone.

They ruled many hippies who came near them by inflicting a subtle terror. I personally felt this as I hovered around them at a pizza parlor on Haight Street after Chocolate George's funeral. One very greasy, leering member of the Angels accosted me for a quarter to "get across the bridge." His demeanor let me know that it would be wise for me to cooperate with his simple request. I wasn't at all interested in testing him and his friends in battle and readily complied.

The twenty-five cents seemed to pay my way to stand by and observe them close-up for several hours. I couldn't help note that in spite of their professed sorrow, they were not particularly heartbroken by the passing of Chocolate George. In fact, they were exuberant. They were high and everyone knew it. Several hippie girls who passed by were grabbed at and aggressively kissed. They responded and smiled whether they liked it or not.

The Angels commandeered what they wanted. Two Angels who were standing around hugging each other and rapping in loud voices were being entertained on the street. A long-robed, beaded, Christ-like hippie played his flute—apparently exclusively for their enjoyment and amusement. He stopped at one point to talk to a passing friend. The Angel turned to him, broke the stride of his discussion, and commanded, "Hey, man, play that fuckin' flute—I like it." The two Hell's Angels decided to go down the block to see a friend and the flutist was commanded to follow along and provide music for their walk.

The Family and Tribal Pads

The main life style of the community is found in the extended (non-related) family life, tribes, communes, and "crash-pads." These living situations honeycomb Haight for a radius of several miles. The pads (apartments) contain what are varyingly called "communities," "families," "tribes," "groups of brothers and sisters," and some "rock music group brothers and sisters." These structures are not too transient, even though people come and go. They are the bedrock foundation of Haight.

One such pad that I visited about six times, with and without Gridley, was a fairly typical "good scene." About eight people lived there regularly and shared as best they could the hundred-and-fifty-dollar-a-month rental cost. The regulars included Bill, who among other things sold pot and acid; Marta, a slightly plump but rather beautiful girl; Bud and Nancy, a permanent couple who "might" get married some day; a fellow named Gerry, and several others. The apartment also served as a "crash pad." Therefore, in addition to the eight "permanent" residents, there were always from four to ten more stragglers sleeping in. At this time Gridley, myself, and the girls were welcomed crash guests. Everyone was very hospitable and we were invited to share in the food and other available benefits of a pad. This essentially included pot and a certain amount of LSD.

Gerry had been a permanent resident in Marta's pad, but he "was thrown out because some asshole lied and said I stole some money." He was tall, about thirty, good looking, and the most cynical hippie I had yet met. Gerry was typical of many hip people in Haight who had come to the scene via a criminal heroin "dope-fiend" and prison background. He had been in jail at least twenty times for offenses ranging from drugs to statutory rape.

His real father was a "drunk and a house painter, in that order," and his mother was "one of those holy-roller ministers who raise their hands and say hallelujah, Oh, Glory Jesus—you know that kind of shit." Gerry's stepfather was in a state prison doing a life sentence.

Also in Gerry's past was a period "devoted to being a male prostitute for wealthy old ladies." At the time Gerry, like many others with comparable backgrounds, was making the hippie Haight scene.

Gerry, like Marta, had lived at Strawberry Fields for a few months. He was a well-known figure in Haight, generally admired by hippie friends as well as certain Hell's Angels. I saw Gerry many times on the street, always "loaded out of his mind." This day at the pad, he sat still for a lengthy discussion with me about Haight Ashbury and his own "bag." Gerry's observations paralleled some of my own views of the total Haight scene. Following are selected excerpts that reveal Gerry's "bag" and life in Haight.

LY–You know, it would be real useful to me if you could kind of run down things you've been doing since you've been here in Haight—after you left Strawberry Fields.

G–Well, actually, I went to Berkeley first, with this chick Diana. I got hung-up shooting smack [heroin] and that wasn't much good. I went right back to that shit again. I was buying it with Diana. I guess I shot smack for a month or so. I said fuck this shit and moved over here.

I started selling roach-holders [marijuana cigaret butt holders] over on Haight Street and decided I dug it over here. I met Marta and she invited me to come on up and stay at her pad.

Now, I'm in a battle and thing with Marta—she won't even talk to me, let alone smile at me. So, that's out. I hassled with her and moved to another pad that was unfurnished. I got beds and all that shit on the street. It didn't take me but five days to get the whole fuckin' place furnished. Wow, ya know, it's just a snap on the streets 'cause everybody's willing to help. We got about eight kids from the street, moved them all in. Ya know, jammed them in rooms. I just wasn't very discreet and I got the wrong people. They all started shooting speed and they wouldn't do anything.

It was a shame that they were fuck-ups, 'cause I almost had a good commune going. I got people who were willing to lay bread on me. I talked to the Quakers or the Friends, or whatever you call them, and they were gonna lay three hundred and ten dollars on me for materials to get the whole commune going. And then bigger than shit, man, they walked up, took one look at the place and those punks, and said, "forget it, man," and walked out.

LY–Are there many communes here?

G–Oh, there's a lot of them. They're all over.

LY–Would you say that most of the groups that are formed up here in Haight have it in their mind to get out of the city, in time? Or are there some that have sort of based themselves here?

G–Oh, I don't know. It's a combination of both. The only thing that I can tell you is just what I do myself. I stay in the city six months, sometimes a year, and I split 'cause I can't stand the city. So, it's sort of back and forth.

LY–What's the main drug scene in Haight?

G–It's pretty simple, man. The majority of it is speed, acid, STP, grass, hash, and that's it, man. There's not much smack.

LY–Just about everyone's turned on to something?

G–Oh, yeah.

LY–Is it easy to get dope?

G–I don't know. It's gonna be tight for a while after this

bullshit thing that happened. As you know, two pushers got killed. It's cut things down a whole lot.

The following excerpt from the *San Francisco Chronicle* (August 8, 1967) highlights the two homicides referred to by Gerry.

HIPPIE DEATHS MYSTERY—
FEAR OF "THE SYNDICATE" ROLE

Persistent reports that an Eastern crime syndicate is trying to gain control of LSD and marijuana traffic in Haight-Ashbury district were given some grim support yesterday.

The body of a man found dead Sunday in a sleeping bag snagged on a high cliff at Point Reyes was identified by fingerprints yesterday morning as that of William E. Thomas, 26.

He was a notorious hippieland narcotics dealer who called himself Superspade. . . .

Marin county detectives, working with San Francisco homicide inspectors, then learned from persons close to Superspade that he had recently been told to join "The Organization" or suffer the consequences.

The information gave a new direction to investigation of the murder of John Kent Carter, 25, another hippieland drug pusher whose mutilated body was found Thursday in his apartment.

Eric F. Dahlstrom, 23, a widely known motorcycle racer, claims he stabbed Carter in self-defense in an argument over some bad LSD, but police were not altogether satisfied with his story.

Carter's right arm had been neatly severed with a butcher knife and was in Dahlstrom's possession when the long-haired motorcyclist was arrested.

"I'm very, very hazy about that arm," Dahlstrom told his attorney, Emmet Haggerty, yesterday. "The principal reason I'm in jail is LSD."

Homicide Inspectors Gus Coreris and John Cotenos pointed out that the two murder victims not only were friends, but were independent operators in the hippie narcotics world. *

**San Francisco Chronicle*, August 8, 1967.

LY–What actually happened to those pushers from your point of view.

G–Evidently Shawn—that's Dahlstrom—burned [cheated] someone. I didn't know his real name. We knew him in the streets as Shawn. I don't feel that he did it, because it's not Shawn's package to burn people. I think that what happened was the guy flipped out and decided he wanted to do Shawn in. Shawn maybe got paranoid and hallucinated. He must have then killed the guy and cut his arm off. He took the arm with him in the car and was arrested in Sebastopol, probably on his way up to the Morningstar commune to hide out.

I don't know. If you've ever lived in the Village in New York, all you're seeing is the Village all over again. I did a lot of time in the Village when I was a kid. It's the same old shit, man. The hippies go to places where everybody's poor because rents are cheap.

Haight used to be a Ukrainian neighborhood. All of a sudden it's turned into another little hippieland, or beatnikland, Bohemia, or whatever the fuck you wanna call it. The natives are really upset about it. It's mostly the older people who complain. The fights come from the outside like bike riders [Hell's Angels] who've migrated here.

The spades from Fillmore come up here looking for a piece of ass or something and it's not happening for them. You know, they hear about "free love" in the newspapers, "free love" on the radio, love-ins, love, love, love. And it's not happening for them. The hippie chicks get up-tight behind it. I'd get up-tight if I was walking down the street and somebody grabbed me and said, "Hey, man, come here—I want to talk to you. How about it?" Something like that. I mean everybody would bum-trip the shit out of me. And this is the class of people that come up here and hit on the chicks in a real crude way. Then a fight breaks out.

Like the chicks are running around without their bras, ya know, it turns me on. I think it's groovy and it's like a nice thing. It's a pretty thing to see. But doing a pretty thing, man, in an up-tight society gets you hurt. A chick running through the secluded section of Golden Gate Park with nobody there but her and a half a dozen hoods; well, you know damn well she's gonna get banged—like it or not.

There's one chick in the hospital now, man, who got banged by six guys in the park. They had to do some operation on her and she's no longer a woman. I mean they had to cut out all her female tubes or something. On top of that the guy shot her. And that shit happens all the time. The whole city just says something like, "Well, she's a hippie, she had VD, so she must've been a whore," and then they dismiss the whole thing. That shit's pretty common down here in Haight.

My biggest bitch is what happened to me Saturday, last Saturday, or a week and a half ago, whenever it happened. The cops picked me up. I was stoned as usual. They took me in and when I got inside they got a little mad at my bad rapping—I said a few nasty things but I wasn't booked for resisting arrest. They slammed my head down on the counter a few times and called me a hippie cocksucker.

One cop held me, the other one slapped my face and then he asked . . . told me to sign my property receipt. I said, "Hell, no. Not until I read it." He signed it himself. Then this cop dragged me by my hair into the cell and stomped the shit out of me in the cell. So ya know, fuck it. There's nothing I can do about it.

I called the HALO [Haight-Ashbury Legal Organization] Society, got a hold of the Switchboard [another hippie aid group], and all they tell me is: "Well, if you've got ten people who've been beaten up by that cop, then we can do something." So I told them, "Fuck it, forget it."

LY–What's been your experience with the Diggers?

G–You walk into the Free Store and you say, "Who's in charge?" And they say, "You are, man." That's about it. Yet there must be some sort of organization. Otherwise, how in the hell would they get the keys to different things. Or how would they get the White Free Store or the Black Man's Free Store going?

Gerry's rap was unusual for a hip person on the scene. He seemed to have a rather negative and gloomy view of the whole movement. I began at this point to probe his personal situation.

LY–Where do you fit into this hippie scene?

G–I'm probably gonna die, ya know. I haven't got a point to life yet. I probably never will have one. The only thing I dig about Haight-Ashbury is I fuck a lot here and I think that's great. Beyond that it doesn't compensate for all the headaches. It really doesn't. 'Cause like there's still no point to living. I still don't do anything creative and even if I do, I get bored quick.

I don't even like acid anymore. The first time I took acid, it was really super great. It was beautiful—no hang-ups, no frustrations, no nothing—just walk down the street and colors were great and things were even nicer and I dug everybody and everybody kind of dug me. But now, I don't know, man. I don't even know whether I'm taking acid. It's so diluted with Meth and other shit. I don't know if it's that or if it's just that my head's changed. Maybe you just can't prolong it—you just can't keep using it. I don't know what it is. Maybe acid is just a one-time thing or a two-time thing or something, ya know. You use it and it does things for you or it doesn't. And after that you just sort of get into a game with it. That's the way it is for me. I don't know, other people have different opinions—different things happen.

What I see is the same thing I saw when I was a kid running the streets in the Village. I see the same thing happening here. Only it's in a greater amount here. In the Village you saw maybe two hundred kids every other week. They would kinda go into the Village and stay there for a while and then split and go on to something else. Here I see just the opposite. I see five hundred to a thousand coming in here every week, in and out, going to different places doing "their thing."

LY–Do you see love here in Haight?

G–I see an attempt at it but I don't honestly see it. I think love is an attempt to understand, live with, or accept your fellow man. And I walk up to somebody on the streets and say like in a greeting, "Hey, I want to talk to you, motherfucker!" And the guy jumps back just because I said "motherfucker." He doesn't jump back because of the sound of my voice or anything. He doesn't give you a chance to express yourself. He's up-tight behind what you say, and yet he professes to be like really for you. He says he really loves. But he doesn't love shit because he's so hung-up over the word game. He's hung-up behind the way you look, the way you talk, the way you come on. And it's a crock of shit. It's not true. I think it's just an attempt at love.

I think they have just discovered that there's a closeness among people and there's a need . . . there's a definite need for a closeness. We've got bombs hanging over our heads and world annihilation and all this shit, ya know. Everybody's gonna try and get closer to somebody. But no, it's not love in the sense that I want to see love.

The Responsible Community

The love that Gerry might be trying to describe is one involving responsibility and concrete human compassion formed into actual deeds. In this context Haight with all of its problems seems to be moving forward. The Haight scene is not all tribes, random sights, sounds, love-ins, and bizarre hippie uniforms. Working close to the surface are an increasing band of leaders and members of the hippie community. These are not outside "do-gooders"; they are integral members of the new community.

The scene has imposed a demand for organization on the hippies. Foremost among these emergent groups are the Diggers, named after a 17th-century society of English agricultural altruists. The Haight Diggers provide free food, shelter, and transportation for down-and-out hippies. (There are unaffiliated counterparts to the San Francisco group in Los Angeles and in the East Village of New York.) Other hippie service organizations are HALO, the HIP Job Co-op, with six thousand names on its part-time employment roster, and Huckleberry's, a home for runaways. There are, of course, many others forming.

The Diggers' Free Stores (both black and white) attempt to make a point regarding love, money, and exchange or barter. They emphasize that all contributions should be given with love. There is a story in their folklore about a wealthy dowager who gave the founders of the Diggers a ten-dollar bill in a snobbish Lady Bountiful charitable fashion. One of the Diggers is supposed to have put a match to the money and said, "We can only accept gifts given with love."

I participated in several of the Diggers' feedings in the Panhandle. The food served to several hundred people out of large cans was good and hearty. Many people in the hip community live off the Diggers on a regular basis.

Another significant group was HALO. It attempted to handle the range of legal difficulties that hippies encountered. I found that almost half of the people I met in my travels had some kind of a court case in process. It usually related to an arrest on illegal drugs.

An apparently useful organization in the area was the Switchboard. This group was housed several blocks from the corner of Haight-Ashbury and worked on all of the issues related to life in Haight. They were attempting to develop a school for hippie children, produce crash-pad space and food for newcomers, assist the Diggers in providing free food, and, like HALO, provide legal aid where necessary and possible.

Al Rinker, a former graduate student in sociology at San Francisco State College, was a founder, leader, and worker on the Switchboard. He described their work as "aiding in any way we can the many displaced youths that enter our community."

Most of these organizations advertised their services with one-page announcements distributed by hand in the community. An example of the type of literature pumped into the community is expressed in the following Switchboard mimeo announcement that was a housing plea for newcomers.

> HELP!
>
> With the summer influx at its peak, the housing situation has become critical. Many of our people are getting busted for sleeping in the park and some are serving 30-day sentences for this. This arresting is not the only hazard. San Francisco weather is not warm and Golden Gate Park is very wet and cold. So if the man [police] doesn't get you, a serious cold will.
>
> We are said to be the "love community" and I believe it. Let us now all show this love and concern by opening our hearts and pads to one or two of our brothers.
>
> If you can possibly house just one person a couple of nights a week then we will have the problem solved—1. Knowing that our heads are in the "right" place. 2. We will be depriving the police of their prime pleasure—and most of all giving the now homeless some sense of comfort and dignity.
>
> If you have the space, call Switchboard Housing Office and give us your address (phone #), the number of people you can house, and for what length of time. We will abide by what you request.
>
> Thank you.
> Love
> Your Neighbor [address & phone #]

A highly significant development in the Haight community was the opening of a Free Medical Clinic founded by David Smith, a young medical doctor. The Free Medical Clinic attempted to bring vitally needed medical services directly into the community. Located on Haight and Clayton in the center of the district, I found it was highly regarded by the residents.

The interior had much psychedelic art work and was managed by hip people and volunteer doctors. According to one client, "Man, you feel right at home and you don't mind waiting. You really are treated with love. I once went to the county hospital with a physical problem and I was treated like a dog."

In an interview with Dr. Smith I asked him about the nature and extent of medical problems in Haight from his viewpoint.

DR. SMITH–First of all, the health problems of Haight-Ashbury are no different than the health problems of any group of young people grouped together in communal living. There are a lot of upper-respiratory throat infections, and common health problems. This group does, however, have additional problems. There is a very high incidence of venereal disease, partly because of the free love philosophy. This is mainly among the younger people. The older hippies don't get venereal disease because they know how to prevent it. They know how to stay clean.

We also see a startlingly high incidence of hepatitis because of the contaminated surroundings. Also the use of a needle by several Methedrine users often produces hepatitis. This is one of the real problems of Methedrine use. Hepatitis is an inflamation of the liver, secondary to a virus in the blood that's transmitted from an infected needle or from people-to-people contamination.

In summary, there is an abnormally high incidence of hepatitis, venereal disease, and of course a very high incidence of drug use!

The Clinic, in addition to handling the range of medical problems indicated, helped people with so-called LSD "bummers." A "bummer" is a situation where a user has "freaked-out" or gone beyond the pale. He may manifest all of the symptoms of hysterical psychosis. The "bummer"-help dimension of the clinic is available on a twenty-four-hour basis through a phone number posted around the community. (The problem of the "bummer" is described in greater detail in a later chapter on psychedelic drugs.)

The integration of the Haight community, in an effort to cooperatively solve its own problems, is expressed in several forms. One consists of standard community committee meetings of Diggers, Switchboard people, HALO, and other such groups. The meetings I attended, aside from the festive hip clothes worn, paralleled inter-organization meetings I had attended in other communities around the country.

A major departure, however, from the "community organization" meetings I was accustomed to was a hippie town-hall meeting I attended. The costumes and dress were far out. The meeting, attended by about five hundred people, was held at the Straight Theater, an old movie house taken over by the "new community." Marijuana smokers almost outnumbered straight tobacco smokers. Young children and dogs ran freely through the auditorium during the meeting.

The meeting was opened (about a half-hour late) by a tall bearded fellow who was rather articulate. He was a leader in the Flame, a hip organization devoted to consolidating all of the hippie "social services" available in Haight. The first subject he raised was a brief comment on the recent tragic murders of two well-known pushers in the community. The leader asked if anyone had anything they wanted to say about one of the victims known affectionately in the community as Superspade. He was really asking if anyone wanted to deliver a eulogy for Superspade.

The first fellow that came up took the mike and spoke in a classic psychotic word salad. Nothing he said made any sense at all to anyone. It was apparent that he had just grabbed the mike to express himself and get some attention. In spite of his gibberish, he was lightly applauded when he finished his diatribe.

The next person who came up to the mike used an interesting ploy. He stood for several minutes and said nothing until he had the group's full attention. When he had complete silence, he delivered a broad smile and his carefully chosen line: "Superspade is in Superspace." This was first met with a long silence, then a glowing approval for the poetry of his comment spread through the crowd. Sounds of "out of sight," "too much," and laughter rocked throughout the audience.

A young man in a floor-length monk's robe, bedecked with beads and wearing about fifteen large bells, rocked with laughter and appreciation. He walked around throughout the meeting shaking his bells. Whenever he was particularly "grooved" by anything said, he would especially ring his bells. After the Superspace comment he shook his bells ferociously. (The sound over-jolted my tape recorder.)

The next one invited to address the group was a young, very hip fellow. He was one of a committee of about ten that was seeking to acquire permanently for the new community the theater we were in. He gave a very hip commentary on the situation: "Like dig people. We got this groovy place, right? Now dig—we want to keep it. Right? It's ours, man. We're getting a permit. *Now.* Let's not mess it up—dig? The dance and music license is coming through—you dig? *Now.* We don't want to mess it up. So smoke your grass outside of here, dig?"

He went on about how it could be messed up by illegal behavior in the theater (the kind that was going on at the moment). At this point in his message another hip young man in the audience seemed to flip out. He emitted several loud, piercing cries that broke the tranquility of the meeting. He shouted, "BULLSHIT! BULLSHIT! BULLSHIT!"

The speaker stopped and challenged the young man to explain his interruption. He came up to the podium, was given the mike, and explained. "Man, if this is really OUR theater, I'll smoke pot here. If this is really OUR theater I'll say fuck here. Like what is this shit about OUR theater? Can we or can't we do 'our thing' here? Either we got freedom or we don't. Do you dig, man?"

About half the audience joined the dissenter with applause.

The two young men were then given separate mikes and they went into a lengthy debate on their respective positions. It lasted for about a half hour. The debate was pretty much a draw.

The mood of the meeting was changed by the next speaker, who went into a rather impassioned and eloquent diatribe against police harassment of the hippie community. He wanted freedom for all hip people to do "their thing." He emphasized how hippie girls were harassed with I.D. age checks when other girls at "straight" high schools certainly would never be bothered. His speech was met with the thunderous applause of approval.

There were many speakers who had minor points to make. Announcements of scheduled happenings in the park, the availability of crash pads, and the opening of what was called the Happening House. An articulate young lady affiliated with San Francisco State College informed the group about an arts and crafts program that was scheduled to be part of the Happening House.

The next speaker given the floor was a frail yet very militant Negro named Scooter. His rap was emotional and threatening. "Most of you know me, I'm Scooter. *Now.* The hip community and the black community should love each other, right? [Applause.] In back of me are thirty beautiful black young men. [He pointed to about thirty young Negroes who had lined up against the wall in back of him.] *Now.* [He said threateningly] We don't want violence or trouble. But we could have it, baby. *We want for our kids the things you people have put down. We want good food, jobs, houses, and cars. Dig?*

"Now. We're selling tickets for a dance in the black community. The honkies downtown, the Birchers and the bigots like they're all buying tickets. None of you hip people buy tickets. Don't you love us? [Applause.] They're a dollar-fifty and the money goes for our kids. Dig?

"We don't want trouble with you people. But we can't control it and really don't want to control it if we don't get what we want. Buy some tickets right now. We black people love you. Do you love us?" [Applause.]

Some tickets were sold. But most of the people claimed to be broke as the young Negroes sold tickets throughout the audience.

Other speakers were coming on, but I had to leave. It was unlike any other community meeting I had ever seen or encountered. The swirl of hippies, staunch regular community ministers, priests, and even a minority of local merchants in business suits were present. There were also several Hell's Angels in full oily regalia sitting threateningly in the background.

I was turned-off by the confusion of no planning, children and dogs running up and down the aisles, and the continuing loud noises of bells and flute playing. Despite some negative feelings, however, I had to admit that it was truly a community representation. The emotionally disturbed, the intellectuals, the profane, and the eloquent were all given the opportunity to speak. All elements of the community participated and in this sense it was a valuable and true town-hall meeting.

I was convinced that Haight-Ashbury had a broad range of hippies and other people interested in and concerned about its problems and development. The people had voices and spoke up for their rights and their positions. The Haight-Ashbury brand of "social worker" was truly a new breed.

A Haight-Ashbury "Social Worker."

An unsung hero of the Haight community who typifies its spirit and the pattern of helping others is a young man named Bob from Roundup, Montana. Twenty-two-year-old Bob describes himself as a troubleshooter in the Haight community. When I met him he was working in the Diggers' Free Store. He related his personal background and the role he played in the new community. He first told me about how he had been in trouble in his high school back in Roundup.

B–My only crime was that I wanted to get a dialogue going between the students, the teachers, and the school administration. For doing this they sent me to a psychiatrist. I went to this psychiatrist for quite a few years. He said that I was insane. He said that I was schizophrenic and psychotic. I told him that I thought that life and everything else works on a micro-magnetic-type principle. And that everything that is manifest must have a positive and negative form. And that the dimensions of everything could be broken down into light and molecules.

[I was not tuned-in to Bob's mystical rap, so I shifted the subject to my reality.]

LY–Could you describe the Diggers' Store and how it began?

B–It began with people who were basically interested in the problem of feeling more. They were also concerned with the fact that a lot of young people from all parts of the country were congregating here and finding themselves with nothing to eat, nothing to wear, and no place to sleep. The press coverage and the songs said, "Come to San Francisco and have a life of love."

Once these people arrived they found the situation much the same as it was anywhere else. Like you can starve on the street. Consequently, a group of people without any interest in making any capital gain went ahead and set up the Diggers and their free stores.

LY–Who are the people who were central in putting it together?

B–Nobody knows. It's all called the Diggers. Nobody can get to the center of an organization and make any trouble for it if the center of an organization doesn't exist. It's all in a state of flux, on purpose. You know, I'm a Digger, but so what.

LY–When you say that you're a troubleshooter in Haight, what do you mean?

B–Well, if there is a hassle where kids aren't communicating with the larger community, I jump in. The people who live up in the hills of San Francisco or Oakland don't know what it's like in Haight-Ashbury. Unless they know, they can't help. They have to look into it and then get into it. Now, they come driving down the street and all they see is cats selling newspapers and cats sitting around ringing bells and beating tambourines, and so on. Then they say, "Wow, all the hippies are insane." But somebody like myself who has been in suburbia and has also been in the middle of this thing can communicate to both groups. If I get a receptive member of the other society to talk with, I can communicate. And I think that if people knew more about what's really happening inside of the hippie colony, I don't think that they'd be as worried about it and as hostile toward it as they are now.

LY–What goes on at the Diggers' Store?

B–Well, we're just a few blocks away from Haight Street. The hippies can walk up here and get free clothes, some furniture and household items when we have them. We are also located in a colored neighborhood and have a Black Man's Free Store. There are a lot of people in the black ghetto who simply don't have clothes or chairs or much of anything. And we're in a position to service maybe a thousand people a week. They come in there and they know that anything they want is free. All they have to do is take it.

LY–Do people steal things here?

B–You can't steal.

LY–I know that, but don't some people think that they are stealing?

B–We used to have a sign that said "Prosecutors will be shoplifted to the full extent of the law." There are people who come into our stores and hoard things. They come in here day after day and take things that don't fit them and they think that they're getting away with something. But, that's all right because they'll hoard it until they get sick of it.

LY–You wouldn't stop anyone from taking anything if they wanted it?

B–No, they could have my shirt if they really want it.

LY–What is your role here? What do you do here? What's your function?

B–I sweep the floor and take out the garbage and . . .

LY–How many folks like that are there here?

B–There are four of us here today.

LY–Four of you and it's sort of a changing group?

B–At this time, it's a relatively stable group, until we get the kitchen open. We're going to have a free restaurant. . . . The other day we took a load of clothes down to the Black Diggers' Free Store in Fillmore. They had a bakery across the street that gave them a truckload of bread. I gave them all of our clothes and they gave me half of the bread. We brought it back and passed it out here.

LY–Is there any difference between the way the Black store operates and the way that this one operates?

B–No, it's all the same principle.

LY–What is the principle?

B–It's a love thing. Love your neighbor. It's like if you could take a step back and look at the whole society, the whole world, you'd find a whole bunch of people living on rich land. There's plenty for everybody, yet they set up negotiations and systems of exchange and they fight over material possessions.

They set up the United States as a capitalistic country. I for one disagree with that. I think that if everybody on this planet shared with everybody else there wouldn't be any basis for war or disagreement.

Haight-Ashbury is comprised mainly of people who are disillusioned by the materialistic society and are searching for love. The "seekers" are here. A lot of them don't have any clothes, are hungry, and don't have a place to stay. This is what the Diggers are here for. The materialistic society won't take care of these people. American society doesn't believe in what we are doing so we have to take care of our own people.

The responsible leaders of Haight were involved in a serious effort to form a vital "new community." A great deal of their energies were devoted to helping the younger people entering the "movement." However, the general problems of health, education, and welfare were enormous.

In this framework, the hip community was beset with many specific problems like venereal disease, hepatitis, poor housing, poverty, some violence, and various patterns of juvenile delinquency. The most pressing "delinquency problem" in Haight and other hippie communities that I could observe, however, was the use and abuse of illegal drugs.

CHAPTER TWELVE

Red, White, and Blue

> . . . The time has come for you to seek new levels of reality.
> Your ego and the game are about to cease.
> You are about to be set face to face with the Clear Light.
> You are about to experience it in reality.
> In the ego-free state, wherein all things are like the void and cloudless sky.
> And the naked spotless intellect is like a transparent vacuum.
> At this moment, know yourself and abide in that state.
> (From *The Psychedelic Experience* by Leary, Alpert, and Metzner.)

ALL OF THE EXPERIENCES AND events I heard about on my trip were somehow linked to the LSD phenomenon. At this juncture in my voyage I therefore decided that it was vital for me to have an LSD experience. Despite my realistic fears about the possible negative consequences of LSD, I felt that a personal investigation was essential in order for me to better understand the many dialogues, scenes, and the people I had encountered on my voyage. And if there was any truth in the power of the LSD experience, my wife had to join my adventure because we wanted to stay together both emotionally and spiritually. So on a Sunday morning at 12:45 a.m., my wife Donna and I very nervously ingested 500 micrograms of LSD each in a special cup of tea brewed for the occasion.

We had prepared for this episode in my research rather assiduously. In addition to a broad examination of the voluminous literature in the LSD field, we both read the "Bible" of the movement, *The Psychedelic Experience.* We were reasonably aware of the potential agony or ecstasy of the trip and had a great anticipation about new vistas of thought and communication that might open up for us.

We chose our guides based on the directive in the book to "select good friends—who would not play any ego games." We had known Arnie Stonehill and his wife Lyn for over a year. During this time we had become very close friends through their participation in a weekly psychodrama group I ran and through many long evenings of very personal and intimate discussion. Both Arnie and Lyn, prior to our friendship, had had several LSD experiences.

Ann, 18, had been living with us for over a year as our foster daughter. Our close friendship had become a loving family relationship. These three people were the guides we had chosen to be present during our trip.

Twenty minutes after ingesting the bluish-purple "high quality" LSD, we were sitting casually talking with our group in the living room of our home when the acid hit. My first sensation was that a finely wound super watch spring of enormous tensile strength was in my gut, had burst loose, and had begun to unwind.

The next set of flashes involved a feeling of sharp crystals bursting in my brain. Everything began to look like sharp-edged crystal snowflakes breaking into arrows. I was filled with awe and became panicky with fright. "Arnie, what have I done? This isn't for me."

I tried to maintain self-control by saying my name to myself, and I tried to stay in the room. For about ten minutes that seemed like a lifetime I fought the power of the LSD. (It was now about 1:15 a.m.) My attempts to maintain control were met with a clear feeling of melting into the floor. I literally felt my backbone, my arms and legs melting like hot lava into the floor. I clutched at my head with my now flickering hands. My head literally felt caved-in! I continued to dissolve into the floor. Waves of nausea and panic engulfed me.

On wobbly legs, with Arnie's help, I staggered into our bedroom, off the living room, and fell onto my bed. I was then alone with Arnie. I began to thrash on the bed, moaning and mumbling. "This is a place I never want to be. What's it all about? I want to be Lew Yablonsky. What's happening to Donna?"

Arnie told me that I must go with it wherever it was trying to take me. I fought a desperate and losing battle. Finally, I let go of Donna, Lew Yablonsky, and a conscious image of the room. This happened partially from the magic phrases that Arnie read to me from *The Psychedelic Experience.*

> That which is called ego death is coming to you.
> Remember: This is now the hour of death and rebirth.
> Take advantage of this temporary death to obtain the perfect state—
> Enlightenment
> Concentrate on the unity of all living beings
> Hold onto the clear Light
> Use it to attain understanding and love.

I distinctly remember Arnie's reading and my facetious comment: "You're the first Hindu I ever heard with a Brooklyn accent."

Two swirls appeared to be available to me. One was an absolutely magnificent, brightly colored red, white, and blue swirl. I saw it somehow as the masculine swirl. The other one was darker and I was convinced it was feminine. I made the decision to go with the Red, White, and Blue, and it encompassed my conscious mind as I melted into it, in a kind of free fall.

At the core of the incredibly vivid and beautifully colored red, white, and blue swirl, I could see the flicker of a shining white light. I wanted to go there because I knew that there was the center of the Universe—My Universe. I traveled through ages and eons of further swirls. The word Excalibur (a word I had never consciously thought of in my life) seared my thoughts. Excalibur became my theme.

I decided to ride on an available silver space ship. (Arnie later told me I distinctly said, "I'm in a silver space ship. Now I can walk among the stars." He also told me I spoke in the Universal Tongues of glossolalia.) Now in space, I floated with great velocity toward the light. My space ship had a brilliant red, white, and blue flag emblazoned on the front.

My voyage was consummated when I arrived at the white light. Its brilliance was astonishing—but I could look directly at it. It flickered between being a shining diamond and a light. The two finally melted together into an almost overpowering bright light. But I felt it was one that I now had in my control. I felt omniscient and omnipotent!

I rose from the bed and informed Arnie that I was one of the greatest patriots of all time. I had Excalibur. I loved America. I loved my friends. I loved Synanon. And I would fight the enemies of my country—those committed to war, false super-patriotism, bigotry, and discrimination.

I kept repeating the word I had never consciously used before in my life—Excalibur!

I realized that I had let my wife go into her spiritual feminine trip and I had been to the peak of my red, white, and blue masculine swirl. I was now ready to join her in the living room. (About 2:15 a.m.)

Our living room, which is a large **25′ x 25′** room, contains a Persian rug and a large fireplace. The room looked remarkable. All of the colors in the room were marvelously brilliant and alive. My wife was more beautiful than I had ever seen her in my life. Her hair was jet black and flickered in the firelight. Her eyes were very oriental. Her eyes and face were framed with startlingly beautiful diamonds and emeralds. Her body and face swayed with a magnificent smile. I could only try to tell her how much I loved her. I chanted what seemed like a thousand times, *"You are the most beautiful woman I have ever known in all the worlds I have ever experienced in all my lifetimes."*

We sat on the floor together staring into each other's eyes and I repeated that phrase a hundred different ways. She found me younger and more handsome than she had ever seen me.

The room became the inside of a Turkish-oriental mosque. There were no sharp corners. Everything flowed together like oriental architecture. Everything swayed with the rhythm of the Ravi Shankar sitar music that was (actually) playing. We devoured each other with enormous electric sensations of touch and sight. If our friends hadn't been present at the moment, we would have made love. These feelings went on for about an hour. (3:15 a.m.)

Suddenly I stood up and declared that I had seen a flash of dawn break through our windows. I pointed out to the rooftops of Paris that shone from our window. It was a very rich and beautiful sight.

Then, for no reason, I shifted to the 1930's. I declared, "Let's all go back to the '30's." I flashed on to thoughts I had had during the opening of my trip. Thoughts about Jack Oakie, Ronnie Reagan, George Murphy, Dick Powell, and Ruby Keeler appeared visually to me. In my mind I saw the movie Vitaphone production, "42nd Street," the swirling girlie movie scenes of the '30's, and especially the college pictures. I wanted some college cheerleaders. It was all gay and magnificent. I was part of the '30's. I was a writer in the '30's.

I began to talk excitedly: "I see all those fantastic college movies with Dick Powell, Patsy Kelly, and Ronald Reagan. Then, of course, Ronnie was really a 'mensch'—he was Reagan at his best, a laughing college boy with a big letter on his sweater. How did he get cast in this new role of governor? He belongs back there singing with Dick Powell in front of the girls dorm the night before the big game." We were all happy and laughing about these thoughts.

Suddenly, for no apparent reason, my focus and mood changed over to merry old England. I said in a mock British accent, "Let's trot along" and demanded of Arnie, who began to look like a devilish circus ringmaster, that he bring me a blowsy Middle Ages "British tart." Arnie presented Ann in this role. She looked beautiful to me—but was too slim for my image at the moment.

Arnie, in the ringmaster role, smilingly produced a variety of images. At one point he parted the room curtains, pointed to his Mercedes parked outside and said, "You want to see a great car? Look!" His car seemed sparkling and magnificent.

Everyone and everything in the room looked fantastic. The colors were deep and pulsating. Donna looked unbelievably beautiful and we decided to return to our Turkish mosque. This move happened several more times. (About 4:00 a.m.)

Nothing in the room had any sharp corners. Everything was curved, carved, rich, and ecstatically beautiful. The fire in the fireplace was brilliant. All of the people were shining images. Despite this enormous high feeling, several times during the night I panicked about being out of control. Part of me resisted being high on a drug.

At several points Ann looked frightened about something. When this happened her arms and legs seemed to shrivel and she appeared like a frightened rabbit. I tried to assure her that there was nothing to fear and she then returned to her original beauty.

Donna and I began to talk very rapidly about our love for each other, our child Mitch, and our friends. At certain moments we conflicted. When this happened her face began to sharpen like a witch's. I would bring her back to her beauty by changing the subject. Apparently there were areas of conflict I didn't want to pursue.

Arnie and Lyn left about this time (about 4:15 a.m.), "now that they knew we were OK." Ann, Donna, and I began to talk about the love we had for each other. Although I had known of my affection for Ann, I realized enormous waves of love for her as the daughter I had never had. At one point the three of us were hugging each other, crying and talking about the home we had all found with each other. It was sad, yet enormously beautiful.

All of our feelings were tremendously sharpened. It seemed rather amazing that Ann, who had taken no drug at all, could stay with all of our feelings and emotions. She wasn't patronizing or removed from our condition. With the exception of the hallucinatory effect of pulsating images, she was emotionally tuned-in. She apparently had what was called, in the LSD world, "a contact high."

We looked at a picture of our 3 1/2-year-old Mitchel, and it began to pulsate with life. He was exquisite.

We went back to our bedroom, where I previously had had my spiritual trip. Donna, Ann, and I began to discuss it. We all agreed I was "true blue Lew—a sincere American patriot." Donna looked at me and said seriously, but with joy, "I really can see it. You love this country." I told her it was true. I was a patriot of the old school. Not a Bircher or bigot, or necessarily an admirer of Johnson's Great Society. I was a patriot in the Tom Paine sense. I wanted to help right the wrongs that existed in the country I loved.

We looked at flowers and oranges that pulsated with life. Donna and I focused on an orange and mutually saw molecules, fetuses, and electrical live pulses.

I looked around the room and became aware of the rich beauty of some of the furniture and the shabbiness of certain things. "That TV and that table are crap. Let's get rid of them and that terrible-looking clock. The rug is awful." I snapped to a game and a battle that Donna and I had played with each other many times in reality. I played the role of a boorish unaesthetic unmaterialistic male disinterested in the home and the beautiful things Donna had brought to it.

I "copped out" to the fact that on a deep level I shared her values and appreciation of handsome objects. I said I would never play that game with her again!

She "copped" to poking at my work, my writing, because of envy and a lack of understanding. She told me that now that she knew of my "sincere patriotism" she would no longer play "the heavy game of subtle interference."

We began to analyze and interpret other frames and imprints in our life. The thirties was for me, we discovered, a period of romance when writers like Hemingway and F. Scott Fitzgerald were kings. Excalibur!

Also I flashed on a scene in my childhood back in Newark, N.J., where I would wait for my mother to throw a dime wrapped in a newspaper to me from a third-story tenement window. The dime was my key to the beautiful movies of "42nd Street" and noble Dick Powell standing patriotically on the deck of a U.S. Navy ship wrapped in red, white, and blue, singing the corny, but beautiful song "Shipmates Stand Together, Don't Give Up the Ship."

Everything seemed corny and magnificent. We looked out from our balcony as the dawn seemed to break, about 5:30 a.m. I literally felt myself in the center of a fantastic Swiss chalet looking over the roofs of a magnificent green countryside. The view was the actual one from our balcony, but it was enhanced a thousandfold.

At dawn I could begin to feel the drug in the pit of my stomach churning as the sharp coil continued to unwind. I felt control of it. We were now about six hours into the trip and I began to feel that I could turn the acid on in order to focus on an idea or a thing at will. I felt that I knew how much was left and that now the amount was finite.

I thought about the book I was writing. And I had a distinct feeling that the carnival, newspaper, flower-child nature of the hippie scene was ludicrous and irrelevant within the framework of the enormous power and potential use of LSD. I felt that acid was wasted on that scene and that it should be in the hands of more responsible people than the kids in the movement. I felt that some of the flower children were destroying themselves with this powerful drug. It was unfortunate because under proper conditions it could be an enormously valuable instrument.

This tripping out on that subject was interrupted by Donna entering and telling me about the resolution of her life-death conflict. She and Ann had discussed Donna's great fear of people dying.

Donna talked intensely and eloquently about not living and loving fully because of a great sadness with the fact that "all this love and devotion disappeared with death." She had flashed on a new thought or insight that "all love goes on into the mainstream of life and that it is never lost." She saw the unity of all things and her connection to the cosmos.

We discussed the male-female delineation and agreed that men and women have a different total life trip. Women have the power of creating life, and this is an area that men will never understand. We agreed that men were more superficially creative than women. Even men intellectually endowed involved in writing books and philosophy were insignificant compared to the power a woman has of giving life through childbirth. She copped out that, as a woman, she didn't fully understand and probably never would how men could focus for long periods of time on intellectual matters.

We happily agreed to let each other do our "own things." We agreed to help rather than to hassle each other. We were now a grand and harmonious duet. (About 6:00 a.m.)

Ann went downstairs to sleep. Donna and I returned to Turkistan and made love to the exotic sounds of Ravi Shankar, the LSD, and our hearts.

About an hour later we took a bath together, ate lightly, and, high as kites, drove the five minutes from our house to the Pacific Ocean.

My car (actually a silver gray 1967 Chrysler sedan) literally felt like a silver space ship zooming over the earth's surface. We cracked up laughing when I truly noticed for the first time that my car's hood emblem was a red, white, and blue cylinder. I simply said, "Excalibur!"

We stopped for coffee at a small all-night coffee shop one block from the ocean. The scene was unbelievable.

Two hood-like motorcycle "wino" young men appeared to me as more evil than any violent delinquent I had ever seen in my life. Despite the fact that I felt they eyed my wallet and money, I had no fear of them because I felt omniscient in my understanding of their plight and problems. I felt enormous waves of compassion for them. Yet I was conscious enough to know that if we spoke to them they would put us down.

An aged woman at the counter looked like a sparrow talking to an old man two seats away. I could actually see the blood coursing through the veins on her gnarled hands. The man was very bent with age but the two of them seemed beautiful together.

We went to the beach. Here we found one of the most awe-inspiring and astonishing sights of the total experience. We both saw the sand as a tan and gold rainbow-colored mosaic of the finest oriental rug in existence. Our bare feet were caressed by the soft, exquisite feel of this grand, pulsating carpet. We looked back and forth at each other and then at the sand, laughing and smiling for what appeared to be ages of time.

We sat near the water. The ocean blended with the sky and both had every color in the rainbow. The air was clearer and crisper than we had ever known it. The fresh air was intoxicating.

This was the magic carpet. We saw the same things simultaneously together and we blended with the unity and beauty of our world.

With this good feeling we went to visit our dear friends Chuck and Betty Dederich and Reid Kimball at Synanon, a few miles farther up the beach. They all looked marvelous.

They tuned-in to our electrical vibrations and we talked at length about our insights, feelings, and experience. Chuck taped some of our conversation.

We went home about 10:00 a.m. and sat in our back yard. An enormous, bright, very blue bluebird perched on the oleander tree in our yard. We both felt he was chirping a message to us and we tried hard to understand it. Donna talked to it. It was friendly and flew around the yard for an indeterminate time.

We went back to our bedroom to rest and couldn't sleep. Our minds were too alive and active. For literally hours we discussed many old and new facets of our relationship and our marriage. We talked into the afternoon, as our high and hallucinatory visions faded out of existance.

In the early evening we knew that we had returned to a non-drug reality. We had dinner and then went to sleep around 9:00 p.m. I had not slept as deeply as I did that night for many years. We woke up the next morning at 7:00 a.m. to what we both felt was a new and better world.

Random Notes on the Voyage

This account of my LSD experience was written about a week after it happened. I have left the report of the event almost in the original form in which it was written in order to convey some of the flavor of my emotions at that time.

The experience was enormously important to me in a way that I find difficult to communicate. It did produce some insights, essentially related to the strong love my wife and I felt for each other. We further had insights into our roles as woman and man. Whether or not this increased self-knowledge will permanently affect our future behavior is an interesting question.

Another issue that I had never consciously pondered in depth was my red, white, and blue patriotism. Somehow my role as a sociologist was clarified. I could better understand how I found it absolutely vital to merge my personal self with my work. The experience also affected my viewpoint as a sociologist. I am more than an observer; I have to assume the responsibility of action to change the society I love.

None of these insights (and many others I see no point in discussing here) may seem enormously important on casual inspection. Yet there was a spiritual and almost mystical quality to the examination of personal problems and issues under the LSD effect that I had never felt in many other "therapeutic experiences" I had in the past.

In spite of the fact that my wife and I apparently had a profound trip, at this time (about a month later) I have no real interest in taking LSD again. I feel that the one experience gave me a considerable amount of personal and philosophical material to work through, and that it will take me a long time to digest the impact of the trip.

I have a resistance against electrically vibrating and shocking my body in this manner. I feel, too, that I can have a similar intense experience in reality without a drug by participating in group methods like psychodrama and the Synanon Game. I enormously enjoy my natural state of being without drugs. I feel I can learn more about my world in a natural state than under the artificial conditions of being high.

One of the most important characteristics about myself and my wife, which was vital to our positive experience, was the fact that we both had some structure of psychological, emotional, spiritual, and intellectual background for constructively framing the powerful experience. I can readily see how people (particularly the very young) who do not have these personality resources would have a "bummer." And I can further see how the ego-smashing dimensions of LSD could produce suicide, homicide, or psychosis in a delicately balanced person.

My personal experience, the issues just mentioned and whatever scientific research information I have absorbed, brings into focus and intensifies two viewpoints I had about LSD usage before my own acid trip. I am even more apprehensive and fearful of the destructive impact of this very powerful drug as it is taken randomly and irresponsibly by people who do not use it in any proper frame of reference. The hippie child's "fun and games" use of acid may produce mind and body shock waves that may be irreparable. (There are, of course, many hospitalized psychotic cases resulting from bad trips to validate this point.)

A second view of mine that is intensified is that if it is properly used (not necessarily under medically controlled experimental conditions), LSD can be a most significant tool in helping many people in a therapeutic fashion for positive personality change. One use that I think would be an immediate boon would be to give people who clearly are dying, like the very aged and people with clearly terminal diseases, access to the chemical. After a careful period of education and preparation if the person voluntarily wanted this experience, I feel it could prove beneficial. The LSD quality of tuning people into an oceanic feeling about the cosmic flux and unity of man might make their immediate lives happier.

I also see LSD as a valuable *aid* to various kinds of formal and informal therapeutic situations. It might help people engaged in personality change and self-exploration move faster.

I can especially see the use of LSD as an adjunct to psychodramatic therapy. A psychodrama, briefly described, involves acting out in a group with the aid of certain techniques a person's actual core life situations. The increased focusing quality of the LSD effect might place a subject more deeply into his critical life drama and help him work it out. For example, in psychodrama with an individual who had a problem with his father, we would have someone role-play his father. In a regular psychodrama, the subject usually feels more or less that he is encountering his real father. With the adjunct use of LSD, I believe he would more intensely accept the auxiliary ego role-playing his father as his real father. It was my observation under LSD that I could almost at will (and at times did) change human forms before me into the images of people I wanted to talk to, like my brother, mother, or father.

Combining LSD with psychodrama is, of course, only one

of the enormous range of possible uses of LSD within the field of therapy. Research into this and other avenues for helping people with LSD should be instituted and developed.

On the hippie scene I can more clearly understand the value of LSD use by the hippie high priests, philosophers, and some novitiates. In fact it does appear to be a vital instrument for tuning-in to the world they are seeking and trying to develop. In the light of my personal experience I can now more clearly and rationally understand the emotional and spiritual feeling states that people like Leary, Gridley, Sonny, Stan, and Gary were trying to communicate to me. I now am more aware of "where they are at" intellectually and spiritually.

In spite of my clearer and greater recognition and appreciation of the leaders' personal trips, I am concerned about the lax manner in which the leaders assume responsibility for the way in which their followers use LSD. There are many thousands of young people following their leaders in a self-destructive way. And despite their disclaimers about being "leaders," they are role models and responsible for thousands of youngsters who might be better off if they were *tuned-out* now and made a reentry into the larger society with all it's faults.

On the basis of my knowledge and personal experience with LSD, it seems to me that more hip youngsters than not simply lack the emotional and intellectual framework for properly tuning-in and using the drug constructively. It is my observation that the majority of hippie youths are using the considerable power of LSD in a self-destructive way. This is unfortunate, since, with proper controls, knowledge, and intelligent use, LSD could become a very valuable vehicle for emotional, intellectual, and spiritual development.

Part Three
Analysis

CHAPTER THIRTEEN

Psychedelic Drugs: The Agony and the Ecstasy

DRUG TAKING IS AN INTEGRAL part of the New Community and its philosophy. The essential drugs used are LSD, marijuana, and "speed" (Methedrine and other amphetamines). LSD and marijuana are prescribed by the hippie philosophy—whereas it is generally believed that "speed kills."

My personal observations of people under the influence of drugs were varied. Some people (especially Gridley) showed limited signs of being high. In fact, with some people I was close to I never could be sure when they were under the influence of drugs or when they were not. In some respects, their natural state was a "high."

At other times, people showed definite indications of being "stoned." Their speech pattern would be sharply halted, erratic, or at times incoherent. Giggling and "cracking up" appeared especially on marijuana. In one situation I observed a very intelligent person I was interviewing slowly become increasingly incoherent as he sucked on a marijuana cigaret.

Marijuana Use and Abuse

Marijuana is the daily intoxicant of the hippie world. Grass is plentiful. The only questions raised about it concerned its strength. It is used without question, guilt, or any self-examination as a staple household item in the hippie world. (Responses to the questionnaires [see Appendix] revealed that over 90% of the hippie world regularly smoked pot.)

Marijuana has, over the years and even recently, been given a seal of approval, even by some of the staunchest advocates of stamping it out. In a New York Mayor's Report, issued in 1944, it was determined that the use of marijuana has no deleterious effects. Dr. William McGlothlin, in a recent series of articles based on his extensive research, concludes that while marijuana is not totally harmless, its possible harmful effects have been blown out of proportion.

In contrast, another researcher in the field of marijuana use for over twenty years, Dr. Constandinos J. Miras of the University of Athens, asserts that he can recognize a chronic marijuana user by the way he walks, talks, and acts. He defines a "chronic user" as one who has smoked at least two marijuana cigarets a day for two years. (From my observation, based on this definition, most hippies I have encountered are "chronic users.")

Dr. Miras alleges that chronic users have "slowed speech, lethargy, and lowered inhibitions." Some become "suddenly violent without any apparent provocation." Dr. Miras' most serious charge is that prolonged marijuana use produces brain damage. His studies with radioactive THC (a chemical known as Tetrahydrocannibinol found in all parts of the marijuana plant) have shown that the substance passes through the brain very quickly. Chronic users, according to Dr. Miras, are prone to anemia, eye inflamations, respiratory infections, and there is also good evidence of abnormal brainwave readings. (It is important to note that Dr. Miras' research is related to Greek marijuana users. There is evidence that the marijuana used in Greece is somewhat different in nature and strength than the type used in the United States and most of Europe.)

Although, as I have indicated, many pot users I have observed in the hippie world manifested no immediate negative reactions, there is a sharp break with reality on the part of many others. Like some drunks, they think what they are saying is much more clever than it really is to an objective audience. Others believe they are more creative than they really are, when their work is measured by some objective test.

A major problem that I see in marijuana use would not be shared by hip people. If the larger society has validity, and I believe it does, then pot smoking is destructive to users since it helps cause them to drop out of the society in varying degrees. On my trip I observed several people drop further and further out with their daily ritual of marijuana use.

Speed

The use of speed (Methedrine crystals, liquid, and amphetamine pills) is a practice that is deplored by the high priests and even the speed addicts themselves in the hippie world. Speed apparently does just that—it accelerates the functioning of the central nervous system. The user does not get especially euphoric—but he does move quicker, become more compulsive, and get an intense feeling of being "high."

In the context of the use of speed, I would categorize a large segment of hippies (almost 50%) as a new breed of drug addict. Old-fashioned heroin addicts (a declining pattern) were locked into a condition from which they generally wanted to escape. Most old-style addicts tried to kick innumerable times. They further attempted voluntarily and involuntarily to find a rehabilitation system. Because the speed freak has a feeble grasp of the hippie philosophy and considers himself a seeker, he is not readily inclined to admit to his addiction. He deludes himself into believing he is on a spiritual trip and this tends to keep him in his drug trap.

The new speed addicts are not the committed priest, or "religious hippies." They are generally younger searchers for Nirvana who have through speed fallen off rather than climbed onto the hippie movement.

Speed freaks walk the streets of Haight bulgy-eyed for periods sometimes of several days without sleep. Their health and brain processes are often severely impaired by the drugs. Hepatitis is a common disease among "Meth freaks" because several people often use the same needle to inject the drug intravenously.

Hippie speed addicts reflect an unusual problem—they are plastic hippies. Their pseudo-thin veneer of hippie philosophy and clothes masks a self-destructive, standard, old-fashioned drug-addict pattern. Even though they live in the hippie world, they find it necessary to "wheel-and-deal" on the borderline of the illegal drug-pusher world to survive.

Speed freaks, unlike LSD and marijuana users, become both physically and emotionally dependent on the drug. Any normative values they hold will be side-stepped in order to get the drug. And, as in other drug addictions, they have great difficulty withdrawing from using the drug. Severe emotional depressions are a standard result of withdrawal. In some cases, according to physicians, permanent brain damage and irreparable damage to the nervous system are found in so-called Meth freaks. Speed users are the clear addicts of the hippie community.

LSD

LSD is used extensively in the hippie world. My research revealed that most people have had several trips and more than half have used LSD at least ten times. Although its use is much abused, the properties of the chemical have an emotional impact which entwines with the hippie philosophy of seeking the Unity of Man and Nature. Despite its use for fun and "highs," the LSD experience can be, under proper circumstances, a deep and meaningful spiritual trip.

The best delineation of LSD, its properties, and its effects that I have found in the literature on the subject is presented in a paper entitled, "Lysergic Acid Diethylamide: An Historical Perspective," written by David Smith, M.D., in *The Journal of Psychedelic Drugs* (Summer, 1967). With his approval, the following commentary in this subsection on LSD is derived almost verbatim from this excellent article by Dr. Smith.

The ergot alkaloids are a group of drugs obtained from the fungus ergot, which grows on rye and gives rise to a great number of medically useful compounds, such as ergonovine and ergotamine. These latter compounds are used to contract the uterus after childbirth, and for the treatment of migraine headaches. LSD was first synthesized in 1938 as an intermediate leading to the synthesis of ergonovine. Its profound psychological effects were completely unknown at that time.

In 1943, Dr. Albert Hoffman, who was one of the people involved in the original synthesis, began working with it again. This time he was seeking a stimulant using lysergic acid (the base of all the ergot alkaloids) in combination with a chemical similar in structure to kikethamide, a central nervous system stimulant.

One day when he was working with this drug he began to have some peculiar psychological effects which he described as follows: "In the afternoon of April 16, 1943, when I was working on this problem, I was seized by a peculiar sensation of vertigo and restlessness. Objects, as well as the shape of my associates in the laboratory, appeared to undergo optical changes. I was unable to concentrate on my work. In a dream-like state, I left for home, where an irresistible urge to lie down overcame me. I drew the curtains and immediately fell into a peculiar state similar to a drunkenness, characterized by an exaggerated imagination. With my eyes closed, fantastic pictures of extraordinary plasticity and intensive color seemed to surge toward me. After two hours this state gradually wore off."

When someone ingests an average dose of LSD (150–250 micrograms), nothing happens for the first 30 or 45 minutes. After the sympathetic response, the first thing the individual usually notices is a change in the way he perceives things. Frequently the first thing he notices is that the walls and other objects become a bit wavy or seem to move. Then he might notice that colors are much brighter or more intense than usual. As time goes on colors can seem exquisitely more intense and beautiful than any he has ever seen before. It is also common for individuals to see a halo or rainbow effect around white lights.

Hallucinations, or a false sensory perception without any basis in external reality, are rather rare with LSD. What is more common are what may be called pseudohallucinations. Here the individual may see something but at the same time he knows his perception doesn't have a basis in external reality. For example, he may see geometric forms of figures or brilliant colors, and he realizes that they don't really exist out there.

There is another kind of rather remarkable perceptual change referred to as a synesthesia—a translation of one type of sensory experience into another. If someone is listening to music, for example, he can sometimes feel the vibrations of the music in his body. Or he can sometimes see the actual notes moving or the colors beat in rhythm with the music. Here there is a translation of one type of sensory experience into another type of experience.

A third area of change is in the area of cognitive functioning, or ordinary thinking. When someone is under the influence of LSD there is no loss of consciousness. Unlike an anesthetic drug, you do not leave the picture. A person is fully conscious and usually remembers most of the experience. Thoughts move much more rapidly than usual. A person doesn't necessarily think in the same logical way or on the basis of causal relations. For example, things that are ordinarily thought of as being opposite can now exist together and are not seen as opposites. Black and white or good and bad frequently become equal. A person can feel heavy and light at the same time. There is kind of a breakdown of the ordinary way of logical thinking; but again, if the person is asked to do something, he usually can perform the task even though he may be annoyed. If he is asked to write his name or take a psychological test, he may say, "I know I can do that but don't bother me now. I just want to go on having my experience."

Time sense is frequently affected. The past, the present, and the future frequently get mixed up. Also, strange bodily sensations may occur. A person's body seems to become much less clear and feels much closer to the universe. Sometimes hands seem to flicker and are almost disconnected from the body. When the person looks at his hands he may say, "It almost seems that they are separate from me." There are certain other bodily distortions such as elongation of the neck and other phenomena of an "Alice-in-Wonderland" variety.

The adverse effects of LSD are largely psychological in nature, and can be divided into acute immediate effects and chronic after-effects.

When an individual takes LSD he may feel that he has lost control of himself. Under this circumstance some individuals panic and become frightened. They want to be taken out of this powerless state immediately. They sometimes try to run away from the situation. At other times they become quite paranoid and suspicious of the people who are with them. They begin to feel these other people are doing something, or may do something, to them, and they may actually lash out at them. Therefore in the acute panic state the individual may try to escape from the situation.

Secondly, individuals under LSD often show very poor judgment. For example, they may have the feeling that they are very light and that they can actually fly. Under these circumstances some LSD users have actually jumped out of windows. Individuals have been known to commit suicide by walking into the ocean, feeling they were "simply part of the universe." Many people have experienced feelings of invincibility and omnipotence. "It doesn't matter if my body dies; my spirit will live." This mind-body dissociation has lead to a variety of disastrous results. Some people feeling this omnipotence have been killed as a result of walking into moving cars and trains.

Adverse effects sometimes occur after the acute effects of the drug have apparently worn off. Some people have had prolonged psychotic reactions. These psychotic consequences do not appear to be totally irreversible; however, in some cases the emotional disorder has lasted for many months.

Another type of adverse side effect is the recurrence of the acute effects of the drug many days and sometimes weeks or months after the individual has taken it. This recurrence of symptoms can have a frightening impact. The person may feel he is losing his mind. The recurrence or "flashback" phenomenon is relatively rare but seems to become more frequent with individuals who take the drug on a regular basis.

The Negative Effects of LSD

Throughout the book there have been many extravagant pronouncements made by hippie leaders or high priests about the great benefits of LSD. Some of their claims about resulting religious and mystical experiences are debatable. However, I saw many valid evidences of constructive personal growth that seemed to result from the use of LSD in the hippie movement.

This positive hippie position is, however, in sharp conflict with a very important and vocal psychiatric-medical viewpoint. This position states that any use of LSD outside of medically controlled experimentation is extremely dangerous. Dr. J. Thomas Ungerleider and Dr. Duke Fisher, LSD researchers at the UCLA Medical Center, and Dr. Sidney Cohen (author of an important book on LSD, *The Beyond Within)* are significant psychiatric authorities who share the belief that uncontrolled LSD use produces illusionary positive effects at best, and, in its more severe consequences, causes permanent personality damage.

The most widely known and respected medical doctor in the field of LSD research is Dr. Cohen. Based on his extensive research, he delineates various categories of LSD users. The following six of his categories parallel use patterns I observed on my trip:

(1) *LSD Explorers*—These are people in theology, philosophy, and students who, in spite of the risk, want to explore their sensory possibilities.

(2) *Social LSD Users*—These, according to Cohen, are people who live in a subculture where LSD is being used. They are encouraged to use the drug because of group pressure.

(3) *Hedonistic Users*—These are young people, very often teenagers or teenyboppers, who are seeking a "kick" or a thrill.

(4) *Magic Pill Users*—These are people with emotional problems who are looking for a magic quick and easy solution.

(5) *Research Use*—In this context LSD is used in a laboratory to study its effects on personality.

(6) *Religious Use*—Dr. Cohen admits that there are people, like Timothy Leary and his *League of Spiritual Discovery* (LSD), who sincerely take LSD for a spiritual or religious experience. (Of course, Gridley Wright and his followers would also fit into this category.)

Dr. Cohen elaborated at length on this last category of use

in a lecture he delivered at a college conference on LSD in 1966. He believes that people who use the drug for religious purposes, no matter how sincere, are misguided. According to Dr. Cohen, ". . . My own opinion is that these people are seriously misguided—or, as the younger people would say, 'hung up.' I believe that there are things to be learned from the LSD experience, and that it poses some questions which have relevance to the religious experience. But the chemical religious experience is not the religious life. To think that the compulsive repetition of this chemically induced state is the way to live is one of the most serious hangups and, in fact, the greatest complication of all. There are young people and a couple of old people who believe this chemically induced state is the most important thing in existence, and it must be repeatedly achieved. If anything that I say today should be emphasized, it's this—that if there is anything to be learned from LSD, it has to be brought down here to this life and applied here and now. People who have struggled to achieve this religious state through living in caves, flagellating themselves, whirling, breathing exercises or meditation, have told us that it's this life that counts, and that the state of self-transcendence is a means not an end in itself."

In another context Dr. Cohen conducted research into the drastic claims of intellectual and creative growth made by many LSD users. He found the claims to be more illusionary than factual. "In measuring alterations in creative thinking following LSD we found that out of 24 LSD subjects, 17 told us that they felt much more creative. However, our extensive testing showed that they were no more creative than the group that didn't get LSD. In brief, as with marijuana highs, the feelings of greater creative ability, omnipotence, and omniscience that seem to accompany LSD use are more illusionary than factual. As indicated, people seem to think they are performing at a higher level than they do in reality."

Dr. Ungerleider and Dr. Fisher have carried out research into the more destructive implications of LSD use. On the basis of his study of an increasing number of patients on bad LSD trips brought into the UCLA Medical Center, Dr. Ungerleider made the following statement at the same conference:

"Beginning in September, 1965, the case load gradually increased from 5 to 20 LSD cases a month. And for every case that came in, we received three or four telephone calls from other people in trouble from LSD. These people did not come in for help. We studied the first 70 patients who came in. They came in most often with hallucinations, secondly with anxiety to the point of panic. Some of the depressed people had suicidal thoughts, some had made serious suicide attempts.

"The characteristics of the group that we studied were as follows: They were predominantly single white young males. Their average age was 21. They came from throughout the Los Angeles area and most were either unemployed or students. Forty percent of the group had taken drugs other than LSD within six weeks of being seen in the emergency room; 36% had histories of chronic marijuana use, but 40% had never taken drugs other than LSD. Our sample contained no professional persons, in contrast to the findings of others where LSD was mainly used by professionals, intellectuals, and upper-middle-class people."

At the conference Dr. Duke Fisher, a colleague of Dr. Ungerleider at UCLA, listed a series of negative impacts of uncontrolled LSD use: (1) Suicide attempts; (2) value system shift, involving dropping out of society; avoidance of obligations; and work no longer seen as necessary; (3) subjective feeling of improvement and an objective loss of function; and (4) a psychotic defense reaction, manifest in an apparent psychotic behavior pattern.

In elaborating on the latter category Dr. Fisher described the following situation: "We talked to one gentleman who is not in the hospital because the 'head culture' supports him. Here is a fellow who took LSD several times and became convinced he was an orange. He withdrew to his room and refused to leave the room for fear that if someone touched him he'd turn into orange juice. The person continues to exist in that state because he is supported by the 'head culture.' He still remains psychotic."

Support of this kind of apparently very disturbed person who has "freaked-out" on acid is very prevalent in the hippie community. It is in some respects laudable to relate to and partially help a person in this condition. In general, however, supporting and defending someone who is obviously pathological reinforces his symptoms and blocks the possibility of his getting desperately needed long-term help. This practice in the hippie world, of absorbing mentally ill people, no doubt cuts down on the statistics on people who have become psychotic from an LSD trip.

Chromosome Damage

One of the most significant research results of the deleterious effect of LSD use is related to reports of chromosome damage. Although the research findings to date are inconclusive, they are certainly worthy of note. At the University of Wisconsin two researchers injected microscopic doses of LSD into pregnant mice. Sometimes no apparent harm was done. But when the LSD was injected into the pregnant mice on the seventh day after the mice were mated, the effect on the unborn mice growing in the uterus was severe. Brain malformation was found in more than half the embryos. They also found abnormalities of the jaw, mislocation of the eyes, and bizarre facial contours. Among 19 litters of mice exposed to LSD on the seventh day of pregnancy, only one seemed normal. The other 18 litters contained not just one abnormal embryo but three or more.

Another significant research project on chromosome damage was summarized in a National Institute of Mental Health publication, *The Mental Health Digest*, which reported the work of Dr. Maimon M. Cohen, of the State University of New York at Buffalo. In cooperation with Dr. Nathan Bach and a graduate student, Michelle Marinello, Dr. Cohen carried out a study of LSD effects on the chromosomes found inside each living cell in blood samples obtained from two apparently normal, healthy donors, a man and a woman. The living white blood cells from these samples were placed in test tubes containing a culture medium that encouraged cell multiplication. The cells were allowed to proliferate for three days. LSD in varying amounts was added to the experimental tubes of cells but not to others. Finally, a chemical called colchicine was inserted to arrest the cells' development at precisely the stage when the chromosomes are most clearly visible. The prepared cells were then viewed on a microscope slide. More than 3,500 cells, containing more than 160,000 chromosomes, were examined. The slides were identified by code numbers so that the examiner could not tell whether the cell he was studying had been grown with or without LSD. Broken and abnormal chromosomes proved to be twice as frequent in the cells exposed to LSD as in untreated cells cultured from the same donors.

In another experiment, Dr. Cohen obtained a blood sample from a patient who had received fifteen LSD treatments for schizophrenia over a six-year period. Three times the usual proportion of broken chromosomes were found in his cells. (It should be noted here that many medical experts report that broken chromosomes can be produced in cells by many chemical substances other than LSD.)

In another research project, Dr. Samuel Irwin of the University of Oregon secured the help of eight Portland hippies who had used LSD several times. They agreed to donate blood for a scientific inquiry. He also obtained nine samples from normal, healthy, non-LSD users and delivered all 17 (identified only by code numbers) to a colleague, Dr. Jose Egozcue. Dr. Egozcue's tests seemed to confirm the Buffalo findings. He found a significant excess of broken chromosomes and other chromosome abnormalities in six of the eight LSD users.

The foregoing summaries of research tend to suggest dire consequences from LSD use in producing chromosome damage. These negative findings, however, have to be counterbalanced by some recent different conclusions reached at an Institute of Narcotics and Drug Abuse, sponsored by the National Institute of Mental Health. The Institute, held in Washington, D.C., in the fall of 1967, was attended by many of the researchers cited in the foregoing summary of research into chromosome damage and by other national scientific figures doing research in this area.

These scientists weighed all of the research completed to date in the field and concluded that *for almost every research project that indicated chromosome damage, there were other comparable research findings that revealed no significant chromosomal damage.*

Another important conclusion of the conference was that the findings of "test-tube," or "in-vitro," research (cells studied outside the human system) in LSD effects on chromosome change cannot be freely interpreted as indicative of the effect of LSD on live human subjects. All that may be said conclusively at this time, therefore, is that the research is suggestive of chromosome damage. Further, the data so far does not prove that birth defects in human beings do occur from LSD. The research is in its opening phase and clear-cut conclusions on the issue may not be available for several years.

The Hip Viewpoint on LSD

In one of our discussions, I mentioned to Gridley the fact that although the data isn't conclusive, there have been some research results which suggest that LSD might cause chromosome damage. His response was philosophical: "Look, man, when you drive a car on the freeway you have a good chance of being killed. Or if you smoke tobacco, you run a good risk of cancer. My use of acid is a calculated risk. It's related to my religious and philosophical goals and no one ever told me it was an easy trip."

Most hippies reject so-called scientific research into LSD impact. They pointedly ignore the recent chromosomal damage evidence as being part of the Establishment's effort to frighten people. For them, formal research settings are bound to produce "bummers." A medical or research environment is considered too plastic a situation for taking a drug that is a "spiritual and religious sacrament" and mind-expansion device. It should, they contend, be used in as natural a setting as possible.

An appraisal of LSD use in the hippie world and a critical opinion of the Establishment's negative position was made to me in my interview with Stan Russell.

S–Just taking LSD doesn't insure that you get any insight out of it. There are a lot of people whom I have met, who have taken LSD, who are just as nutty as they can be. I have seen people blow their minds from LSD. People whom I was very close to and living with. The experience of stepping out of the social structure is a very liberating experience, especially if the structure has been oppressive and has made them distrustful of their own inner nature, or uncomfortable with their own inner nature. To step out of that is a pleasant experience. For some people getting out is an end in itself. That's all they are interested in doing. They keep stepping out, and stepping out, and stepping out.

Each time they do, they give up their personality, or ego, or whatever you want to call it. They see shedding their ego as a virtue because it feels good. They have set up a structureless personality for themselves. That leads them to become relatively passive people, who don't have the perimeters of a personality. They have what might be referred to as "blown minds."

They have to restructure themselves if they want to come out of this. Most of them convince themselves that there is nothing they can do. They don't believe in anything. I met a guy who had taken two hundred acid trips and he didn't believe in anything. That's what he told me, but actually, what he did believe in was that there is nothing to believe in. Do you follow me? And that was something that he had imposed upon himself and then conditioned into himself.

Now he was on a closed circuit where there was nothing to believe in. "There is nothing to believe in." And he just keeps taking acid and believing in nothing. And he tends to be cynical and unhappy.

On the other hand, if you take acid with the proper preparation and in the proper setting, in order to go inward and with specific goals to accomplish, it's fantastically effective. It can assist you in making any changes that you want to make. If your body is not well, it can place you in harmony with your body, so that your body can heal itself. If you are locked in very heavy ego games you don't understand, you can step out of those games and look at them and see what's happening, and then step back into them and act in a different way.

LY–What's your opinion of Dr. Sidney Cohen's opinion on hippie patterns of LSD use?

S–Cohen is on a Sidney Cohen trip. He is out to be *the* expert on LSD. He's going to be the Establishmentarian expert. No matter what happens or what is determined, he is able to channel it into the Establishment's viewpoint on LSD.

The mass society would like to hear that LSD is the answer to all of their dreams, which it is. But there are a lot of people in political power who want people to keep coming to work every day at nine o'clock and stay there until six. Then they can go home and watch TV until they fall asleep. And then come back the next morning at nine and work there the whole day. They should also wear white shirts and neckties. If these people started taking acid, they wouldn't do that anymore. LSD could liberate these people but they won't let that happen. Many professionals are rewarded by the Establishment with grants, professorships, and awards to say what they want to hear, that LSD is no good and it will kill you. LSD could liberate many more people than hippies, but the Establishment won't let it happen.

A Balanced Viewpoint

The most lucid and well-balanced observer of overall drug use in psychedelia that I met on my trip was Dr. Smith, the founder of the Haight-Ashbury Free Medical Clinic. Dr. Smith has seen much of the bad and some good effects of drugs on the hip scene. His views corresponded most closely with many of my own observations and positions. The following interview I had with him, in my view, places the total psychedelic drug scene in a realistic and balanced perspective.

DR. S–The free clinic had its philosophical origins primarily from a concern of mine to have adverse drug reactions treated properly. As director of the Alcohol and Drug Abuse Screening Unit here at San Francisco General Hospital, and in my research role at the U.C. Medical Center of central-nervous-system stimulants, I became clinically involved in the drug abuse problem throughout the San Francisco area. We noted an alarming increase in adverse reactions to drugs in people from Haight-Ashbury.

We felt that the social milieu of Haight almost required that these drug reactions be treated improperly. When someone is high on a central-nervous-system stimulant, they have very marked paranoiac characteristics. The act of being brought to a regular hospital many times can precipitate a bad trip, or at least complicate and aggravate it. We felt that a regionalized clinic in the community would be of great value.

At first we primarily dealt with bad LSD trips. However, the pattern has shifted rather dramatically. We're seeing a startling increase in the use of Methedrine, a more toxic substance. Methedrine is a general central-nervous-system stimulant. It suppresses appetite and interrupts sleep patterns. Taken intravenously, it produces tremendous physiological and psychological damage.

We're seeing a lot of young kids that are attracted to the flame of Haight-Ashbury, like moths to a light, and these kids don't have any idea what the hippie philosophy is all about. They have the ornaments of a hippie with the long hair and the clothes, but they don't know any of the positive philosophical aspects.

They only know the alienation that they feel, along with their attraction to the flame; and they come here primarily interested in drugs and sex.

As I mentioned, many of these young people get involved with intravenous Methedrine use, and this produces tremendous physiological and psychological damage. Some of them just don't like the effects of LSD. LSD makes them think too much. Methedrine just makes them high. They can stay stoned all the time and that's really what the teenybopper appears to be after.

These kids have no idea of hippie philosophy. The hard core of hippies in Haight-Ashbury that bravely try to put their philosophy into effect have little effect on the kids. They're surrounded by masses of all sorts of people that are just there for kicks or exploitation, or to get in on the drug market, which is an enormously popular and profitable business.

LY–I detect that you are sympathetic to some of the overall patterns of hippie philosophy.

DR. S–Well, I think when you view the problems of today, and you view the extreme alienation that now exists in youth, you conclude that the hippie philosophy and its involvement can be appealing. The problem is to get the philosophy into effect. Getting it into operation is quite difficult, particularly in a society like ours where there is such antagonism toward the questioning of middle-class values.

LY–One view that I have is that the hippie community has its own drug-addiction problem. That drug problem is

Methedrine. Pot and acid in the hippie community is not related to drug addiction. The "Meth freaks" are the drug addicts of the hippie world. Is this true from your viewpoint?

DR. S–In the hippie philosophy, there is no place for Methedrine. Methedrine is not a social drug. For example, marijuana is the alcohol of the hippie culture. They use pot like straight society uses alcohol. They smoke marijuana and have their parties with it.

On the other hand, LSD is the philosophical and religious drug. The drug that they use to scramble the circuits, so that they can forget all the social nonsense they were taught by their parents and society. LSD reconditions them so that they can live the hippie philosophy.

The hippie philosophy, however, is a very difficult thing to live. It's very hard not to want to earn as much money as you can. It's very difficult to rid yourself of racial biases when you've been raised in a racially biased community. It's very difficult to believe that you can overtly love your neighbor, without being suspected of being a queer, a sex fiend, or something like that. It is very hard not to believe that hate, violence, and war will always be with us. And this is how the hippie uses LSD. He uses it to recondition his mind and have a vision of how life ought to be.

LY–Could you elaborate a little bit more on these drugs? Don't worry about popularizing any of the medical terms for me for our purposes here. For example, when you say "LSD scrambles the circuits," what do you mean?

DR. S–In the sub-cortical structures of the brain, there's an area called the reticular activating system. The reticular activating system is that part of the central nervous system that codes incoming sensory stimuli, and people are conditioned to respond to sensory stimuli in different ways. For example, at a very loud cocktail party a mother may hear her baby cry, and the intensity of the cry is much, much lower than the general mass of noise that's going on. And maybe nobody will react to, or even hear, that noise but the mother. She will react and go to the child's aid. This is how conditioned responses or habits are formed.

Now, LSD sensitizes the reticular activating system—sensitizes it to the point where the code is broken up. You perceive all incoming sensory stimuli, and many times this perception is distorted. If one wants to de-condition themselves then, through a drug like LSD, it is possible to produce this de-conditioning effect.

Herein lies the Leary philosophy of turn on, tune in, and drop out. The philosophy states that the individual begins by having a feeling of alienation toward society and then makes the first move toward dropping out of society. He *turns-on* by taking LSD as a sacrament, as a way of having a new vision and breaking with the old. In effect, the philosophy states that they've been brainwashed, and that they are trapped by their own mind.

Once this is done, then one must *tune-in* to a new way of life. The philosophy also clearly states that LSD drug usage is necessary in the beginning, but continued usage is not essential. In fact, it states that the really "in" thing to do is to be turned-on without drugs. Being continually turned-on and tuned-in without drugs is the Nirvana of the hippie.

LY–How many people do you feel have reached this state?

DR. S–When you're dealing with subjective phenomenon as abstract as this, how can you tell? When I see someone wandering around saying, "I'm turned-on and tuned-in," I don't know whether he's mentally ill or has achieved this state of being. The line between mystical experience and mental illness is a fine one. This is one of the problems of the hippie population that has created so much confusion about Haight-Ashbury and the drug scene. It is a very new situation to have thousands of young people taking powerful psychoactive drugs. Never have we had such a large group of young people so involved with mental processes, not just intellectual processes, but emotional processes. They have been described as the "Freudian proletariat." They spend a great deal of their time scrutinizing their emotions, examining intellectual phenomena, and going on the assumption that the potential of the mind is limitless.

Here, in part, is one of the reasons there are so many health problems in Haight-Ashbury. They're so involved with mental processes that they, in effect, neglect and ignore their bodies. Their bodies are just vehicles for their emotions and their minds.

LY–What's your opinion, personal and professional, about the real effect of what the hippies say is happening to them?

DR. S–I've seen what I consider to be valid converts. People whose lives have changed for the better. Again, you have to get down to define where the good is occurring. The good seems to occur at the individual rather than the social level, because a society of happy people is not necessarily the most productive society. As we know from books like *Nineteen Eighty-Four* and *Brave New World,* sometimes a society needs a war for maximum output.

Many hippie converts that I know have quit high-paying positions. They've gone from a life of relative unhappiness and quiet desperation to lives of happiness and aesthetic development. Their economic level has dropped down three or four notches. Instead of a big home, they have a small apartment, and maybe one old car. But they seem much happier, more artistic, much more turned-on to life.

When you're under the influence of LSD, you feel like you want to help your fellow man. The question is, "Does this feeling of wanting to help your fellow man, rather than take advantage of him, come from the psychedelic drug experience or does it merely create this impression?"

Now, whether this illusion lasts or not is the real issue. Whether you can take this momentary peak experience and translate it into terms of individual or social good is where the question arises. I've seen people do it. But a majority of people do not have the psychological facilities for undergoing this dramatic mental alteration.

LY–We really don't know yet, do we? I mean we may know in ten years if these people are really tuned-in to beauty or headed for destruction.

DR. S–No, we don't know the long-term effects, particularly the results of uncontrolled LSD use for non-medical purposes. Dr. McLoughlin, of UCLA, did a study where he gave to three groups of people at UCLA a placebo, 25 micrograms of LSD, and 250 micrograms of LSD. He then tried to determine what their long-term attitudinal changes were. He found that there was a statistically significant tendency toward the aesthetic in the 250-microgram LSD dosage group.

Also, with alcoholics, there have been some studies to indicate that LSD breaks up compulsive patterns and helps make them drug-free. It cures their compulsion and it doesn't matter whether the compulsion is alcohol or to make a million dollars. Compulsions tend to make one unhappy. If you can break up compulsive behavioral patterns, then it can be of value. There's no question in my mind about that.

LY–A central figure in my book is a man named Gridley Wright. He started a community called Strawberry Fields. I've observed him over several months. I've more or less lived with him and his group. He has been taking LSD in small dosages about every four days. What's your reaction to this practice, which seems rather prevalent?

DR. S–I think this is a very foolish way to take the drug. First of all, what you're after is the peak experience, and if you take it too regularly, even though you really aren't addicted, you develop a heavy tolerance. So you would have to take a progressively higher drug dosage to achieve the same effect. There's a very high tolerance in all central-nervous-system stimulants, and the psychological dependence on frequent LSD use minimizes the ability to achieve a peak experience and then correlate this peak experience with real life.

LY–Can you take a deadly overdose of LSD?

DR. S–The LD 50 of LSD is 2 mgm per kilogram. [An LD 50 dose is the amount necessary to kill an experimental animal.] You would have to take about a thousand times the standard 250 microgram dosage to overdose. The problem that results from an overdose of LSD is convulsions.

LY–Do people die from it?

DR. S–No, but people have died from LSD-related effects. These are primarily suicides.

LY–Would you elaborate on some of the negative results of LSD use you've seen, or as hip people call it, a "bummer."

DR. S–LSD alters perception. About one hour after you take it orally, you start to see perceptual alterations. It also causes alterations in cognitive functioning and alterations in value judgment. It also causes a phenomenon of increased focus, so that you might, for example, suddenly become attracted to and enamored with the significance of a red rose. You lose the connotation that "a rose is a rose, is a rose."

One of the important things about the psychedelic experience is that it redefines all sorts of psychological phenomena. A rose is not a rose, if you're under the influence of LSD. It may become the most important, significant thing in the universe at that moment in time. The alteration of perceptual function and value judgment may work in the reverse direction. You may see something that really freaks you. You may be hallucinating and suddenly the hallucinations become real to you.

For example, a nineteen-year-old girl who took LSD and had severe perceptual alterations came to the clinic. She looked in the mirror and her face turned almost to that of a mummy and she just blew her cork right there. She had panic reactions—screaming, yelling. All she could think about for days was this vision in the mirror.

In another case, a girl who had taken a trip became sick to her stomach and began to vomit. She was sitting on the john. The spots on the floor turned to spiders. And she cracked right there. When they break, many times it's a very acute panic reaction.

Some people, however, are predisposed to longer-term psychological disorders or perceptual disorders from LSD use. There are basically two types of long-term perceptual disorders that result. Some people have a continued long-term alteration in perception, halos around lights, flashing lights, or recurrent perceptual disturbances or hallucinosis. Dr. Ungerleider has described it as "flashback phenomena." We call it a recurrent hallucinosis. It's the same thing, a trip scene without a drug.

Then you have the long-term emotional effects which are of the greatest concern to us. Long-term depressions and feelings of an inability to communicate. Psychotic states of being.

We used to think that the only people who had long-term emotional problems were those who were somehow disturbed beforehand. And people went to great lengths to find out a person's past disturbed pattern. It becomes obvious that if you look at any of our backgrounds, we find something that could be made to appear as a past disturbing pattern. It has become obvious to us in our research that personalities within normal limits, that is, almost anybody, if they take LSD under improper circumstances can develop a long-term emotional disorder.

I'm seeing a boy now—a twenty-year-old Jewish boy. He was very hard-working, came from a well-structured Jewish family, had good grades, was moderate and temperate in all things. He took LSD in the back of a car and the car kept stalling in traffic. He said it was the most horrible experience in his life. All these cars and buildings and people and everything looked meaningless. And he hasn't gotten off that "meaningless thing" feeling. His statement now is that he can't communicate and he's so depressed that he's made suicide attempts.

LY–On the flashback phenomenon, chronologically, is it your

view that this is a continued psychological set, or is it that the LSD is still in the system and keeps up its "hold" periodically.

DR. S–No. LSD leaves the system one hour after ingestion. In fact, you can hardly find any more LSD in the body when the actual drug reaction begins. It sets off something in the central nervous system. Flashbacks, at least according to our current thinking, are definitely psychological phenomena. There is the small possibility that LSD does some sort of microscopic brain damage that accounts for this pattern. These theories are being tested. But until something very specific comes along, it appears to be just a vague alteration in the EEG [brain wave] pattern.

LY–What about the incidence of bad trips. Can you cite some numbers or statistics related to your clinic?

DR. S–The number of admissions and visits for bad trips is not astronomical. There are about five a day here [San Francisco General Hospital] and maybe five to ten a day at the Haight-Ashbury Free Clinic. It breaks down to about fifteen a day in the places where I work.

As I mentioned, bad trips on LSD have gone down recently and Methedrine problems have increased. Methedrine stimulates the central nervous system, depresses appetite, and interferes with body functioning to the point where the individual may suddenly become acutely anxious, and can even hallucinate. He develops a toxic psychosis of the type I described. This occurs in association with some significant physical impairment. The toxic psychosis of Methedrine is similar to that of LSD in that the toxic psychosis of Methedrine has a lot of hallucinatory material. But the toxic psychosis of Methedrine is much worse because of the extreme paranoia and motor stimulation.

We've done some animal research to verify that Methedrine also produces a tremendous amount of hostility in the animal. He becomes very aggressive, he attacks. And this is what we're seeing in the kids, too. They become very paranoid, very frightened, very aggressive, and act impulsively.

LY–Is it quite different from the LSD?

DR. S–Somewhat different, but it's in the same direction. Methedrine is primarily an intoxication phenomenon. Withdrawal is actually a state of complete exhaustion.

Here's a good example to reinforce this in your mind. If a heroin addict and a Methedrine addict are in your waiting room, and if the heroin addict has his maintenance dose of heroin, he's on the nod, and drowsy. A heroin addict who has his maintenance dosage of heroin is hard to tell from anyone else, looking from a distance. He's anxiety-free and he might be sitting there very calmly. Whereas the individual intoxicated with Methedrine is agitated, disturbed, and maybe hallucinating. He can't sit still. He'd be walking around, in motion. But as the Methedrine wears off, the Methedrine addict goes into a state of exhaustion and he may go to sleep. Whereas when the heroin wears off, the addict becomes agitated. He has cramps; he can't sit still. Here you have a good example of intoxication and withdrawal and how the drug effects are just exactly opposite—one hundred and eighty degrees opposite.

LY–What is the problem with the Methedrine addicts? Is it that they have taken it for a long period or that they have received an excessive dosage?

DR. S–Both. They get an excessive dosage and they have an anxiety reaction for long periods of time.

LY–What about psychotic effects?

DR. S–Two special characteristics of this community are, first of all, that the hip people deny that mental illness exists in Haight-Ashbury. You might have an acute bad trip, but that's considered to be a temporary phenomenon. They try to minimize the fact that any mental illness exists.

You have to be in the situation in order to realize how difficult it is when a hippie brings in another hippie who has some bad effects from an LSD trip. The patient may be catatonic, have inappropriate effects, may be visually hallucinating, and may even have auditory hallucination. I'm thinking of a specific case now, where they brought this boy in to see me because they wanted some medicine to help him come down. He had been up for about a week or week and a half, and he was still out of it. I said, "Well, I think the boy has some severe mental problems. He needs to come into a mental hospital for a long period of time." They said, "No, he's not mentally ill. He's where it's at, but he's just having trouble coming down. He's having a re-entry problem, but he's not mentally ill."

And you find that this is very, very difficult for you to handle, because they have become so involved with mental processes that the fine lines between mental illness, ecstasy, and Nirvana have become blurred.

I've been thinking of writing up a theory of mine in which I describe things in our terminology about a circular theory of mental illness. A person takes LSD and starts in one direction and another person has a schizophrenic process that starts in the other direction. At all times, it's both an *individual* and *social* value judgment as to whether "I am, or I am not ill."

In Haight-Ashbury, they just don't evaluate people who are high on drugs as being mentally ill; whereas in the larger society we would. But in the stage of the hundred-and-eighty-degree culmination, both the LSD extreme intoxication person in a catatonic state of mind and the non-drug schizophrenic person are incapable of making individual value judgments. They can't say whether they are mentally ill or not mentally ill. They can not form any sort of value judgment and it becomes purely society's decision. In Haight-Ashbury they just happen not to call it mental illness and it becomes a very arbitrary phenomenon. One in which the individual is so far out that he has no say in the matter. If someone is freaked out for a week or more, we would have to diagnose him as psychotic.

CRITIQUE

Unquestionably psychedelic drugs have the power to produce severe and lasting changes in human personality in several directions. On my reality trip, I saw disturbing results of individuals freaked out—staring into space for long periods of time. Some youths, to my eyes, were slowly killing their egos, spirits, and bodies with continuing LSD abuse. Young children from the ages of four to ten who had been given LSD and pot by their "doting" hippie parents had glazed and vacant looks in their eyes.

American society may be building up a large mental hospital population of psychotic "bum-trippers" from the new movement. In the clearer cases of personality destruction, it seems recently that at least once and usually twice a week there is a report of either a bizarre LSD-caused suicide or homicide.

In a life-giving direction LSD has been hailed by Leary as the ultimate sexual elixir. In one of his interviews he described the sexual power of LSD as the "untold secret," and "what LSD was really all about." He indicated that the sexual orgasm was magnified thousands of times through the heightened electrical sensations produced by the chemical.

On my research trip, several individuals reported to me that LSD had solved their sexual impotency problems. "The elimination of the up-tight ego by acid puts you into a clearer state of enormous pleasure." My personal experience with LSD led me to conclude that it would unblock people who had sexual inhibition "hangups." However, for sexual partners who were free from inhibitions in reality—without the drug—the sexual experience was improved, but not to the enormous degree that Leary claims. The power of the drug in helping one focus intensely on the subject (sexual partner) at hand and the increased ability for sexual partners to communicate and interact seems to enhance the pleasure of sexual intercourse.

Also, in a positive direction, I personally saw people who

had apparently been rather firmly entrenched criminals, neurotics, and some psychotics flip over into a more meaningful way of life as a result of LSD use. I remembered Sonny with twenty suicide slash marks from the past on his arm, now smiling, happy, and articulate with his psychedelic drugs.

The ecstatic new hip world use of LSD can't be quickly dismissed. As Stan Russell described it to me: "When you have the acid experience and you get up there in the clouds, and suddenly the clouds part, you get a flash of what is undeniably heaven. And that heaven came right from within you. You can have that flash all by yourself. It isn't given to you by other people. If there is somebody else there, and you share it together, then it is indeed the most ecstatic experience that you can have. And there is no doubt in your mind when you have the experience that it is ecstasy, pure and simple."

In spite of these flashes of ecstasy, however, no one, not even the staunchest hippie high priest, can block out the living agony of certain LSD bummers. In counterpoint, not even the most severe medical or square critics of LSD use can totally ignore the positive loving personality and intellectual gains made by some users of psychedelic drugs. The issue, however, appears to be most confusing and baffling in the middle-range area.

The Alice-in-Wonderland Effect

Some people clearly appear to have enlarged their intellectual ability and happiness by the use of psychedelic drugs. In other cases there are clear-cut destructive results taking the form of psychosis, suicide, and homicide. Another kind of situation has increasingly emerged among psychedelic drug users. Many, after prolonged drug use, seem to find themselves in the dilemma of living between several worlds, and not fitting clearly into any one of them. They are part of the psychedelic complex, they are attempting re-entry into the straight world, and thus they exist in an *Alice-in-*

Wonderland condition. The following case example may articulate this issue.

A 19-year-old, rather attractive girl, whom I will call Alice, appeared with her mother at my weekly Psychodrama group. She was bright, vivacious, and when she began to act out her scene I quickly determined that she was "high." Her high was a carry-over from an LSD trip she had had the day before in San Francisco. She had come to Los Angeles to visit her mother directly from a five-month engagement as a "house-mother" in a Haight-Ashbury hippie pad. For the most part she claimed to have had a good, loving experience in hippieland.

She left Haight partly because "the 'Meth freaks' who had recently moved into my pad were getting further and further out." She finally decided that one of them, who was partially her boyfriend, was definitely "crazy" when for no reason he attempted to stab her with a bread knife. She acted the scene out in Psychodrama, and from her viewpoint it was clear that there was no argument or provocation for his act of violence. This Methedrine addict, after apparently a long run of using the drug, simply and suddenly flipped out into a paranoid state and attacked Alice with a knife. Fortunately, there were other people present to restrain the would-be killer or else another LSD headline tragedy might very well have occurred. This incident, and others like it, had changed her positive feelings about the Haight scene and she left.

A positive effect she had developed in Haight was the feeling that she could now really love her parents. This combination of negative and positive feelings brought Alice back to her broken home in Los Angeles.

In subsequent Psychodrama sessions, however, we learned that her new-found "love" derived from a five-month run of LSD, Methedrine, and marijuana use, and was not powerful enough to produce any significant communication or real love between Alice and her parents. They were divorced and she had tried to live happily with each one. It simply did not work.

In one intensive Psychodrama session, she acted out a recent scene in her room at her father's house. In describing the room, it was revealed that she was attempting to recreate her "Haight scene" here in Los Angeles. Her mattress rested on the floor, posters were on the walls, and she had painted her room in psychedelic colors. *Perhaps most important was the fact that although she had not used any drugs for several weeks, she was now beginning to hallucinate and "flash-on" visions and images she had once experienced under LSD.*

She saw eyes staring at her, the walls at times pulsated, and she could see the shape of people's faces change. As she sat on the floor of our Psychodrama stage in the middle of her scene, with two auxiliary egos playing the role of the staring eyes, and another member of our group as her mother, she looked up at me and asked the key psychedelic question in a calm voice: *"Are these images and hallucinations a result of my past drug experiences, or am I just going crazy?"*

I had no answer to her question then, and still don't. This unfortunate girl had tried the only two worlds available to her and was turned-off by both. Life in the upper-middle-class "square" world of her super-straight parents and the societal opportunities of schools and material objects they had to offer her was an apparently unacceptable way of life. She had also tried the hip life of Haight and was disillusioned with the phoniness, hypocrisy, and the violence she found in this other world. Neither of these worlds was attractive to her and now—with the help of the after-effects of the psychedelic drug bombardment of her psychological system—she was drifting into an Alice-in-Wonderland existence.

To conclude on the case of Alice, I felt that my once-a-week Psychodrama, although useful to her, was not adequate enough for this girl's long-term resolution of her problem. She required, I felt, a full-time life situation that would bring her back to some reality. I recommended that she enter Synanon. In this drug-free environment, I felt that the work she would be assigned, the intensive group sessions, and the opportunity to encounter interesting people from all walks of life on almost a twenty-four-hour-a-day basis, might possibly tune her back into a real world that she could accept. She did, in fact, enter Synanon and seems to be making progress.

Alice's experience is very typical of many young people who have tried the seductive temptations of the psychedelic drug scene. The non-demanding life style of the psychedelic world and the fantasy quality of the drugs have a magnetic attraction for young people disillusioned with the admitted hypocrisies and plastic characteristics of American society. My observation, however, is that for many "flower children" the hopes they had for a happy hippie life soon become corroded by the chaotic realities of the scene.

Many hippie youths soon find, as Alice did, that much of the hippie philosophy and way of life is even less satisfying, more hypocritical, and more plastic than straight society. At this juncture, re-entry into the larger society is often very difficult because the original problems they had are compounded by the *Alice-in-Wonderland* fantasy effects produced by psychedelic drugs.

The possible deleterious effects of the psychedelic drug bombardment of the human physical and emotional system is an area deserving enormous research attention. In my view, at this time, the medical and other professional experts shouting "total destruction" and the hippie priests shouting "total salvation" are both extremists. Time, the reports of personal experiences, and careful scientific research investigation will hopefully produce answers to the vital questions related to the impact of the psychedelic drug scene—a revolution that has in a relatively short span of time caused so much agony and so much ecstasy.

CHAPTER FOURTEEN

C.E.D. on LSD

CHARLES E. DEDERICH, FOUNDER of Synanon, was one of the early experimental test cases of LSD. In 1957 he had two powerful LSD experiences as a member of a group of ex-alcoholics who were given the chemical in a UCLA medical experiment. He believes that his LSD experience was profound and drastically changed his life style in a positive way; yet he raises some serious questions about what is happening with uncontrolled LSD use on the hippie scene. As a pioneer in the LSD experimental field, his viewpoint sheds considerable light on the controversial issues surrounding LSD that are currently under scientific investigation.

Chuck is an earthquake of a man. In 1958, after about forty years of a riotous life that included alcoholism and several aborted efforts as a business corporation executive, he founded the Synanon movement. This new family of men, women, and children was guided, primarily through his energy and his genius, over the past ten years into the creation of a human organization that has helped thousands of people. Many of these people had serious problems of crime and heroin addiction. Recently a handful of ex-hippie addicts, who were destroying themselves with drug abuse, have benefited from Synanon's anti-drug posture.

The two LSD experiences he had more than ten years ago were helpful, according to Dederich, in changing his life from one of egocentrism and destruction toward a direction of great service to his fellow man. Chuck's LSD experience seemed to propel him into a life style of greater compassion, human involvement, and social action.

As described in greater detail in my book, *Synanon: The Tunnel Back,* Chuck founded Synanon with a thirty-three-dollar unemployment check. In a short decade, this minor capital outlay combined with his spiritual and intellectual force skyrocketed Synanon into a significant national organization. In addition to its work with crime and addiction problems, Synanon as a social movement has recently been joined by thousands of normal "square" citizens in Synanon Clubs around the country.

Chuck, from his own LSD episode, his past highs as an alcoholic, and his peculiar experience of founding and heading an organization that has separated more addicts (some former hippies) from their addiction than any other intentional program in the country, has a unique view of hippie organizations and LSD. Following is his considered appraisal of his experience and viewpoint as it relates to the new scene.

C–Let me tell you where I think the hippies are in the use of LSD. In 1957, as we celebrate in song and story, I became a member of a group of people who were taking LSD under pretty good, controlled conditions. In the first place, the number was very, very limited. It was being handled over at UCLA with some doctors. These were competent medical men like Dr. Sidney Cohen and Dr. Keith Dittman. The people who took LSD along with me were mainly in their thirties and forties. The experimental group was rather unstable. They were recently recovered alcoholics, people who had been sober in the AA from one to four years. At that time I had been sober about eighteen months.

My first experience was in August, 1957, and I digested it on an intellectual level. Prior to the experience, I had been told by the administering people there that they would prefer that I *not* read Huxley's two books, *Doors of Perception* and *Heaven and Hell,* until after I had the experience. I was a good patient and did exactly what they told me. I read those two books plus many more on the subject right after the first experience. I digested the LSD experience for about four months and then had one more. The second one didn't produce much more for me. I was just high.

Now I'm an old hand at getting high. At that time I was a middle-aged man and I had been a good professional alcoholic. I knew how to have more fun than most people have with alcohol. It was only for about three or four years before my last drink that it turned to garbage. But for many years I knew how to get high. I knew how to enjoy myself with alcohol by going way out in an unusually uninhibited way.

The second LSD experience was a fair-to-middlin' Wednesday night kind of drunk you might have by inhaling eight or nine martinis and then throwing a steak dinner on top of it at midnight. You know, a good working salesman's way of spending a Wednesday night when he's out on the road somewhere.

This is important; unlike the hippie kids of today, I never felt any need again to take an LSD trip. I have no fear of taking another trip at all. It's quite possible that under certain favorable conditions I'd sit down some day with a bunch of my friends and take an LSD trip. But I have no need to do it right now. I wouldn't walk across the street for the opportunity.

The LSD trip that I took back in '57 corresponded to all the things I read about later. It had a hold of somewhere between two and three months. The experience doesn't end when you come out from under the immediate intoxicating influence of the drug. It stays with you and you go through all sorts of changes and insights. I had all of those.

Memories of things came up out of my past that I had completely blocked out. During the first two months after taking LSD I had possibly about half a dozen deep emotional experiences. I would go to my room sometimes in the middle of the morning or the middle of the afternoon and cry. In a sense, I cried for the world. I was also very joyful about the world. You know, the universe is an extremely fantastic experience. Consciousness was exquisitely painful and exquisitely the opposite—comically pleasurable and enjoyable.

I seemed to have the experience of resolving *"the paradox."* Life was very good and also very bad. Good was so good you couldn't stand it. And bad was so bad you couldn't stand it. These feelings were fantastic sensations.

Here are some other things I observed from my experience. Even under the controlled conditions that had been set up under the UCLA program, I saw some pretty tragic situations develop.

I saw a very brilliant kind of guy, who was a real 1967 hippie in 1957, fall apart before my eyes. He was a highly educated person, about thirty-two, and came from a wealthy family. Like most of the contemporary hippies, he also was a gently reared young man. He had dropped out. He didn't make it through Harvard; however, he had the most beautiful Harvard accent I've ever heard. He could talk that way. But, in the middle of a sentence, he had this fantastic ability to flip over to a real funny and hip kind of "street talk." He was a pretty fantastic and likable guy.

One of the things we did together after our experience was to read some basic books on Zen. We also dug around and got one of Alan Watts' books and some others. I somehow seemed to understand the Zen situation as being basically a set of injunctions and hints and suggestions and so on to a strictly subjective, moral life. One that would pay off in a better existence.

I found Zen to be no different except in some insignificant details to the great philosophies of Christ, Mohammed, Shakespeare, Freud, Dante, and many other great minds.

My friend's interpretation of Zen, however, threw him into a state of omniscience and omnipotence. He had been an alcoholic for many years up to the LSD experience and had been off of alcohol for two years. Feeling omnipotent, one of the first things he did, of course, was to start drinking again.

He didn't last very long. Before I knew it, he was in bed and howling all over the place. I went over and tried to argue with him and I took this Zen book that he had interpreted. I said, "Jack, this is ridiculous. You've gone a hundred and eighty degrees off to what seems to be said here!" He couldn't see it. He wound up with the screaming meemies climbing the wall, and he destroyed himself. He was a big, healthy, good-looking, brilliant, sensitive human being. That was the end of him. In one year he was dead!

My LSD experience was extremely important to me, mainly because of the fact that I was very conscious before it, in certain ways during it, and of course gave it considerable attention for many years after. Yet, in retrospect, I don't really know whether it was any more important than getting royally drunk on some weekend seven years before.

Here's the point I would like to make. Going back to the summer of 1957, when I had my first trip, I saw what seemed to me then and what seems to me now some very destructive things happen. I no longer know anything about the people who took the LSD with me. They've all disappeared. As the years and months went by, I heard that some of them got drunk again. No positive change seemed to have happened in their lives.

People are now experiencing en masse what I saw go on in the microcosm of that UCLA experiment. What seems to be happening now in a totally uncontrolled way is that the hippies are taking this highly unpredictable drug and all of its cousins and shooting it into human organisms that have absolutely no hook into reality. Most of them are disappointed children. Some of their leaders are even beginning to question the notion that everybody should take LSD.

Here is one of the problems of the hippie leaders. When I took my LSD in August, in September I was still in the experience resulting from that one injection of LSD. I, of course, thought at that time that the best thing that could happen to the Congress of the United States would be to give everybody in the United States LSD. I was convinced that the world's evils and wars would be over if we could give everyone in the United Nations LSD.

I thought that the heads of all large corporations should take it immediately. I went around bellowing and beating my chest that this was the panacea for everything. Now, of course, I realize that I was under the influence of a drug. When I shouted these asinine suggestions in September and October, several months after taking LSD, I was still under the influence of a powerful drug.

The hippie leaders don't realize that LSD has what the street kids call a "hold"—a long hold. The hippie leaders, although they're beginning to suspect something is wrong, are making all these wild, missionary statements under the influence of the drug.

I would have told you, and perhaps convinced you, during the time I was high on LSD, that you only had a few days to live unless you took LSD. I would say, "Wake up and live! You'll find God. And you will talk to your inner ear and your third eye will be entertained beyond your wildest dreams," and so on. At that time, just like these kids are today, I was simply under the influence of a powerful drug.

LY–Let me comment, briefly, on what I've observed about LSD in the last two months of my travels. And then I'd be very much interested in your commentary.

In recent months I have talked directly to well over a hundred hippie people and, less intensely, to about five hundred in New York, up and down the State of California, in camps and cities. First of all, one fact is clear. Almost everyone I talked to on the hippie scene, with the exception of maybe a few people, has had some LSD. I would say that this is a scientific random sample because I didn't push myself in any special direction. I floated with whatever was happening.

At a minimum I'd say about half of the people I talked to, people who ranged in age from fifteen to thirty, had somewhere around four to twenty LSD experiences. You can throw the term "dosage" out the window because nobody really knows the power of the acid they're getting.

The majority of hippies who have had a large number of LSD experiences are all rather grim and dramatic about it. They're exploring. They feel they have found something earth-shattering and very important in their life scheme. The other half have been on from twenty-five to two hundred LSD trips. And by the way, these are not exclusively New York or California hippies. These are kids from Ohio, Michigan, Montana, New Mexico, Texas, and Georgia. The large trippers speak slower and more methodically. They've done some reading. Many have a clear conception that there is such a thing as a "cosmic reality" and a "collective consciousness."

I don't know how they were before their LSD experience, but at the moment they seem very intelligent and rather well read. They talk about being tuned-in to infinity and a universal mind. They smilingly tell you that when they meet another "head" they can see it in the look of the eyes. Their religious orientation is oriental, and they talk about reincarnation. Their high priests say they are not mad at the Great Society. They're striving toward the formation of small primary group communities where people can take LSD and smoke pot without any penalties.

They want to be left alone, as they say, "to do their thing" in freedom, in a tribal situation.

They use the concept of "my trip" and "your trip." If you play the sitar and I like to go into the woods for two months at a time, you know, that's your trip and the woods is mine. Another fellow likes to "screw" almost everything in sight. All of these things are okay with them. They talk about their trip as a "social experiment." Many view LSD and pot as sacraments in a new religion in which they are prophets and philosophers. They talk lovingly of Christ, Buddha. . . . They believe in the unity of all men. . . .

C–They talk about "holiness" that's wholesome. If they haven't come to the conclusion that if there is one person left in the United States who can't enjoy the "good life," then of course they can't enjoy the good life. They are the ones that talk about the oneness of all mankind and all living things and so on. They have fallen into a trap which is very human—a trap of snobbishness. The test of their life style is "Can all two hundred million people in the United States do it?" The answer, of course, is no. The particular world culture that we have now with all these billions of people cannot exist without Chevrolets, bulldozers, highways, plumbing, and so on. It cannot exist without it, you see. Or we would find ourselves in a terrible mess. We would find ourselves beset with starvation, famine, plague, and disease.

The interesting thing to me is that they say their experience is a cosmic, oceanic feeling of oneness with all living things. Of course! I had that for many years. I lived with it, sleeping and walking. I have it, to a degree, today —ten years later. It is infinitely multiplied over the little mickey-mouse high that I had in 1957. And I am impelled not to drop out and let the guy across the street and in Flagstaff, Arizona, starve to death. This is impossible for me!

My experience, my non-dichotomous, devised experience under LSD, lead to action. Now, see, you can't have these cults "till all men have Paradise." They do not comprehend the notion that the words "wholeness" or "holiness" are the same word. They don't comprehend that, you see? When their investigations lead them to dropping out, who brings them their food? Who makes it for them? Who paves the highway so that daddy's car can bring the hippie to sit there and drop out?

During my experience, which I suspect, lasted somewhere between two and four months, I thought exactly like they do now. There's a cliche that comes out of the newly born LSD nut. His standard response to everything is, "It doesn't matter, it doesn't matter."

"It doesn't matter," they chant like idiots. That's the first stage. Then, of course, one somehow doesn't retain this notion that it doesn't matter. *Unless you keep on staying loaded all the time, something else begins to dawn on you.* Oh, yes! It doesn't matter, to be sure. But in chorus with that, in close harmony to that howl, is another howl —a quiet voice that begins to gather volume. "It matters exquisitely; it matters exquisitely." Of course, it doesn't matter at all, but you see, it matters exquisitely. The homogenization or the emulsification of these two notions exists simultaneously in one area of your being.

I became somewhat like the Zen people. Cement mixers must mix cement. Writers must write. Aggressive, howler monkies must howl. I'm a howler monkey, you see? I love to face the ocean with my ass to city hall and howl and beat my chest about human injustice. That is my nature, you see.

LY–Here's something else I would like you to comment on. If you raise the issue with hippies about the social problems of violent crime, race riots, or the war, the comment made is, "I cannot change anybody else. I can only change myself."

C–Let me comment on that matter this way. I like to play God. I like to create. So I have addressed myself to creating an environment, like Synanon, where it is possible for a person to change himself.

I'm somewhat like a fellow who has a little oasis, rather well equipped, in the middle of a desert. And there's someone out there who, because he's thirsty and has nothing to eat, and his clothing isn't proper, and he's getting all the skin burned off the top of his head and back, needs a change of environment. He stumbles into my oasis, where there's water, food, tape recorders, hi-fi's, motion picture equipment, paint and pallets, pens and pencils and paper, and all those things. He walks into my environment and, I suppose, he changes.

He cools off and he eats a hearty meal and, you know, he's no longer the object you saw in the desert. He's a totally different organism. His blood is running in different directions and at a different rate of speed, and the rest of his juices and glands are beginning to function properly.

Then of course, quite obviously, this oasis can't let him come in and glue himself, let's say, to the hi-fi for twenty-four hours a day, because there are still some people in the desert. He can't be holy as long as part of his own body is diseased. Lao-tsu, one of their gods, said, "*It is a sound man who recognizes other men as part of his own body.*" Now, if they don't know that, then of course, they might just as well not have taken LSD.

Total anarchy may be possible, come the millennium, when every single human organism on whatever planet it occupies is totally, one hundred percent aware of the Golden Rule. A concept that is part of the folklore of every civilized culture. It's there in the folklore, but the true meaning of the Golden Rule is not available to our species yet. You know, it really isn't—not even to the enlightened ones—not in its true and deep meaning.

The Golden Rule cannot be practiced by a person who says, "I will take your Chevrolet to get me to hippie-land, and I will take your electric guitar which makes *me feel good,* but I will give you nothing in return." That is a decaying orbit, and a decaying orbit can only end in a crash. You see? The whole story is right there.

LY–They are doing some valuable things. For example, let's take the Diggers' Free Store. I sat in the Diggers' Free Store. It's a beautiful concept that protests against money, and makes a lot of sense within its own context.

C–Synanon opened up as a free store. It gave away food, shelter, education, medical attention, and so on—to the people who wanted all of those things. Now, in addition to that, as long as eight years ago, we began to distribute our surplus because whatever Synanon is doing attracted more than we could use of certain items. We were giving to the Salvation Army, to Goodwill, to the St. Matthew's Thrift Shop. We gave milk, cream, clothing, shoes, and so on.

After the Watts riots—we don't publicize this, we've never even written about it—our pickup truck, loaded with food, clothing, and everything else, was down there when the city was still smoking. As poor as we were, our warehouses were available to those people.

We don't, of course, address ourselves only to the needy because we don't think that there's that much difference between human beings. If a millionaire walks into Synanon today, he sits down to dinner with us like he did ten years ago when we began. He eats a little bit better now, because we eat a little bit better now. But, you see, we ran the first free store—a totally free store. The Diggers, God bless them. If somebody comes in and takes a loaf of bread, where is he going to eat it and where is he going to sleep to digest it? You see, if somebody comes into Synanon and takes a loaf of bread, he eats it on our premises, goes to bed in one of our beds, and develops a career for himself over a period of a lifetime, if that is what he wants to do. Once again, we always come to this concept of the totality or the whole.

LY–Another angle of the Diggers that is interesting is that they claim to accept gifts only if they are given with love.

They don't accept gifts given in a Lady Bountiful, charity fashion.

C–That is right. Now you talk about arrogance. Who, in the name of God, is going to judge whether somebody is giving something with love or in a Lady Bountiful way. Now a great teacher who they all think seemed to have it on the ball said, "Judge not, that ye be not judged," you see. So some goddamn Digger looking over a broad coming in with a hundred-dollar check says, "I am going to decide whether this woman is giving me this check with love or with patronage." This is ridiculous. Once again, the word is wholeness and totality. . . .

As we've been talking here, Lew, I wrote something down. *The fetal experience of the womb is God's LSD for every man.* Now the experience of leaving the womb starts with a slap on the ass. This may be the first dichotomous emotional and physical experience. It is both inhalation and expiration. You see, a fetus doesn't breathe. There is no dichotomy that is breathing. Oxygen and nourishment come in through the umbilical cord. It is a non-dichotomous thing. And you can say that the experience from conception to birth for nine months is a non-dichotomous experience, a kind of LSD-type of experience for every man.

Then, of course, life goes on. One is expelled from the womb and someone—some adult—has to do something. He has to play God. He helps create life by slapping that organism sharply on the rear. He plays God. He hangs it up there by the feet and says, "I'm going to make this one start life on earth." And, whack! He slams it in the rear, and the child goes into its first dichotomous experience—inhalation and expiration. And that continues until the person slips on a banana peel or reaches three-score and ten, and lies down and dies without his boots on.

Here's the problem of the hippies in a nutshell. Here's what I see. Leaders must have the guts to play God. No group, no human gestalt, can exist without someone to make some decisions and say, "Let's go." And this, of course, is anathema to the leaders of the hippie movement.

The hippie movement is, in part, a logical outcome of a very asinine notion that has come up in our time, possibly in our whole world culture—more probably in the Occidental culture. It is the leveling off of our heroes and the development of the anti-hero. You see. There aren't many heroes, and we will not permit hero leaders to stick their heads up and say, "You cook the food, and you empty the garbage, and you drive the truck . . .

Now the hippie movement is partly a logical outcome of the anti-hero, anti-leader, notion that has appeared for a hundred years in our literature. The assumption that adults are no different from children and an educated man is no different from an uneducated man, and a cripple with malnutrition is just as strong as a guy who can pull a crosscut saw all day is unrealistic nonsense.

The potential leaders are going to be the worst casualties of the whole hippie movement because they ought to, by God, know better. They have to take the responsibility of playing God and making decisions for their people who can't make decisions.

There was a great philosopher, a real square named Harry Truman, who said, "The buck stops here!" Unless the hippie leaders learn that simple truth about responsibility, their whole movement is doomed to extinction.

CHAPTER FIFTEEN

Significant Dimensions of the Movement

THE HIPPIE MOVEMENT BEneath the surface carnival is a valiant attempt by a segment of American youths to achieve an intense condition of human creativity and LOVE. That their aspirations fall far short of their lofty goals may be more of a commentary on the spiritual poverty of the society in which the effort is taking place than on the feeble attempts at love acted out by the young affluent participants in the movement.

To freely paraphrase Voltaire: "If the hippies did not exist, we would invent them." The fact of the movement's existence reflects at least two conditions. One is that American society has failed to hold the life-style attention of a sizable number of youths who, although they have access to most of its material opportunities, remain frustrated and uncommited. The other condition is that the hippie movement fills a spiritual and religious vacuum for its adherents and fellow travelers not satisfied by the overall social structure. Here Tim Leary's flippant comment on American religiosity is pertinent: "Religion is not a bunch of people getting up on Sunday morning, going down to a mortgaged building, and staring at the back of somebody's neck." The deeper human relationships of tribes, families, and friends are, in his viewpoint, more fundamental religious situations.

America might invent a hippie movement if it did not exist because apparently the yearning for creativity, humanism, and love, no matter how deeply buried in the plastic heart of the most robot-like psychopathic American, is a Homo sapiens trait that cannot be extinguished. There is a surge in this direction found in every record of society in human history. And the hippie movement may signal the beginning of a new American Renaissance of humanism.

A Lesson from History

Lao-tsu said, "It is a wise man who knows he is part of all men." Rather than persecute that part of ourselves in our society that is seeking in this direction, we should respect and attempt to learn something from their struggle. If Roman society had studied and tried to understand, rather than attempted to kill their Christian hippies, that civilization might have flourished with room for the Christians in it. The history lesson here may be one of tolerantly understanding and learning from a natural, spontaneous experimental social movement that has emerged in our society in our time.

Learning from an experiment does not necessarily mean advocating or supporting its principles and behavior. It does not imply believing the hippie priest "high" on LSD who declares that the movement is the only hope left for American society. Nor does the learning posture advocate legalizing psychedelic drugs to make the hippies' trip easier. Most drug-control laws in this country (with an easing up in certain areas) are apparently useful to the totality of American society. Certain citizens, especially youths, require the external controls of law to help protect them from a possible dangerous drug binge during their radical decision-making years.

The new drop-out movement should be seriously examined even if it has a short life in its present form. It may tell the larger society a great deal about where "it's at" with reference to the fundamental human traits of compassion and love, held up as a banner by the new youth movement.

The experimental voyage engaged in by around a quarter of a million young people is a perilous trip. Later re-entry into the society they may help to change (possibly for the better) could be impossible. Some participants in the hippie movement may find themselves physically and emotionally foundering on drugs for the rest of their lives. Those who do not fall victim to a potential drug brain scramble may become casualties through time lost in the experiment. Several years' absence from demanding social interactions may render them helpless as successful role- and game-players in the formal structure of American society.

Most Americans do not question the validity of our social structure. Many who do question it refuse to run the risks of dropping out, perhaps because they are not sufficiently dissatisfied, frustrated, or desperate. Those who have made a commitment to hippie life could some day be viewed as heroic Americans who made a valuable contribution to this society's growth and development. Innovators, no matter how radical, often contribute to the knowledge of a society.

The Emerging Movement

The hippie phenomenon has emerged rather spontaneously on the American scene. There was no specific leader who collated the interests of the current participants. The hippie movement, in this respect, is *unlike* two powerful hate-love developments of our time—the Nazis and the civil rights movement. Both of these movements had recognized and powerful leaders.

In a negative social movement, Adolf Hitler began initially with a group of disgruntled World War I German ex-soldiers and molded them and a fanatic group of citizens into the most destructive social and political juggernaut in the history of man. In an opposite and positive direction, Martin Luther King rose above the Negro crowd in the early 1950's to crystallize Negro sentiment into a constructive vehicle for drastically changing American society through the civil rights movement.

The hippie movement was not spearheaded by any powerful, definite leader. It emerged more as a consequence of great unrest and frustration felt simultaneously by a large number of youths.

If, however, there is a recognized leader and founder of the hippie movement, it is probably Tim Leary. Beginning with his scientific social-psychological psychedelic drug experiments at Harvard in the early '60's, Leary attracted at first a core group of co-experimenters and students. This coterie of psychedelic pioneers developed two later organizations. One was known as IFIF, Institute for the Investigation of Inner Freedom, and the other LSD, League for Spiritual Discovery. Neither of these organizations flourished.

Leary, LSD, and marijuana at first merged with the earlier beatnik situation (including random followers of the poet Allen Ginsberg). The spontaneous overall hip movement grew to epidemic proportions by 1966, and hit a peak in 1967.

Leary facetiously admits that he is a hip Billy Graham and over the past years his evangelistic efforts have brought his act and dialogue to campuses and civic auditoriums from coast to coast. In the process a reasonably specific policy (turn-on, tune-in, and drop-out) has emerged along side of a widely accepted creed or set of principles. (See "The Hippie Creed," Chapter 2.) This creed has been widely and, in a surprising way, coherently transmitted to the hippie troops around the country.

The hippie movement therefore has emerged rather spontaneously. It gathered momentum around the slogan of LOVE and a rejection of middle-class materialism, hypocrisy, and dishonesty. The participants were running away from a plastic society—at the same time they were running toward the difficult-to-define and even more difficult-to-live-by human ethic of love. Most participants have been "running away" from American society faster than they were "running toward" the new community.

The movement has had an enormous velocity. In reality it is only an infant in its present form. Already an intellectual snobbishness has emerged among some of its would-be leaders, who deny they are hippies and want to assume the presumptious title of "Free Men."

Semantically, in my opinion, the term *hippie,* at first used by its own adherents and later picked up by the press, is very appropriate to the scene. The term hippie derives from "hip." It roughly means emotionally and spiritually wise or in-group and has a clever, light, and airy semantical connotation. It seems apt for a movement with a gay love-in, colorful, fun, not totally serious ethic. Yet recently in Haight-Ashbury there was an attempt to have a symbolic hippie funeral to bury the hippie concept.

The funeral of the hippie was spontaneously produced by a handful of leaders in Haight-Ashbury. They sparked a group of several hundred hippies to carry a casket full of hippie artifacts, clothing, and trinkets to a final resting place in Golden Gate Park. The explicit idea was to bury the hippie image, as they put it, "produced by the mass media" and to signal the birth of "The Free Man." This rather snobbish effort indicates that the social movement (that I choose to continue to call the hippie movement) rather than being buried is perhaps entering, as social movements do, into another phase or cycle.

The Nature of the Movement

The hippie phenomenon fits the sociological model of being a social movement. It is in this conceptual scheme that I believe a great deal can be learned about it. Turner and Killian succinctly describe a social movement as: "A collectivity acting with some continuity to promote or resist a change in the society or group of which it is a party."* And similarly Blumer describes a social movement as: "A collective enterprise to establish a new order of Life."† Both of these generalizations apply to the hippie constellation.

*Ralph H. Turner and Lewis M. Killian, *Collective Behavior* (Prentice-Hall, 1957).

†Herbert Blumer, "Social Movements," in A. M. Lee, *Principles of Sociology* (Barnes and Noble, 1951).

Hoffer, in his excellent analysis of social movements *The True Believer,* identifies, among others, two pertinent characteristics of joiners of social movements. They are generally dissatisfied, alienated, and frustrated participants in the formal society looking for a change. "It is a TRUISM that many who join a rising revolutionary movement are attracted by the prospect of a sudden and spectacular change in their conditions of life.*

People who join social movements tend to manifest characteristics of discontentment, frustration, and have a sense of alienation. They believe, perhaps correctly, that the institutionalized social system holds no promise of fulfillment for them. They are in the hippie argot "turned-off" by the larger society. In this context Hoffer's observation is pertinent:

> A rising mass movement attracts and holds a following not by its doctrine and promises but by the refuge it offers from the anxieties, barrenness, and meaninglessness of an individual existence. It cures the poignantly frustrated not by conferring on them an absolute truth or by remedying the difficulties and abuses which made their lives miserable, but by freeing them from their ineffectual selves—and it does this by enfolding and absorbing them into a closely knit and exultant corporate whole.†

Another general characteristic of participants in mass movements that is relevant to the hippie phenomenon is an *extravagant faith* in the new order. Hippies, especially under the influence of drugs, have an unshakable belief in the correctness and perfect character of their new life style.

Extravagant faith is especially characteristic of religious movements. In many respects modern hippies are comparable to the early Christians. Their dress and hair styles are apparently close to the early Christian mode of attire. The early Christians, like the hippies, had fantastic visions of a beautiful life in the future. Participants in both movements felt they were escaping from a decadent society into

*Eric Hoffer, *The True Believer* (Harper & Row, 1951), p. 13.

†*Ibid.*, Hoffer, p. 44.

a new community based on religious and spiritual freedom. And the hippies, like the early Christians, feel and experience legal and social persecution from the larger society of which they are a dissonant part.

The similarities end sharply when it comes to leadership. The hippies have no Jesus Christ. We could speculate, however, that LSD is to the hippie movement what Jesus Christ represented to the early Christians. There is a blind faith, complete belief, and worship of the chemical that will tune them in to love, compassion, and the unity of Man with the Universe. Some hippies claim that under the influence of LSD they feel so omnipotent that they can almost walk on water. Also, LSD has been given credit by many hippies for miraculous and immediate emotional and physical cures.

Fanaticism is another general characteristic of social movements that is a dimension of the hippie scene. Hippies, especially high priests and novitiates, are fanatics in their beliefs. In one respect this is reflected in their resistance to any suggestion that their trip is dangerous. The constant theme of resistance and rationalization of the potential threat of prison, physiological (chromosome) damage, psychosis, and disease reflects a fanaticism that is hard to shake, at least on the surface. These patterns are very comparable to the unshakable beliefs of the early (and some modern) Christians.

The *extravagant faith* of the hippies, the early Christians, and modern "holy rollers" may be an effort to overcompensate for deep feelings of underlying insecurity and emptiness. Such insecure and lonely people often attempt to throw themselves into the arms of omnipotent religious movements or drugs. Hoffer's commentary on the fanaticism of *The True Believer* is revealing in this context: "The fanatic is perpetually incomplete and insecure. He cannot generate self-assurance out of his individual resources—out of his rejected self—but finds it only by clinging passionately to whatever support he happens to embrace." *

**Ibid.*, Hoffer, p. 80.

The Movement and Near-Group Structure

The small groups that form the total hippie movement are structurally similar to gang organizations I studied in New York.* My research revealed that gang collectivities were neither cohesive stable groups nor were they ill-defined mobs of youths. In terms of organization they fell midway on a continuum from mob to cohesive group. I referred to these midway collectivities as near-groups. This concept was helpful in describing gang phenomena with greater insight and accuracy, and I believe it will be a useful conceptual tool for better understanding the hippie movement.

Unlike a true group, I found that near-groups characteristically had the following properties: (1) The roles of members were not precisely defined; (2) the organism had limited cohesion and tended to be impermanent; (3) there was a minimum consensus among participants about the entity's norms; (4) the members and participants were constantly shifting; (5) leadership was often vague and confused. *All of these factors are applicable to the smaller group organisms found in the overall hippie movement.*

Another dimension of the near-group concept applicable to the hippie scene is the fact that there are differential levels of commitment to the movement. There are *core* participants (complete drop-outs), and *marginal* participants (partial drop-outs).

Most true groups have a greater consistency of commitment. Members are clearly committed and belong to the group. In near-groups there is a greater allowable range of involvement or commitment. In the near-groups of the hippie movement *core* or central participants would include the "high priests," and "novitiates." In a more *marginal* part of the group would be teenyboppers and hippie fellow travelers.

Members of the movement can be recognized or placed at

*Lewis Yablonsky, *The Violent Gang* (Macmillan, 1962, and Penguin, 1966).

different levels of commitment to the movement and being dropped-out from the society. For example, high priests are totally involved in the movement and totally dropped-out of American society. Novitiates, even though they are living in the movement, are still emotionally working out their status in their "new" and "old" world. Teenyboppers and fellow travelers are physically and emotionally marginal participants living both in and out of the movement.

All of the qualities and properties of the near-group seem to be applicable to the small-group constellations of communes, tribes, and "families" found in the overall hippie movement. For this reason I would apply the near-group concept to this host of small collectivities that comprise the total movement.

The personality structure of "permanent" near-group participants generally varies from that of people who relate to "true groups." People who have a limited personal ability to perform adequately and responsibly in more demanding and definite true groups gravitate toward participation in near-groups. Because a near-group is vague, impermanent, and has diffuse normative definitions, people with personality problems and defects find it a more compatible adjustment than trying to remain in a true group.

Many occupational, educational, and social groups in American society are too demanding for certain individuals. The hippie movement and its many near-group pockets is an attractive organism for youths with the limited social abilities to perform adequately in the inclusive society. On the hippie scene they can do their "own thing" (even if it is a borderline psychotic syndrome) in the sanctuary of the near-group forms that comprise the total movement.

A large number of youths, perhaps 20–25% of the total movement, are clearly emotionally disturbed youths who use the malleable near-groups of the hippie movement as their syndrome.* The traditional Napoleon, God, Christ, and oth-

*It is important to note that all of my references to "psychosis" or "emotional disturbance" are in terms of the probable diagnosis of a standard psychiatric or psychological clinician in American society. The hippies, er psychotic delusional syndromes so popular over the years may have been replaced by the *hippie syndrome* for many youths who have severe personal problems.

It is a convenient group syndrome for many disturbed youths. Membership in it places their behavior in a more acceptable and rational framework. Being a hippie is even exaggerated and envied by many representatives of the larger society. In brief, adopting the hippie role and life style provides a sanctuary for many severely disturbed youths and other youths who are seeking a refuge or a temporary amnesty from encountering the demands of the more coherent groups of the inclusive society.

Personality Characteristics

Aside from their claimed loftier motivations of seeking LOVE and spiritual unity the reason many youths join the hippie movement is because they do not seem to be able to find the possibility of full human expression in the larger society. Many other hippie converts are simply social rejects.

Extravagant social movements like the hippie phenomenon are often joined by what Hoffer calls "social misfits." Hoffer divides "misfits" into two categories: "temporary" and "permanent." Temporary misfits are people who have not yet found their place in life but still hope to find it. Adolescent youths, unemployed college graduates, veterans, new immigrants, and tne like are in this category. According to Hoffer, these people are restless, dissatisfied, and haunted by the fear that their best years will be wasted before they reach their goal. They are receptive to the preaching of a proselytizing movement and yet do not always make staunch converts. They are not irrevocably estranged from the self and do not see themselves as irremediably spoiled from participating in the larger society. For many temporary misfits, any evidence of progress or success will reconcile them with the larger society.

---

of course, do not accept the establishment's viewpoint. Pathology or "emotional disorder" is part of the "psychiatric establishment bag" that they reject.

The *temporary misfit* is very evident in the hippie movement. These are the teenyboppers, Clark Kents, and other part-time hippies who, given certain opportunities, readily move back into the straight world. Many become "summer hippies" for want of something better to do. "Comes September" and most move back to school and straight society. These people are on the periphery of the hippie movement.

Heavily involved in a core way in the hippie movement are individuals who may be more *permanent misfits.* Straight society and its complicating demands are beyond their scope, ability, or interest. Permanent misfits are often people who because of a lack of talent or some seemingly irreparable emotional defect go through life constantly pursuing unattainable dreams of glory. No achievement, however spectacular, seems to give them a sense of fulfillment.

The drug-influence variable makes it difficult to precisely diagnose the hippie personality. Most hippies that I encountered were under the influence of drugs more often than not. This makes it difficult to ascertain their "true personality" in a drug-free condition. I could only go by the behavior that was manifest and this seemed more bizarre than most youths I have known in other situations. Even though the drug cloud tends to obscure the issue there appears to be a disproportionately high mental illness rate among hippies than that found in the general population. (Another evidence of this was the statistics I gathered regarding post hippies who had been incarcerated in mental hospitals or had received psychiatric care.)

The higher incidence of emotional disturbance or psychological problems is also reflected in the enormous emphasis on internal psychological explorations (with and without drugs) manifest among hippie youths. Most youths are self-conscious, but hippies appear to be extravagantly self-analytic. They are continuously and persistently concerned with "hangups," "personal freedom," paranoia, and emotional self-examination.

Drugs, particularly LSD, are used as vehicles for the exploration of this "inner space." Under the guise of hippie philosophy many youths in the movement appear to use drugs more for changing their reality feeling state (even for kicks) than for their avowed religious and philosophical goal of mind expansion.

Gridley Wright, of course, claimed and (I am convinced) on one level sincerely believed that he used drugs for a religious experience. We conflicted many times when I asserted that he often used psychedelic drugs, especially marijuana, when he was "up-tight" or depressed. I charged that his drug use was an attempt to *escape* from his problems. He claimed the drugs helped him to *solve* his problems. The argument was a stand-off since it would be difficult to prove either case.

Transcendence, hallucination, mysticism, religious fervor, and psychosis are such comparable manifest states of being that it is difficult to sort out one from the other. For example, in one case that came to my attention a young man who had used LSD determined that he could speak directly to God. In all other behavioral areas the young man seemed normal. Yet this quirk and belief placed him in a mental hospital. He was hospitalized for this "breakthrough" sought by religious leaders in all societies since The Beginning.

Many youths who would ordinarily be hospitalized for their behavior find sanctuary in the hippie world. For example, Gary's description of his disintegration of a butterfly under LSD and the spiritual quality of the paranoid-schizoid reactions of other hippies are easily absorbed into the mysticism of the movement.

Being a Christ-like figure in the hippie world is much safer than being one in American society. The hundreds of hippie-legitimate Christ-like figures in full regalia walking up Haight Street would all probably be hospitalized for manifesting this appearance and behavior prior to the existence of the hippie movement.

In contrast with the possibility that the hippie syndrome or adjustment obscures the traditional symptoms of neurosis and psychosis there is some evidence of remarkable personality "cures" within the hippie framework. Sonny and many other stars on the hippie scene seem to have had their suicidal and in some cases homicidal tendencies arrested by LSD and their new life style. Leary told me about a random survey he made of Haight-Ashbury which revealed that a host of youngsters whose backgrounds were pointing them toward delinquency and prostitution had had these possible symptoms deflected by becoming hippies and joining the movement. In many cases the adoption of the hippie syndrome is clearly the lesser of two evils.

On a loftier level of "seeking," many hippie high priests appear to be compassionate, loving, positive goal-oriented individuals as a result of the hippie vehicle. Many are involved with the Eastern religious view of becoming loving human beings and aspiring to Nirvana. Others are intrigued with psychological goals of becoming super humane, empathetic, and "self-actualized."

In this context, for example, the psychological theories of Dr. Abraham Maslow are often discussed on the scene. Maslow's view of what constitutes a self-actualized person is an idealized model personality aspired to by many hip people. According to Maslow:

> Among the objectively describable and measurable characteristics of the healthy human specimen are: (1) clearer, more efficient perception of reality; (2) more openness to experience; (3) increased integration, wholeness, and unity of the person; (4) increased spontaneity, expressiveness, full functioning; aliveness; (5) a real self, a firm identity, autonomy, uniqueness; (6) increased objectivity, detachment, transcendence of self; (7) recovery of creativeness; (8) ability to fuse concreteness and abstractness, primary and secondary, process cognition, etc; (9) democratic character structure; and (10) the ability to love.*

Though most hippies fall far short of these lofty personality aspirations, their goal seems to be a valid pursuit.

*Abraham H. Maslow, *New Knowledge in Human Values* (Harper & Bros., 1959), p. 127.

A major problem of the hippies is comparable to that of other movements and groups, including standard American society. Idealized goals are often sharply different from reality. Ideal-type personality goals on the hippie scene are often remote aspirations when measured against the empirical reality of the situation. Although they talk a great deal about love, compassion, and being turned-on intellectually, most participants in the movement, including the leaders, seldom achieve these lofty goals.

The near-groups of the hippie movement are resonant with the personalities of many of its participants. For most, little is really expected of others and little is given. Personal responsibility and expectations are minimal. Impermanence and transiency are institutionalized patterns. These patterns of irregular and irresponsible personality structure fit with the human demands of most of the near-groups found in the total hippie movement. This credibility gap between lofty emotional and spiritual aspirations and actual practice, however, is not too different on the hippie scene from the hypocrisy and discrepancy found between the goals set forth by American religious leaders and the practices of the mass of church-goers.

Stratification

All human organizations evolve some hierarchical pattern. At this time the hierarchy of the hip movement has not crystallized. However, with pressure from without and the need for some organization from within, a status system is emerging. Although status or class systems are anathema to hippies (this is part of the reason they have dropped out), looking in from the outside there appears to be a vague yet observable class system.

Stratification is related to qualities and values reversed by a particular group. The revered idealized traits of the hip world include love, philosophical sophistication, "proper use" of drugs, freedom from personal hangups and "ego-game-playing," and the ability to verbalize the philosophy. Although on the realistic level most hippies fall short of living in these terms, the leaders or true hippies are considered to have these virtues.

The "upper class" hippie is totally dropped-out of the inclusive society. They appear to be hangup-free from "hassles" or role-conflicts with the society. They manifest a loving posture which is not triggered by hostility or disappointments in critical situations. They claim to love all humanity and nature, including American society. They are able to articulate the hippie creed or the policy and philosophical view of the movement. They claim to use drugs religiously as a means to Nirvana rather than as a sedative or a kick-oriented experience.

In the next identifiable class are the novitiates, who are informally in training for upper-class status. They form the predominant middle-class of the movement.

At bottom, in the lower-class group, are assorted teenyboppers, part-time hippies, and "speed" drug users. Lower-class hippies are generally naïve, inarticulate, and use drugs like "speed" essentially for emotional excitation or kicks.

This brief analysis of the stratification system is, of course, only that of an outsider looking in on an emerging movement. Hippies have an aversion to any hierarchy or superior-subordinate dichotomy. To them, philosophically, all men and women are equal in the movement and there are no leaders. In practice, the phenomena of "social-climbing," "status-hangups," and people on "ego-trips" for self-aggrandizement is almost as rampant as it is in the larger society.

Leadership

Hippies reject the concept of leadership found in American society. To them, "No one should lay his trip on someone else." The disclaimers of hippie leaders about being leaders appears to be one of the core problems of the movement. Being a spiritual center or role-model is fine for symbolic goals; however, if anything productive is to happen, someone in a group has to assert his authority and assume some responsibility. (As Dederich commented, "Someone has to play God.")

The hippie leadership rejection of formal organization is a reaction formation against the bureaucracy of the "plastic society." The cold-blooded "pushy" leader is a part of the reason they have dropped out. Yet some organization is a necessity for group development. Committees, the division of labor with some located authority, formalized meetings involving the discussion of specific topics such as health, wealth, and wisdom appear to be vital factors in the growth of a social organization. The total hippie reaction-formation to all of this phenomenon may be a major factor blocking the development of the movement.

The role of relating to the hostile and friendly groups that surround a movement is a function that has also been abdicated by the non-leaders. The hippie view of the leadership role requires revision if the movement is to develop. This factor may be a central determinant of the future life or death of the total movement.

Tribes and Communes

Most hippie leaders when pushed to define the major conditions of the movement will comment as one did: "Basically we want to work out a different relationship to the land than the plastic society." This goal is lofty and almost necessary for a mechanical society that has choked the land with cities, highways and over use—and, in fact, with the same impact filled the air with smog. They also reject the vast, anonymous (secondary group) mass of faces in the crowd found in American society. The hippie dream is to return to the tribal position of the American Indian or the more satisfying life of a more closely knit extended-family—a situation where adults and children can live more intimately and humanely in a cohesive, face-to-face primary group. The goal, therefore, is a more cohesive, emotionally closer, fundamental human unit living in a more natural state.

The hippie view that we have in our motorized, mechanized society moved too far away from each other and the basic quality of the natural environment is well taken. The middle-class suburban family moving to their apartment-type house with a 9′ x 9′ plot of green yard where they barbecue neatly butchered meat on a chromium-plated electrified barbecue machine may in a more tortured fashion than the hippie be reaching back into history toward the simpler life of the cave. The hippies who buy their buckskin jackets, rough leather boots, and sleeping bags at the Army surplus store and move onto a mountain may more blatantly and dramatically have the same underlying yearnings as the barbecue man. Both are trying to turn back history and seem to be failing.

A principle of group behavior is that part of one's self must be given up to the group; in return, the individual receives a degree of protection, security, and other rewards of cooperative activity. The major problem of most hippie communes, tribes, or "family" situations I have observed is related to their inability or unwillingness to sacrifice any personal autonomy to the group.

The hippies drop out partly because they feel they have given too much of their "emotions and body to the society." They want to onanistically do their "own thing" and heavily resent *any*, even slight, intrusion on their autonomy or "freedom." They claim that if everyone does his own thing the work will magically get done. The result is not a group—but a near-group—of egocentric selfish individuals participating minimally in the collective condition. This is one of the main problems and reasons for the failure of the glorified and idealized hippie tribes, "families," and communes. The hippie failure provides some clues and insights into the failure of the original "tribe," the traditional American family.

Socialization of the Children

Every human organization has to evolve a method for socializing its young. The hippie philosophy dictates certain patterns of child-rearing that are being crystallized at this time. The following statement about bringing up children in the hippie world was made by Gridley Wright, and it summarizes some of the central hip views on child-rearing:

"I maintain that children are born with a spiritual consciousness. The effect of this culture's ignorance of the nature of a spiritual life is to render us incapable of knowing or accepting spirituality in infants and children. The culture and homes into which children are born are devoid of a spiritual atmosphere. Competition, status, and materialism are watchwords. Children are given plastic toys, and the television set is the national baby-sitter. A spiritual atmosphere is characterized by a deep respect for all forms of life, a recognition that all is perfect because it IS the present manifestation of Life, not in potential, in the fantasy future, but NOW. Infants and children are not respected. They are treated as slightly imbecilic and moronic, a different species to be guided along until they become like adults."

He goes on to point out that "adults should not lay their trip on kids," especially not in the "circumcision violation, or in any other areas." In brief, he almost calls for a total parental hands-off policy and treating the child as an adult's equal in interaction. Gridley's viewpoint is representative of many hippie parents.

Gridley's idealized beliefs about child-rearing are interesting, perhaps even experimentally sound, but not true of what actually takes place on the hippie scene. Most children in the hippie world are idealized and treated more like toys or objects than like human beings. I have observed what may be termed "selective relating." The parents deal with the child and take care of its basic needs mainly when it suits the adult. "Selective relating" ignores a basic requirement of the socialization process. A baby, a raw bundle of emotions and physiological drives, requires someone to "lay its trip on." The child's almost total dependence on an older and hopefully wiser person is a fundamental need that has to be met if the child is to mature. In fact, at this stage of development, the child is far from being an equal. He seeks and requires the limits and core provided by one or more adult parents. He needs to emulate an adult role-model.

Of course the pattern of relating to children by whim is as rampant in the larger society as it is in the hippie world. A major difference, however, is that hippie children, at this time, grow up in wilder and more disorganized situations. Moreover, the nomadic quality of hippie adult life appears to produce a constant wrench on the child's security. Care and feeding is sporadic at best and children are often left to their own devices by drug-loaded, freaked-out parents for days at a time.

Although hippie parents constantly talk about "not laying their trip" on anyone, especially their children, they often do precisely this with their children in one area of their life. Many encourage their children to use drugs at an early age. In one case a four- and a six-year-old were taken from a mother who had turned them on to pot. This case was not atypical.

In another situation I spent some time with a four-year-old who had been given LSD. The child seemed psychotic. She stared bug-eyed and from time to time jumped around in circles emitting sounds of stark terror.

The parents who do this to their children claim to sincerely want to give their children the benefit of their beautiful experience. They ignore the obvious fact, among many others, that a child has a limited intellectual, emotional, and physical framework for absorbing the powerful impact of psychedelic drugs. The child is involuntarily put-upon by parents who are perhaps in some tortured way of reasoning trying to justify their own drug problem. The convoluted assumption I heard several times was: "If it's good for me, and I think it it, then pot and acid are good for my children, too."

In summary, the following problems exist for children socialized in the hippie world. Their parents are nomadic drug users. The children are thus often placed in an unprotected, difficult, and unpredictable environment. Child care and feeding are sporadic and at the whim of the parent. There is very little consistent care. Psychedelic drugs are often given to these children by "well-meaning" but obviously confused parents. Children are ill-equipped emotionally and intellectually to have their system shocked or affected by the impact of psychedelic drugs.

The final results of this pattern of socialization of hippie children has not been fully recorded because of the short existence of the movement. I would predict, however, that over a longer period of time, there will be many casualties produced by the psychedelic movement. The hippie parents' failure rate in creating problem children may prove to be even higher than that produced by the larger society.

Work Patterns

> Most men, even in this comparatively free country, through mere ignorance and mistake, are so occupied with the factitious cares and superfluously coarse labors of life that its finer fruits cannot be plucked by them. Their fingers, from excessive toil, are too clumsy and tremble too much for that. Actually, the laboring man has not leisure for a true integrity day by day; he cannot afford to sustain the manliest relations to men; his labor would be depreciated in the market. He has not time to be anything but a machine.
>
> THOREAU

This view of work in the overmechanized society, so poetically described by Thoreau, parallels the hippie viewpoint. They abhor the "Protestant ethic" generally adopted by American middle-class society. The "Protestant ethic," as presented by the sociologist Max Weber, makes a religious virtue of individualism, frugal living, thrift, and the glorification of work-practices that favor the accumulation of wealth.

Hippies generally consider "nine-to-five work" in the technological Establishment of American society as spiritually, emotionally, and physically harmful. Despite their general reluctance to work in the Establishment, there is fair effort at work in arts and crafts. Jewelry, leather sandals, and clothes of various sorts are hand-made by some people on the scene. Hand-made jewelry, beads, roach-holders, posters, and other trinkets are made and sold by the hip community.

If music is considered work of a sort, there are, of course, innumerable acid-rock bands. Many of these, like The Buffalo Springfield, Big Brother and the Holding Company, and the Jefferson Airplane, have become big business and have been adopted by the larger society.

Part of the drop-out protest is the rejection of society's work pattern for the sake of more "natural or spiritual work." Hippies glorify natural work but in practice they do not often glory in doing it. Hip people in a drug-induced state of consciousness talk endlessly about various projects and work they are going to do, particularly in a natural environment, when the conditions are right. Conditions seldom are right and despite the idealized aspirations very little real work is done on the hippie scene.

The drug reverie apparently gives the individual the satisfactions of work—without doing any. The dream of working in a commune in the country is often eloquently presented off the top of a marijuana puff of smoke. It all sounds fascinating and "like wow." However, the reality is usually slovenliness, laziness, and disorder.

As they claim to be in so many other areas of the society, hippies may be Veblen's avante-garde leisure class in an automated society. One hippie leader told me once with complete sincerity, "American society is definitely going to be fully automated some day. The hippies know how to live under that condition without work. One of the lessons the society can learn from the new community is how to fill up each day in a meaningful way without work."

Patterns of Violence

In terms of a philosophical viewpoint, violence of any

kind is deplored on the hip scene. It is considered and, of course, is a gross violation of the love ethic.

Despite this, there is a considerable amount of violence in the love culture. Part of it is the result of excessive drug use. Methedrine or "speed" in particular sometimes has the effect of producing paranoid feelings of persecution. The "speed" victim may then strike out at the nearest human object. (Some medical research with Methedrine given to rats reveals that they become paranoid and violent in this described pattern.)

The "death of the ego" under the influence of LSD also has in many dramatic cases unleashed violent reactions that may have been simmering for a long time deep down in a person. There are an increasing number of cases of homicidal and suicidal violence reported on the part of people under the influence of LSD.

Another reason for a heavy incidence of violence in the hippie world is that as a kind of separated sub-culture it is left to its own devices to handle the violence that emerges. Personal internal controls are often the only available means for suppressing violence. No police are available or would be called when an act of violence erupts on the scene. Also in the hip community people will seldom intervene in a violent interaction. There is a tendency to let people "do their own thing" or a fatalistic "let what has to happen, happen," even if the happening is assault. Some will literally say that a violent person should be free to "do his thing."

Several nights before we visited the Ben Lomand, Holiday Lodge commune, violence had erupted. Gary, the leader, received wounds requiring several stitches in a fight that occurred when he was attacked by several drunken gang youths from the local town who raided the commune "for kicks." There were around twenty commune residents actually observing the assault on Gary. It was not until a critical point in the attack that the group finally decided to interrupt the assault. No one intervened until it appeared as if Gary was actually going to be killed!

The urban slum areas where hippies have moved pose some special and complicated violence problems for the movement. The conflict situations usually emanate from difficulties felt and acted upon by the older resident population.

A common problem of hostility is the older residents' resentment of the seemingly blatant and looser sexual morality of the hippies. Their hang-loose ethics and more open sexual freedom produce an up-tight feeling and an envy that often produce aggression. The fun and games of the hippies without working also generate hostile feelings in many urban slum dwellers who are working hard toward success in an achievement-oriented society.

Some subterranean conflicts also exist between the older-urban-area minority residents and the new minority group hippies. The violence that is generated may be related to the fact that the hippies have had and have rejected the very goals that the minority groups are seeking. The middle- and upper-class hippies walked away from material affluence and available opportunity channels to American success in jobs and symbols. The anger of the minority group urban dwellers, although perhaps unclear in their own minds, may stem from the frustration of seeing this wanton rejection of things they are taught daily to desire by the mass media. They have accepted the value system that validates the pursuit of materialism as the major way to achieve the "good life" in America.

The crass rejection by the hippies of deified material objectives is a threat to the dreams of minority groups. They may have to question whether the goals they are working and battling for are really worth the struggle. If these people (the hippies), *who had it all*, can so easily walk away and enter conditions of poverty even more severe than their own, it raises the issue that perhaps their valued goals—such as the color TV, the new car, travel, and the house in the country—are not worth the struggle.

In summary, the hippies present a challenge to the way in which minority groups rationalize their own suffering. To them the hippies are implicitly saying that the god *material success* is a false idol. A partial result of this caldron of value confusion, frustration, and anger produced by the hippies, is the acting out of violence.

Love

The assumption in the hippie ethos is that the capacity to love exists in all people. As Leary states it, "Love is where it's at." A "beautiful person" in the hip world is really a loving person. Drugs are used to reach a state of love and compassion. Hippies are preoccupied with love. Yet, as in so many other areas of their life style, there seem to be some discrepancies between their idealized concept of love and the practice of love in the hippie world.

A working definition of love is presumptuous. However, I would define love as the ability and the desire to assume the role of another person close to you and to act in his or her behalf without any selfish concerns. Love entails a large measure of self-sacrifice, responsibility, and behavioral action.

Love on the hippie scene tends to be egocentric and onanistic in practice—even though vast universal feelings of love are felt in a general way. In the psychedelic drug reverie the individual is loaded with oceanic feelings of love and compassion; but in action, aside from a casual embrace or a sexual act, little concretely is done in the terms I have indicated. Very little action is unselfishly taken for another or others.

The paradox may be stated in the following terms. To feel love for everyone and everything is to love nothing. To love one person fully, responsibly, and by action is to reveal the capacity to love everyone and everything. Hippies are seldom able to fully act out love for one person in a total way.

A hippie often ecstatically told me about his connection to the universe and his oceanic love for all people. Yet I saw very little fulfillment or action. Like other hippies, his amours with women were many and spaced out over short periods of time. Children, friends, and "wives" with whom he had established "love associations" would literally be left at a moment's notice for the intrigue or attraction of a new person or a trip.

The *feeling* of love was seldom translated into concrete commitment or *action.* The value of *feeling* in the hippie world sometimes seems to suppress action. Simply "feeling love" is enough, and satisfies the need to act. Therefore "love," in the movement, tends to be hedonistic and selfish.

One view of love on the hippie scene was expressed in a vignette reported to me by Gridley. When we were in Big Sur together, Gridley pointed out an enormous man with a beard, dressed in hippie clothes. The fellow, according to Gridley, had during his lifetime been on "a heavy criminal assault trip and probably killed a few people." In fact, I later learned he had been convicted of homicide and had spent a long term in San Quentin prison. Gridley told me how he had personally turned the man on to LSD and changed his life. In the throes of his first beautiful LSD trip his "new partner" told Gridley, "You son-of-a-bitch, I really love you more than I can say. Not in a homo way but really true love. Like, if you ever want anyone killed—you just tell me. That's how much I love you!"

Freedom

Complete freedom is implied by the expression "do my own thing." This phrase is used repeatedly in the hippie world. It ideally refers to being an individual free from the encumbrances, "games," or "hangups" of the society.

Again the goal is lofty. Few would disagree with one's right to do "one's thing." Questions arise when you begin to examine the "thing," or its effect on other people. In many cases it seems to be a drive for a partial or complete psychotic state. A position of total disengagement from responsibility, expectation, or duty to other people. In some cases "the right to do my thing" is a plea for being left alone to be insane.

This value is a debatable core-value issue in American society. Does someone have the right to commit actual or emotional suicide? Should the body politic intervene in the case of a person desirous of self-destruction? These are some of the issues raised by the total anarchistic notion of "doing one's own thing."

The reaction-formation reason for seeking this "total freedom" is in most cases apparent. The youngster who has felt himself being suffocated by middle-class values moves on to the hip scene with a tremendous appetite to be left completely alone.

Yet the values implicit in the superordinate-subordinate relationship are the ones that drive American society. Teacher implies student. Parent implies child, and society implies citizen. In all cases, in hippie parlance, "someone's trip is laid on someone else." The goals are positive even if the results are sometimes disastrous.

The hippie demand to "do his own thing" is asking for a value orientation in direct conflict with the superordinate-subordinate complex of American society. It is a core-value shift and makes one wonder if perhaps our society has gone too far in "laying its trip" on youth. The right "to do one's own thing" is a central battle orientation of the new movement. Perhaps American society has become too authoritarian in imposing its value uniformly and oppressively on our youth. This orientation probably caused the extremist reaction-formation of the goal of complete freedom.

An important step toward freedom is an emancipation from "ego games." An ego game is essentially a culturally prescribed act that is institutionalized. It can be anything from a total job situation like the "professor game" to the "status game" of someone involved with prestige. Ego games are rejected in the hippie world. The goal is to transcend this state of being and stop, to the best of one's ability, being a "heavy game player." Movement away from society's ego games is at the heart of the drop-out movement.

American society to the hippie is one big "ego game." In *The Psychedelic Experience* an effort is made to define "ego games" as they are viewed in the psychedelic world:

> Games are behavioral sequences defined by roles, rules,

> rituals, goals, strategies, values, language, characteristics, space-time locations, and characteristic patterns of movement. Any behavior not having these nine features is non-game; this includes physiological reflexes, spontaneous play, and transcendental awareness.*

There is a recognition that a person cannot be totally removed from game playing, but the goal is to play as few games as possible. The cessation of all games is the goal of the psychedelic experience. The elimination of "game playing" and the death of the (phony) "social ego" are resonant with the hippie drive "to do one's own thing."

In brief, the "battle hymn" of the hippie republic urges fight for freedom from society's oppression. The idealistic hippie seeks emancipation from the chains of bondage to what they varyingly term the "oppressive," "bureaucratic," "game-playing," "robot-like," "plastic" American society.

*Timothy Leary, Richard Alpert, and Ralph Metzner, *The Psychedelic Experience* (University Books, 1964), p. 13.

CHAPTER SIXTEEN

The Plastic Society

> The fate of man threatens to become that of the dinosaur in reverse. The dinosaur may have perished because he extended the power of his organism in excess of its usefulness. Man may perish because of reducing the power of his organism by fabricating robots in excess of his control. The conclusion is that as parents and creative agents we produce more perfect robots than babies.
>
> J. L. Moreno*

THE CAUSES OF DROPPING OUT of American society into the hippie movement are not the same for each individual. Some hippies are relatively healthy, intelligent people who chose to engage in an exciting new movement. Although they may deplore many dimensions in the plastic society, they do not totally reject it. Other youths have some complicated neurotic involvements with their personal family and find the hippie movement a valid and useful adjustment. Another segment of the movement is comprised of youths who have severe emotional problems and find the

*J. L. Moreno, *Who Shall Survive?* (Beacon House, Inc., 1953).

hippie syndrome a more compatible role adjustment than one that would confine them in a mental hospital.

It would be presumptuous of me on the basis of my data, and my trip, to present a complete causal explanation of the hippie movement. What follows are some generalizations and speculations on some of the causal factors that seem most pertinent to me in explaining the movement. This analysis will not account uniformly for all types of youths involved, but the generalizations made will be applicable to many people and aspects of the movement that I have researched on my trip.

The Plastic Society and the Hippie Reaction-Formation

Most hippie drop-outs have a strong sense of alienation or disaffiliation from the larger society. In fact, their primary warm-up to drop-out status has been the same feeling of alienation that resulted in a lack of commitment to the larger society. LSD for many of these youths is a trigger to help them tune-in to a sense of "cosmic-consciousness" and a new, more loving way of life. These exorbitant goals may be a reaction-formation of many hippie converts.

Their extremist reaction is an attempt to escape from their deeply felt sense of loneliness and alienation. Through LSD, love, and the new community they are trying to feel part of the universe. Their *reaction-formation* to their former *alienated condition* is so strong that they feel the necessity to move themselves to the opposite extreme of attempting to become part of the *Total Unity of Man and Nature.*

Many youths who become hippies seem to encounter the extreme conditions of the plastic society's machine-like quality and its super-rich affluence. These youths claim they are overwhelmed and frightened by an American society machine that spits out such an enormous amount of facts and figures. The overwhelming number of alternatives and potential opportunities of the "robot" society turns them off. The possible choices of jobs, material goods, and other machine alternatives are increasing at such a remarkable rate that these youths feel a compulsion to turn off their relationship to the rapidly expanding and overwhelming machine. Their emotional and intellectual computers seem to freeze and lock when they play with the almost infinite number of choices offered by the bureaucracy. They then run in the opposite direction to nature, mysticism, and psychedelic drugs.

Also, many feel, perhaps correctly, that no one is really there to help them with the infinite choices of the plastic society. This may in part account for their sense of loneliness and alienation. The hippie drop-out thus gravitates toward the psychedelic illusion of love and freedom—away from the machine.

The plastic society that confronts them is essentially a maze of ahuman bureaucracy. Part of this bureaucratic machine they have to encounter in the "game-playing system" is cogently described by Merton:

> . . . Bureaucracy involves a clear-cut division of integrated activities which are regarded as duties inherent in the office. A system of differentiated controls and sanctions are stated in the regulations. The assignment of roles occurs on the basis of technical qualifications which are ascertained through formalized, impersonal procedures (e.g., examinations). Within the structure of hierarchically arranged authority, the activities of "trained and salaried experts" are governed by general, abstract, clearly defined rules which preclude the necessity for the issuance of specific instructions for each specific case. The generality of the rules requires the constant use of categorization, whereby individual problems and cases are classified on the basis of designated criteria and are treated accordingly.*

The bureaucratic plastic social structure approaches the complete elimination of personalized relationships and of non-rational considerations (hostility, anxiety, affectual involvements). It exerts a constant pressure upon people to be "methodical, prudent, and disciplined."

Bureaucracies, in order to operate successfully, must at-

*Robert Merton, *Social Theory and Social Structure* (The Free Press, 1949), p. 126.

tain a high degree of reliability of behavior and an unusual degree of conformity with prescribed patterns of action. Sharp discipline is as highly developed in a religious or economic bureaucracy as it is in the Army. Discipline can be effective only if the ideal patterns are buttressed by strong sentiments which entail devotion to one's duties, a keen sense of the limitation of one's authority and competence, and methodical performance of routine activities. The machine-like system, in brief, requires total adherence to the prescriptions of the machine and ultimately the total squelching of human feelings.

It is this type of society that many affluent American youths are rejecting for, at minimum, the promise of more meaningful personal associations on the hippie scene and, at maximum, a personal integration with nature, God, and the universe.

Anomie and the New Deviants

This pattern of rejection of the plastic society is not equally felt by all young Americans. Most young people from the lower-class situation still buy the great American dream of success. In this important respect their reaction is markedly different from the hippies. Examining this differential response between the hippie from an affluent background and the more traditional delinquent from a culturally and materially poor background helps to illuminate the hippie condition.

The hippie movement of deviance from basic American values and institutions is fundamentally different from that of lower-class delinquent youths. It is a much more basic and potentially destructive rejection of the goals and values inherent in American society. It portends an increasing condition of *anomie*. Briefly, anomie is a situation in any society where the normative system no longer controls behavior.

The concept of anomie was first presented by the noted sociologist, Emile Durkheim. In describing two categories of need, physical and social, Durkheim made the point that physical needs are satiable, whereas social gratification is "an insatiable and bottomless abyss." *Thus when men's goals become unlimited the "norms no longer control men's actions" and a state of "normlessness" or anomie exists.*

Robert Merton elaborated on and refined this proposition. In Merton's speculation anomie (normlessness) and the breakdown of social control emerge not because of "insatiable goals" alone but because of *a lack of fit between the goals and the legitimate means for acquiring the goals of society.* Merton stated that aberrant behavior may be regarded sociologically as a symptom of dissociation between culturally prescribed aspirations and socially structured avenues for realizing these aspirations.

The American ideology of "equal opportunity for all" is an empty myth for those who find themselves cut off from legitimate pathways to upward mobility and achievement in the society. Because lower-class groups are generally blocked from upward mobility, the pressures toward deviant behavior are greatest in this segment of society.

The traditional delinquent (not the hippie deviant) may therefore be accounted for in terms of the following set of conditions. The disparity between what lower-class youths are led to desire and what is actually available to them is the source of a major problem of adjustment. Faced with limitations on legitimate (legal) avenues of access to society's goals and unable to revise their aspirations downward, these young people experience intense frustrations. These frustrations often cause them to turn to a delinquent or deviant adjustment. Briefly, youths blocked from achieving through the normative avenues for success in a highly achievement-oriented society will select a deviant path. The "deviant path" for many lower-class youths means the traditional delinquent activities of violent gangs, assault, and theft.

This traditional delinquent pattern has become an integral adjustment pattern in most modern technological bureaucracies in the past century. Blockages in opportunity channels for segments of the society have been a part of all societies of this type. There have always been have-nots who could not achieve the lofty goals aggrandized by their society. In a sense, the goals and values of these societies are confirmed by the fact that there are such people who will go to unusual means to win these rewards. Delinquency in the modern technological society is partial proof that the structure's values and goals are attractive and people will go to any means including theft and violence to achieve what the society prizes.

Some traditional delinquents are so frustrated by not being able to achieve success that they retreat. In a sense, the old-style drug-addict delinquents took drugs (and many still do) to console themselves about their lack of achievement of the goals of the society. The drug reverie is in part an escape from the addict's failure to succeed American style. This is in direct contrast with the psychedelic-drug addicts who are trying to scramble their circuits to eliminate from their consciousness both the total social game-playing scene (the paths to achievement) and the goals of American society.

The causation explanation of anomie, in the context described, does not explain the reason why middle-class hippies deviate from the norms. The new deviants in the hippie movement have excellent access to the goals of the society, and are not at all reacting to blocked opportunity structures *In contrast with the traditional delinquent, the new deviants, the hippies, reject the means, the goals, and the values of the society.*

The hippies' deviant behavior and posture reflect a much more devastating attack on the basic structure of American society than the traditional delinquent pattern. Traditional American delinquents *accept the goals* of the society even though they find it necessary to pursue them in a deviant way. *The lower-class American delinquent, therefore, is really affirming the validity of the goals of American society by striving for them at any cost. Traditional crime and delinquency in this context is a tribute to the goals and values of American society.*

The hippie reaction, in contrast, is a condemnation of the total American system. Most youths who drop out into the hippie movement have access to and usually can have all of the cultural prizes of American society. Their condemnation and rejection is total. They reject the American family, religion, education, government, and the economic and materialistic prizes of American society, and more than that they reject the "game-playing" approach for their acquisition. This total rejection of America's basic social institutions by its more affluent and more highly educated youths deserves closer examination.

The "Plastic Institutions" of American Society

In the broadest sense, a social institution refers to an organized way of carrying out some fundamental function in a society. The basic institutionalized patterns of any society include: (1) Religious forms—ways of relating spiritually to other people, the universe, or God; (2) Economic forms—the manner in which the wealth of a society is accumulated through work and then distributed; (3) The family—a human arrangement for experiencing a primary group, loving situation that will properly procreate and socialize children into the norms and values of the system; (4) Government—a patterned social organization granted the authority and power by individual citizens to administer many basic internal and external affairs or matters; and (5) Education—organizations designed, through the pursuit of truth, to transmit fundamental knowledge about the arts and sciences from one generation to the next.

All societies have evolved institutionalized patterns for handling these basic human requirements. The existence and functioning of a social institution implies that individuals are willing to give up certain almost inalienable rights to a collective authority. In a real sense, to have a society with defined institutions requires that individuals be willing to give up a part of themselves. A contract is made with the authorities drawn from the society to administer and manage certain dimensions of the citizen's life situation. The social contract further implies that the authorities can control the freedoms of and punish those who violate the norms of the society, especially those written into law.

The hippie movement is a blanket total rejection of all of these fundamental institutions. Implicit in the hippie life style is not only a total rejection but a statement that the laws promulgated by the society are ridiculous and no longer binding. In a Nietzschean sense hippies have placed themselves above all of the laws and restrictions of American society.

The hippie movement's posture of *total rejection* places it in a unique position as an American social movement. Most small and even powerful social movements in America have been geared to modify only part of the social structure. The Townsend Plan movement, for example, was essentially related to a greater distribution of the wealth to older people. The civil-rights movement essentially has had the objective of acquiring equal civil rights for all people regardless of race or creed. Even the most militant "black power" advocates live their daily lives American style. The new left and other campus political activist groups had and have limited political goals. The labor movement sought a particular kind of arrangement and relationship to management. *Unlike these efforts at partial changes in the society, the hippie phenomenon, although fetal and relatively powerless, emerges as the first American social movement that totally rejects the American social system.*

The arguments voiced by hippies against "the hypocrisy" of America's fundamental social institutions have been recorded in various hippie "raps" or dialogues throughout this book. However, it may be useful here to summarize this unique and significant hippie reaction to each of the basic institutions of American society.

Religion. According to the hippies, the spiritual and emotional quality of the religious experience in traditional American religions has died along with God. Churches and temples for them have become materialistic mockeries of an affluent society. Rather than catering to the spiritual needs of the people, religious leaders (priests, rabbis, ministers) have become quasi-businessmen, lawyers, accountants, and "social directors."

People go to church in expensive clothes and cars to show off their affluence. They are unaware of and unconcerned with fundamental spiritual or religious emotions or experiences. They simply participate in a religious situation (when they do) as a matter of proper form.

The hippie youths and their leaders tend to turn almost completely away from the "hypocritical Western religions" toward the Eastern religions. Despite their fragmentary knowledge they claim that the Eastern religions of *today* still emphasize LOVE, helping your fellow man, relating to God in your own way, and, most important, seeking a deep religious experience ("through drugs or meditation").

The only real Christian identification found by most hippies is an involvement with the trials, search, and tribulations of Christ and the early Christians. Many fluently quote and read the New Testament. Also the hip style of dress is often geared to the simpler clothes of the early Christians.

Government. Hippies generally view the rights and controls of any government as "total insanity." The assumption that anyone should have real granted power over another person is a complete violation of the hippie ethic of "doing your own thing" and being a "Free Man."

The student on the new left, or the "political activist," is not a pure hippie. These partial movements seek to replace the current government with a different, more liberal form. Hippies deplore and reject all forms of government—even minor attempts in their own communes or tribes. The true hippie is a complete *anarchist*.

A dimension of government that is considered "complete insanity" by the hippies is the governmental power to make war and kill people. One of the most flagrant hypocrisies noted by the hippie leaders is the spectacle of an American government that talks peace and makes war. This governmental hypocrisy appears to be so deeply felt as an obvious indication of America's spiritual bankruptcy that most hippies refuse to even discuss the issue.

In my view, the hippie reaction to and total rejection of government is the most limiting dimension of their movement. Their reaction-formation to government, formal organization, or controls is so strong that it defeats any effort on their part to do anything as a group. Their assumption is that if an issue is not spontaneously resolved, or a positive act of work does not simply emerge, they are better off without it. Consequently, most hippie attempts at communes *without government* are chaotic failures, at least by American standards of evaluation. Their bitter rejection of government and their embracement of total anarchy is thus a major difficulty of the movement.

The Family. The American institution of the monogamous family is viewed by the hippies as arid and sterile. There is, according to them, no real love, no real communication, and no meaningful, satisfying sexual relations. Also, in the family, they believe children are in bondage. Most hippies base their viewpoint on their own personal experiences in their own families.

Here again the hippie reaction is extremist. In their "families" of communes and tribes an effort is made toward almost a continuing self-conscious super-love. They constantly talk about love and try to express the emotion as much as possible, to the best of their ability.

A hippie assumption that is apparently true is that super-communication exists when people get high together on drugs. Even if it is only illusionary, there is a strong sense of deep communication in the drug condition.

The sexual freedom of the movement may be an extreme reaction-formation to the covert and guilty sexual practices of the average middle-class family. Sex in the hippie family or commune is definitely freer and more wide open. Couples often have sexual intercourse in view of other members of a "tribe." This dramatic reaction to middle-class mores may be another way they blatantly declare their freedom from the middle-class, bankrupt institution of the traditional family which they personally experienced.

Economic. The American competitive system of free enterprise is clearly rejected by the hippie movement. The Diggers' effort at barter and trade, rejecting the use of money wherever possible, is a concrete part of this reaction-formation situation.

Affluence is consciously and often methodically replaced by poverty in the hippie movement. As one young lady in the East Village told me, "I joined the hippie scene because I wanted to experience the emotion of poverty." She came from an extremely wealthy family in the Midwest.

Begging on the streets of Haight-Ashbury and in New York is a clear part of the hippie rejection of the American work pattern. Hippie beggars do not appear to be self-conscious or guilty, like other American beggars. Their flagrant demonstration of begging attempts to say that people should share with each other.

Another statement by the hippies related to America's vast and powerful economic institutions is their life-style declaration of rejecting technological machines. Hippies are attempting to move from America's great industrial, technological, and economic system back to the land and an agrarian way of life. This is clearly evidenced by the valiant but generally unsuccessful attempts at farming, making one's own clothes and food, and the natural life efforts in the rural communes.

Education. The hippie view of the hypocrisy of the American educational megalopolis is most clearly evidenced by its college drop-out pattern. A majority of hippies have experienced the college or university life and then dropped out. Some dramatically demonstrate their strong negative reactions by going through a university up to their senior year and then quitting the system.

The major complaint is that they feel they are IBM cards in the vast educational system. They do not, as has been stated, "want to be folded, spindled, or mutilated by the machine." Large anonymous classes, professors disinterested in teaching or relating personally to students, and value-free compulsive administrators give the hippies their rationales for leaving the cold bureaucratic educational system.

Another perhaps valid feeling expressed by many hippies about American higher education is that it educates people only to perpetuate American society. The emphasis is on acquiring knowledge to "fit in better" and to learn how to produce rather than to lead a happy life. The quest for truth, the "holy grail," or knowledge-for-the-sake-of-knowledge is dead in American education, according to the hippie drop-out.

He believes that through LSD, pot, and becoming emotionally "open" he will learn more on the new scene than in our chromium-plated universities. Hippies claim to be more interested in learning how to live happily and spiritually than in "cluttering their brains with useless knowledge."

The use of drugs for acquiring knowledge is a highly debatable issue. Due to the euphoric, omniscient impact of psychedelic drugs, hippies may feel they are learning more than they really are. There are few shortcuts to emotional insights, Nirvana, and truth.

In brief, the hippie movement is both a rejection and a rebellion against the basic institutions of American society. Despite their claims to the contrary, the hippies are very much involved in a subtle, sub-rosa way with the society in which they exist. In placing most of what they are trying to do under the microscope for analysis we can see that many of their patterns are a reaction-formation, in the opposite extreme, from the basic institutions of the alleged "plastic" American society.

The foregoing reflects the view many youths in America have toward their society. A closer examination of the youths involved and how they appear to drift away from the "plastic society" and into the "Hippie Syndrome" tends to illuminate the *gestalt* or totality of the problem.

The Hippie Syndrome

Youths drift into the hippie movement for a variety of reasons. Some intellectually and emotionally precocious youths confront the "plastic society" and then on the basis of reason and rationality decide to try the hippie adjustment. Other youths gravitate to the radical hippie condition because it is a more comfortable adjustment than accepting the "neurotic" or in some cases "psychotic" label and treatment they would receive from the larger society. In the hippie world their pathology or social inability is responded to with greater tolerance and in many instances with greater understanding and helpful attention.

Many youths, therefore, who enter the hippie world do so with "their eyes open" to the leap into the beyond that they are making. Most hippies are not emotionally disturbed. However, others—especially those who have had enormous psychological pressures in their personal lives—are seeking out a syndrome that will afford them some respite from the pressures and demands of the straight society.

The rejection of the plastic society and the drift by many disturbed youths into the hippie syndrome is a complicated transition. Given certain circumstances, youths with emotional problems fail progressively to maintain an adequate level of participation in the larger society. According to Cameron, writing about the general problem of psychological drop-outs, "they become socially disarticulated and very often have to be set aside from the rest of their community to live under artificially simplified conditions." * Hippie near-groups, thus, may serve as a "simplified" withdrawal syndrome for "disarticulated youths" who drop out from the more demanding society.

A group formation that structurally parallels my near-group concept is what Cameron calls a "paranoid pseudo-community." According to Cameron, the drop-out situation develops in this way:

> As he [the youth] begins attributing to others the attitudes which he has toward himself, he unintentionally organizes these others into a functional community, a group unified in their supposed reactions, attitudes, and plans with respect to him. He in this way organizes individuals, some of whom are actual persons and some only inferred or imagined, into a whole which satisfies for the time being his immediate need for explanation but which brings no reassurance with it and usually serves to increase his tensions. The community he forms not only fails to correspond to any organization shared by others but actually contradicts the consensus. More than this, the actions and attitudes ascribed by him to its personnel are not actually performed or maintained by them; they are united in no common undertaking against him. What he takes to be a functional community is only a pseudo-community created by his own unskilled attempts at interpretation, anticipation, and validation of social behavior.†

Cameron's paranoid-pseudo-community concept seems to fit the model and world of many hippie youths. It is especially descriptive of the previously described Alice-in-Wonderland syndrome of hallucinogenic flashes produced by psychedelic drugs. The wavy world of psychedelic drugs and life in a near-group hippie situation are all patterns that are analogous to Cameron's paranoid-pseudo-community mode of existence.

*Norman Cameron, "The Paranoid Pseudo-Community," in *American Journal of Sociology* (July, 1943), p. 32.

†*Ibid.*, Cameron, p. 34.

The Sequence. In summary form, the processes of drift that propel and involve youths (especially those who are emotionally disturbed) in the hippie movement may take the following sequential pattern of development:

Phase I: *The Plastic-Society Impact.* The complicated socialization defects of the plastic society with its alleged hypocrisies and inconsistencies produce youths with a limited ability to relate to others. They are turned-off from relating to the Establishment. These youths have a sense of being dehumanized and ahuman. They feel an overpowering need to break out of their plastic robot-like shell and experience the human warmth and love they do not feel able to get from the larger society.

Phase II: *Alienation and Disassociation.* Such youths tend to become disconnected and alienated from the plastic society they now feel they were forced to encounter. Their negative self-feelings of "difference," social ineffectiveness, and rejection become reinforced and hardened by the "unloving plastic family and society." They feel they no longer have the ability or the desire to succeed according to its conditions of success. They reject and drop out of the plastic society.

Phase III: *Dropping-Out into Psychedelia.* In the hippie, psychedelic world their former feelings of alienation and weakness are replaced by the drug-induced (especially LSD) states of illusions of grandeur, being God-like, fusing with Infinity, the Universe, and feelings of oceanic love. The hippie scene and its drugs give these youths a continuing illusionary ego strength in another, more amenable social context—the hippie world.

The hippie near-group movement of both reality and unreality thus becomes for many youths a convenient pseudocommunity—a community that is functional in at least temporarily alleviating their personal inadequacy and the need to participate in the oppressive straight society. The structure of the new near-group situation, with its flexibility of size, roles, and delusionary possibilities, makes it a most convenient and socially acceptable escape-hatch for many youths seeking an emotional solution to their problems.

Another incentive to adopting the hippie syndrome rather than being a disturbed youth in the larger society is its acceptance by many people from the larger society. The worship of the hippie movement on an underground level by many people (often parents) in straight society helps to validate the hippies' belief system. Most deviant behavior is stigmatized and/or charitably sympathized with. Not so the hippie movement. The general community response of intrigue, and in some fashion covert envy and aggrandizement, reinforces the hippie scene as a most desirable, stigma-free pseudo-community for many drop-out youths. The "straight" community's almost positive response to this deviant pattern may be partially accounted for by a traditional American worship of aggressive, adventuresome, sexually free heroes who "go it alone" ("do their own thing") unencumbered by social restraints or standard moral conscience.

Another possible speculation about the seeming general acceptance by the larger society of the hippie syndrome is related to the assumption that pathological or *deviant behavior* is restricted only to *individual behavior*. It can be argued that if one individual commits a bizarre act he is considered emotionally disturbed; however, the same act committed in a large, somewhat coherent movement provides the individual actor with a degree of immunity from being considered "sick." The appraisal of collective behavior patterns gives some clue to this element of group legitimization and sanction for bizarre mass action. Lang and Lang make this point in a discussion of "crowds." They comment that certain aspects of a group situation help to make deviant acts and emotions more generally acceptable:

> . . . The principle that expressions of impulses and sentiments are validated by social support they attract

> extends to collective expressions generally. The mere fact that an idea is held by a multitude of people tends to give it credence.
>
> The feeling of being anonymous sets further limits to the sentiment of responsibility. The individual in the crowd or mass is often unrecognized; hence, there is a partial loss of critical self-control and the inhibitions it places on precipitate action. There is less incentive to adhere to normative standards when it appears to the individual that his behavior is not likely to provoke sanctions against him personally.
>
> . . . Each person sees himself acting as part of a larger collectivity which, by inference, shares his motives and sentiments and thereby sanctions the collective action. In this sense the crowd is an excuse for people all going crazy together. . . . *

In brief, many youths drop out and become hippies to rationally escape from a society that undeniably has many plastic, ahuman characteristics. However, many other youths who join the hippie movement do so because they are already in one degree or another emotionally disturbed rejects from the larger society. In a sense they are displaced persons, refugees, whose emotional condition was produced by a society that has no acceptable solutions for their treatment.

The extreme feelings of love, "belonging," and being part of all men and nature produced by psychedelia and its drugs provides an illusion existence that is at the opposite extreme from their former sense of loneliness and alienation. In a desperate search for this alternate and more immediately gratifying mode of existence, many socially disabled youths adopt the hippie syndrome.

A Summary of Significant Characteristics of the Movement

The general hippie phenomenon may be summarized in the following brief descriptions of significant dimensions of the overall movement:

*Kurt Lang and Gladys Lang, *Collective Dynamics* (T. Y. Crowell, 1961).

1. The hippie phenomenon may be viewed as a vast live social experiment that reflects many youths' dissatisfaction with the basic institutions of American society.

2. Study of this youthful reaction-formation can provide insights into the current condition of American society.

3. The hippie phenomenon can be viewed as a broad social movement attempting to operate under the banners of love and human compassion.

4. Unlike most social movements that seek partial changes in the society in which they emerge, the hippie movement constitutes a total denunciation of basic American institutions.

5. The near-groups of tribes, communes, and "families" in the overall hippie movement are very compatible with the dominant personality of the hippie participant. The condition can be summarized by specifying the following general propositions about near-groups:

(a) Participants in near groups are very often disturbed personalities, with a minimal ability to relate responsibly and effectively to others in a true group. (b) The near-group situation for these individuals is often a compensatory paranoid pseudo-community, and serves as a more socially desirable adjustment pattern than other pathological syndromes available in the community. (c) Individualized roles are defined to fit emotional needs of the participant. People can "do their own thing." (d) The definition of membership is diffuse, and varies with each participant. (e) Behavior is essentially emotion-motivated within loosely defined ego boundaries. (f) Group cohesiveness decreases as one moves from the center of the collectivity to the periphery. (g) Limited responsibility and social ability are required for membership or belonging. (h) Leadership is vague and diffuse. (i) There is some consensus among participants in the collectivity as to its functions or goals; however, in action behavior tends to be highly individualistic and egocentric. (j) Membership is in a constant state of flux. (k) There is a limited consensus of normative expectations for behavior, and there is a loose set of ethics. (l) Norms and behavior patterns are often in conflict with the inclusive social system's prescriptions. (Drug use and sexual patterns reflect legal and moral violation.)

Briefly, therefore, the hippie movement in total is comprised of many near-groups: communes, tribes, and "families." Near-groups are not as demanding social entities as true groups. People with both minor and severe personality problems with limited social ability can belong to a near-group. Because of the flexibility of a near-group, participants can project any image on to it that fulfills their personality needs of the moment.

6. There is apparently a higher incidence of emotional disturbance among hippies than youths in the general society. The lax, loose, and non-demanding way of life of the hippie movement is a reasonable adjustment situation for many youths with such personality difficulties.

7. The psychedelic drugs used in the movement give the hippie the illusion of being self-actualized, spontaneous, and tuned-in. Actual performance, however, is often dissonant or in conflict with the drug-induced illusions.

8. Despite attempts at avoiding status hierarchies, there is a vague stratification class structure observable in the hippie social movement. The "high priests" are upper-class, "novitiates" are in the largest middle-class. "Teenyboppers," "Meth-freaks," and part-time hippies are lower-class. There is, however, the opportunity for upward mobility.

9. The American superordinate-subordinate concept of leadership is rejected. There are, however, individuals who are considered to be "spiritual centers." They are accepted as leaders. A major problem of the movement is the unwillingness of the "leaders" to assume responsibility for "their people."

10. Tribes and communes are essentially feeble efforts at moving toward a more "natural" fundamental way of life. The hippie who wants to do his "own thing," however, has great difficulty in giving up something of himself or his personal freedom to the group. This inability seems to limit the functioning and development of the overall movement.

11. An attempt is made by hippies to socialize children in an anarchistic fashion. Their method is to let children grow up permissively, without "laying heavy adult games on them." In practice children are usually not properly taken care of and are treated as objects for the projection of hippie "adult games," such as drug abuse.

12. "Natural work" related to arts, crafts, and farming is idealized but seldom assiduously practiced. Music and art forms, however, in rare cases are unique and creative.

13. Violence is rampant in the love community. Some of the violence is drug-induced. In other cases, the urban-slum-community complex produces violence against hippies.

14. Love is worshiped as an ideal, but real love involving responsibility and compassionate behavior is seldom acted out. The feelings (partly drug-induced) are experienced, but they are essentially philosophical, mystical, and onanistic.

15. Total personal freedom is aggressively sought. Generally the right "to do one's own thing" is the license to remain free from relating responsibly to other people.

16. The concept of "ego games" is almost a pseudonym for society. Ego games are essentially the rights, duties, and obligations of role-players in American society. Game-playing is rejected by hippies. Dropping-out in part implies the refusal to "play games."

17. Dropping-out is essentially caused by:

(a) Anomie—a condition, in this case, where the goals and values of American society are rejected, and the norms are no longer binding; (b) a sense of human alienation from the plastic bureaucracy of American society; and (c) a reaction-formation and rejection of the hypocrisy of America's basic social institutions of the family, government, religion, the economic system and education.

18. Traditional delinquents, predominantly from a lower-class position in American society, become deviants because their opportunity channels to America's values and goals are blocked. In a sense their deviant and extreme striving for American success is a validation of the society. In contrast,

the new deviants, the hippies, by philosophical position and behavior totally condemn America's fundamental values and achievement goals.

19. Many youths enter the movement and the hippie syndrome on rational grounds in order to reject what they feel is a plastic ahuman society.

20. Others who have emotional problems drop out into the hippie syndrome because they believe it is a more compatible alternative to the one they confront in the larger society.

21. The sequence of events that leads to this type of hippie adjustment by many in the movement may be summarized as follows:

(a) Youths subjected to many emotional pressures focus on the plastic society and its many dislocations and defects as the source of their problems. (b) Confronting the demands of the society are too difficult. When they do this their sense of alienation and frustration is enormous. (c) They drop out into the psychedelic movement. Here they find the amenable near-group of the commune, tribe, or hippie-type family a more resonant and "happier" adjustment. The feelings in psychedelia of uniting with other people, nature, and God are a reaction-formation to the youths' prior feelings of loneliness and alienation.

The Future

Many radical speculations have been made about the future of the hippie movement. Hippie leaders, high on psychedelic drugs, predict the demise of Western civilization as it now exists—and an obvious take-over in a rather short period of time by the hippie ideology. In contrast the mass media, whose original focus was on love-ins and gay, happy flower-children, have shifted their focus to the violence and death which in my view have always been part of the scene since the inception of the movement. The nature and history of social movements in general may provide some valuable clues for determining where the hippie movement is "at" and where it might be heading.

Most social movements go through four phases of evolution:

(1) *Unrest* is the first phase of a social movement. The leaders of the American Revolution, for example, correctly observed and acted upon the sense of unrest felt in the society. This produced the early surge toward freedom. Unrest reflects a stirring in the society for change—for a new order that will enlarge the scope of man's potential and provide more satisfying, more meaningful relationships, and a more effective social system.

(2) *Excitement* is usually the dominant theme in the second phase of a movement. In the excitement phase lofty, beautiful plans and hopes for the future appear in the hearts, minds, and transcendental expressions of the revolutionaries. No hope, belief, or faith is impossible. When the goals are secured, all people everywhere will benefit and enjoy the fruits of their enormously exciting movement. The excitement phase in the American Revolution produced such remarkable and idealistic documents as the Bill of Rights and the Constitution.

(3) *Organization and Administration* are the dominant themes in the third phase of a movement. This is the creative hard-work stage of development. It involves the transformation of extravagant faith and hope into a workable human organization—based on reality. Human and physical structures must be built to house the necessities for implementing the goals of the movement. A governmental structure involving policy-makers, "legislators," and administrators must evolve if the revolution is to succeed. Active, responsible leadership is a vital quality of this phase. In this context the American Revolution produced one of the most elaborate and efficient systems of government in human history.

(4) *Survival or Dissolution* is the next critical phase of any movement. If the human structure that has emerged out of

the revolution is to survive, it must be nurtured with a vital human spirit and it must prove functional. Life and spontaneity must be continuously fed into the human machine or it will dissolve.

Here the battle of spontaneous man versus the robot emerges as the crucial issue of survival. Moreno brilliantly posits the issue of spontaneous, creative man versus the human and technological machines he has created in his aptly titled classic book, *Who Shall Survive?* The survival of a movement depends on a continuous opportunity for the development of the spontaneous, creative, aspiring, searching qualities of Man. When a movement or a society calcifies or loses these essential qualities, it dies.

These phases and factors about human social movements in general reveal some specific issues related to the hippie phenomenon in America. First, I would repeat the generalization that the hippie reaction is a rather direct response to the plastic American society of automations and robots. The plastic American society may be changing drastically because the machine is winning the battle over man's more basic human qualities of spontaneity and creativity, and the hippies' development may reflect this change. In a sense, the hippie reaction may be a barometric indicator of the decline of American society.

Secondly, viewing the hippie phenomenon as a movement in its own right, apart from its role as a spiritual reaction-formation against American society, it appears to be locked into a particular phase as a movement. Phase I, *unrest,* may have generated the hippies into Phase II, *excitement.* However, their inability (perhaps because of the drug impact) to lead themselves into any viable human organization, a requirement of Phase III, may lead to its rapid disintegration.

It is, of course, also conceivable that, like the people locked into the Limbo of Dante's *Inferno* forever, the hippies may remain in a perpetual Phase II, *excitement* state.

Even though the movement appears to be frozen in the excitement phase, or perhaps because of this, it appears to be growing in size, scope, and quality. For example, in a recent personal exchange, Leary told me that the size of his audiences at personal appearances were growing larger. Also, the questions he was asked were increasingly at a higher philosophical level of sophistication.

Young people and the general public seem to be tuning-in to the movement, in a dramatic way, in growing numbers. The psychedelic shops, books, and record businesses are phenomenal. Also, if mass-media coverage is a barometer of general public involvement, the hippie movement is of tremendous interest to a large segment of the public. Almost every major mass-media publication has had a cover story on the hippies.

This enormous involvement with a movement that has directly involved only a small percentage of the total population may reveal something fundamental about the nerve-end it strikes in American society. The hippies, at least in their basic idealized form, stand for love, compassion, sexual freedom, and the right to do "one's thing," whatever it may be. These issues apparently intrigue a society engaged in "heavy game-playing," mass production, and bureaucratic bondage.

American interest in people of "free spirit" has existed since the country's founding. As Thoreau stated, "The mass of men lead lives of quiet desperation." It is perhaps because so many Americans yearn for the freedom the hippies seem to enjoy that there is such an enormous involvement with the movement.

The poetic words of Emerson, Thoreau, and Whitman blend with the hippie attempt to move back to the more natural posture of early America. A closer merging with the natural beauty of our streams, mountains, and the land strikes a chord with many Americans who have become part of the more recent, machine-like society.

The views and feelings of the mass of people in American society are a crucial factor related to whether the hippie movement stands still, lives, or dies. If the texture of American society becomes more humane, loving, and compassionate, there would be a diminished need for the hippie scene. Most of the youths now in the movement would be able to find humanistic avenues of expression by living in the overall society.

The hippie movement thus seems to have struck a resonant chord in the feelings of many Americans. Despite some surface negativity, there is a covert and overt approval that supports hippiedom. It is characterized by the responses of many middle-class parents of hippies who overtly deplore their child's drop-out behavior yet send money and often add some subtle reinforcement to his revolutionary behavior. Some openly admit that in the inner recesses of their thoughts they believe their child has found a more satisfying way of life than their own.

The movement has already served the latent and useful function of helping to illuminate some of the hypocrisy, contradictions, and machine-like trends of the society. In brief, the future development of the movement is related to several key issues. One is the degree to which the hippie movement strikes a continuing, responsive, and approving chord in the middle-class "squares" of American society. Another significant issue is whether or not the bureaucratic, plastic thrust of American society changes (perhaps by manipulation) from its current machine-like trend into a more humanistic direction. All of these issues are important. However, the life or death question about this new youth movement is related to its potential for truly fulfilling its idealized humanistic goals of compassion and love.

Part Four
Appendix

APPENDIX

The Questionnaire

THE BASIC RESEARCH approach in this study involved participant-observation, depth interviews, and dialogues in action situations. An adjunct to these methods of gathering information was the use of a detailed questionnaire that attempted to elicit pertinent, core data about: hippie vital statistics, family background, drug-use patterns, arrest and custody records, drop-out behavior, the general hippie philosophy, and attitudes about American society.

Approximately seven hundred questionnaires were filled out by hippies in the major hippie centers of San Francisco's Haight-Ashbury, New York's East Village, and the Los Angeles areas of Venice, Fairfax, and Sunset Strip. Questionnaires were also filled out in several communes in California. There were about 400 responses from California and 300 responses from the East Village in New York City. Specific hippie respondents were predominantly from New York and California; however, the total sample came from 44 states in the United States (see Table 2).

An effort was made to acquire a random sample of subjects; however, because the total hippie population is not known and neither well defined nor static, no claim is made that this is a true random sample. The difficulty of being more definitive is related to the question: Who is a hippie?

For the purposes of this facet of the overall study, questionnaires were given to individuals, at random, who were in hippie areas, had a self-concept of being a hippie, and were dressed in hippie attire. Hippie locales included: the street scene, hippie pads, tribes or communes, in both rural and urban situations. The use of the foregoing criteria, the fact that we had respondents from 44 states, and my own observation of a reasonable percentage of the total respondents leads me to conclude that we acquired, to the best of our ability, a reasonably representative random sample of the hippie universe.

The interviewers did not obtain any specific data as to whether the respondents were Negro or white. There are very few Negroes in the hippie movement. My observation is, however, that we did acquire a representative number, about 2% of our total sample.

The questionnaires were given out by three sociology students of mine (two rather hip) and five hippie young people who had some college training and were clearly part of the new movement. All of my interviewers received a lengthy indoctrination from me on how to best administer the questionnaire in the context of the overall research effort. I have every reason to believe that the responses to the questionnaire were honest.

About twenty questionnaires were eliminated because the responses were obvious attempts at being humorous or were simply hostile to this "Establishment technique." Not all of the respondents completed all of the questions. Consequently, the N or Number varies in different areas of the study report. Specific data on facts and figures are presented in Table form. The more open-ended essay-type questions (e.g., How do you feel about American society?) were all closely read, content analyzed, and then written up in essay form.

The data acquired through the questionnaire was a valuable aid to me in directing my overall research trip. The generalized findings of the questionnaire are integrated into the body of my overall presentation. However, it was my judgment that directly inserting too much specific data would impede the natural flow of the book.

The questionnaire and its specific findings are presented here as coherently as possible. It is my hope that this data will help illuminate particular areas of special interest to the reader.

A. THE ACTUAL QUESTIONNAIRE

(Appropriate space was left after questions on the original questionnaire.)

> The information requested below is for an honest book on the new "happening," "drop-out" scene. The goal of this questionnaire is to find out something about the people, where they come from, how they feel about this world, and what they are doing. It is not necessary to identify yourself. A sizable number of copies of the book will be distributed to people on the scene, free of charge, when it is published. Thanks for your help.
>
> Lew Yablonsky
San Fernando Valley State College
Northridge, California

1. Age——Formal education——Male——Female——
2. Family's Residence—— —— Family's religion——
(city) (state)

2a. Father's Occupation——Father's Yearly Income——
(roughly)

3. What is your own definition of "dropping-out"?
4. Have you "dropped-out"?
5. Why did you "drop-out"?
6. State rough date of your "drop-out"———, ———
(month) (year)
7. Give your opinion of some of the problems or "hang-ups" on the new scene.
8. Would you attempt to define the philosophy or general viewpoint of the new scene in a few sentences?

9. How do you feel about "American Society"?

10. Check the drugs listed below that you have used.
Pot—— Used Often—— Sometimes——
LSD—— # Trips— Used Often—— Sometimes——
Methedrine—— Used Often—— Sometimes——
"A" or Speed Pills— Used Often—— Sometimes——
Other drugs—— Used Often—— Sometimes——
State rough date of first use of any drug——, ——
(month) (year)
What was the first drug used?

11. Are you working in some way for legalizing drug use?

12. Have you ever been locked up?——
If yes, check the appropriate box or boxes below and fill in dates and circumstances.
Jail——————
Mental Hospital————
Prison (over 6 mos.)————
Other—————

13. Any other general comments or observations:

B. TABLES

1. Age:

Age	*N*	*Age*	*N*	*Age*	*N*
15 and under	22	25	23	35	3
16	37	26	13	36	1
17	61	27	17	37	1
18	97	28	10	38	1
19	105	29	6	39	1
20	76	30	7	42	2
21	54	31	4	46	1
22	46	32	3	53	1
23	42	33	5	56	1
24	42	34	3	58	1
					N=686

Median=19.6 Mode=19 Mean 21.1

2. Family Residence:

Alabama	3	Mississippi	1
Alaska	2	Missouri	2
Arizona	2	Nebraska	1
Arkansas	2	New Hampshire	2
California	169	New Jersey	34
Colorado	4	New Mexico	1
Connecticut	17	New York	173
Dist. Columbia	5	Ohio	14
Florida	19	Oklahoma	1
Georgia	4	Oregon	1
Hawaii	3	Pennsylvania	18
Idaho	3	Rhode Island	2
Illinois	21	South Carolina	1
Indiana	7	Tennessee	3
Iowa	3	Texas	12
Kansas	2	Utah	1
Kentucky	2	Vermont	1
Louisiana	3	Virginia	5
Maine	2	Washington	10
Maryland	2	West Virginia	2
Massachusetts	30	Foreign	5
Michigan	6		N=603
Minnesota	2		

3. Formal Education.

Level	*N*	*%*	*Level*	N	*%*
9th grade or less	26	3.9	2 Yrs College	108	16.2
Some High School	123	18.5	3 Yrs College	36	5.4
High School Graduate	180	27.0	4 Yrs College College Graduate	61	9.1
1 Yr College	108	16.2	Some Graduate Work	11	1.7
			Graduate Degree	13	2.0
				N=666	

SUMMARY:

77.6% have graduated from high school.

50.6% have attended at least some college.

The category "Some High School," it should be noted, includes individuals who are not old enough to have finished high school. (8.9% of those individuals answering the age question, above, are 16 or under.) The same condition would apply to the higher educational levels.

4. Sex.

Male	506	75.5%	
Female	164	24.5%	
	N=670	(This male-female ratio is the approximate one observed on the overall scene.)	

5. Family's Religion.

	N	%
Protestant	202	34.8
Roman Catholic	164	28.2
Jewish	102	17.6
Mixed	23	4.0
None	67	11.5
Other	19	3.3
	N=577	

6. Family Income.

$ 4,000 or less	23	4.8
$ 4,001 to $ 7,500	76	16.0
$ 7,501 to $14,999	167	35.1
$15,000 and over	170	35.7
None	10	2.1
Dead	30	6.3
	N=476	

SUMMARY:

70.8% report a family income over $7,500.

7. "Have you dropped out?"

Yes	476	72.3%
No	182	27.7%
	N=658	

8. "State rough date of your 'drop-out.' "

Less than 6 mos	71	15.9
6 to 11.9 mos	64	14.3
1 to 1.9 yrs	89	19.9
2 to 4.9 yrs	126	28.2
5 to 9.9 yrs	49	11.0
10 yrs & over	21	4.7
From birth	27	6.0
	N=447	

9. Drug usage:

Marijuana	Often	475	69.0
	Sometimes	149	21.7
		N=624	90.7
LSD	Often	216	31.4
	Sometimes	253	36.8
		N=469	68.2
Methedrine	Often	89	12.9
	Sometimes	228	33.1
		N=317	46.0
Amphetamines ("Speed")	Often	113	16.4
	Sometimes	279	40.6
		N=392	57.0
Heroin (total only)		19	2.8
Other	Often	96	14.0
	Sometimes	289	42.0
		N=385	56.0

(Percentage figures were obtained by dividing reported usage, in each category, by 688, the total N of those reporting their age.)

LSD: Number of trips

1 to 10	168	42.7
11 to 25	85	21.6
26 to 50	59	15.0
51 to 100	39	9.9
over 100	42	10.7
	N=393	

10. "State rough date of first drug usage."

Under 6 mos	29	5.7
6 to 11.9 mos	42	8.2
1 to 1.9 years	95	18.5
2 to 4.9 years	200	39.0
5 to 9.9 years	104	20.3
10 yrs & over	43	8.4
	N=513	

SUMMARY: First usage was 2 or more years ago: 67.6%

11. First Drug Used:

Pot	426	70.4
LSD	38	6.3
Meth, Speed	48	7.9
Other	87	14.4
Heroin	6	1.0
	N=605	

12. Working for legalization of pot:

Yes	103	16.6
No	519	83.4
	N=622	

13. "Have you ever been locked up?"

Yes	326	49.4
No	334	50.6
	N=660	

14. Type of lock-up:

Jail	270
Mental Hospital	87
Prison	33
Juvenile	40
Military	6
	N=436

C. RESPONSES TO OPEN-END QUESTIONS

1. *Define dropping-out. Have you dropped out?*

(Because they are so closely linked, the responses to these two questions were merged.)

Respondents defined "dropping-out" and stated their reasons for having "dropped" in terms of escape and rejection of society, or of searching for better, more meaningful ways of life. Many indicated a combination of both motives. Replies ranged from terse statements of bitter rebellion to a fervent quest for brotherhood and union with God.

Escape From

Bitterness and blame were expressed by a 30-year-old male, who wrote, "I dropped out because historically the main function of society is to break down the fiber of the individual." Having indicted society, he then blamed his parents and the police by giving his family religion as "career Jews" and indicating that he had been in New York jails "for stealing when *not* a cop."

The most common scapegoat for bitterness was the total society. A 19-year-old male from Sharon, Massachusetts, who has been using drugs since December, 1966, stated, "I was bounced out." He defined dropping-out as "leaving bourgeoisie society." Similarly, a 15-year-old boy from Beverly Hills, California, stated, "I couldn't stand the ideals of society, its customs and traditions." He tossed in a barb at his family by indicating that his only experience of being locked up was "by my damned parents."

Society was named as the villain by respondents from all parts of the country. A Detroit youth, using drugs since 1962, dropped out because he was "tired of eating society's bullshit." A youth from Venice, California, tersely states, "The Establishment is fucked." A Boston youth responded, "I detest the degeneracy that America has evolved to." "I dropped-out because society sucks" was the bitter response of a 17-year-old boy from Compton, California.

Some expressed a vague bitterness. A 21-year-old male with a record of being locked-up in jails, a mental hospital, prison and other unspecified institutions said that dropping-out was "getting so tired of all the shit you say fuck it and then become your own person." A boy from Boston wrote, "They though me out becouse of my aperence [*sic*]." The ubiquitous and nameless "they" are the "bad guys" in his life and he has decided that their actions were based upon a very unfair judgment of his appearance.

A hopeless placement of blame was that of a 24-year-old male from Chicago who evidently wanted to drop out of the whole world because he "finally realized the world is full of shit and hate."

Some were not as rebellious, but had decided that living in this society was futile. Hopelessness with a touch of bitterness pervaded the response of a 30-year-old male with an M.A. degree who decided he was "abandoning any hope of rocking society's bag from within."

Quiet disillusionment is indicated by two female respondents. One, 19 years old, stated she had dropped-out because of being "sickened by much I saw around me." A 24-year-old, who has used drugs since 1956, called dropping-out "leaving a schizophrenic existence."

The desire to escape or withdraw from society was often expressed with a touch of humor. For instance, a 22-year-old male who has used drugs for 12 years gave his definition as "dropping outta line headin someplace you don't wanna go and go in your own way." He dropped-out, "cause the other guys in the line kept steppin' on my toes so i split."

While both seek only escape, there is a remarkable difference between the intellectual modes of expression of an 18-year-old from Compton, California, and a 21-year-old from Darien, Connecticut. The former states that dropping-out means "Don't work. Don't vote. *Just exist*." And he says he dropped because "I don't dig society." The latter gives this complicated reaction: "Abandoning the archaic linear perception and thought-systems of 'straight society' (though there is a necessary paradox here as such classification is part of the systems being abandoned) and accepting a total oscillatory wonder and receptive innocence."

Escape is the goal of a 32-year-old son of a Texas oil importer. His dropping-out meant "being completely free of any system." Sardonic humor comes into play in the statement of a 26-year-old male from New Jersey who expresses his desire to escape by defining dropping-out as "leaving the social contract due to the statute of limitations." A desire simply to withdraw is expressed also by a male of 21 from Los Angeles who has been on pot and LSD for three years. He says dropping-out is "ceasing to have intercourse with the established society."

Hedonism coupled with superficiality is expressed by a girl of 17 with a record of being in jail for prostitution and two years of drug use, who stated she dropped-out because "It was the 'in' thing to do." Her attitude was not unlike that of a 15-year-old boy, also with a jail record and a heavy user, who said he dropped-out "for kicks." Escaping for his own comfort seems to be the goal of a 22-year-old male who has used drugs since 1964 and was for some time a patient in a New York mental hospital. He stated, "The world is up-tight and in a lot of trouble; I just don't want to get involved."

A young man who uses pot every day and has used many other drugs, including opium, since 1960 dropped out because of the hypocrisy of American society. "To me," he wrote, "dropping-out means to reject the dominant moral, economic, and social values of one's society. I dropped out because the values (dominant) in our society have become obsolete. We are no longer a farming civilization or a society of small independent proprietors. We no longer have such rural institutions as a large and close family structure and a strict rural morality. We are a society with laws against abortion and one million illegal abortions a year; laws against pot and ten million illegal pot-smokers; etc. Our society is simply full of internal contradictions between its values and the reality of what people actually think and do. I am a drop-out because I believe that most of America lives in a world of myths. Forty percent of America is terribly poor and yet we have tried to hide this from ourselves and the world because the dominant American middle class has interests in perpetuating this myth."

Escape To

Many respondents indicated not only a desire to withdraw from the present social system but coupled this with stated goals they sought to achieve. The goals ranged from self-indulgence to seeking "spiritual rebirth" and "ultimate truth."

A 14-year-old girl from Venice, California, says, "It helps me tune-in to something else, more meaningful." She defined dropping-out as "dropping-out of everything that is meaningless in your life!" It is interesting to note that this girl's father was on welfare. An almost identical attitude was expressed by the 16-year-old daughter of an orthodontist with an income of roughly $100,000 annually. The latter, from Brooklyn, defines dropping-out as "being free to accept and discard what you want." Her reason for dropping-out: "I began to think about all the horrible things around me and all the beauty there was to be had."

Bitterness and disillusionment are expressed in varying degrees by those who reject society for a stated or implied goal. A 17-year-old male, with a record of having been in juvenile shelter for glue sniffing and runaway, and in jail for burglary, says that dropping-out means "to overthrow the chains society has put on you and become yourself and say the hell with what society says about it." Without disclosing just what his philosophy is, he states that his reason for dropping-out was that "I won't throw away my philosophy to get along with society."

Milder disenchantment is revealed in the response of a 21-year-old male from Los Angeles who stated, "To drop out is to live from inner truth and knowledge with a love to all from all. Western society is very hung up in tradition and dogma and is *afraid* to change." A 22-year-old female who has used drugs since 1959, with a record of four arrests and jail terms served for drug possession, defined dropping-out as "dropping into my essense [*sic*] and out of the duality games." She gives her reason for dropping-out as "To be." It is interesting to speculate whether her having had over 250 LSD trips is a factor in forming her attitude. A similar drug experience, "no idea how many LSD trips," and a similar record of having been jailed, was indicated by a 20-year-old girl from Kansas who desired to "shed middle class mores and adopt a new religious ritual." A 20-year-old male who used pot and LSD often said, "Dropping-out is leaving the entanglement of fear defenses in your mind, and returning to the reality of your soul."

An implication of disillusionment is coupled with a creative purpose expressed by a 20-year-old male who defined dropping-out as the "end of masked multi-effortal social robot ego games, beginning of cosmic consciousness and to be born."

Not all respondents indicate either a desire to "escape from" or "escape to" something. A few gave superficial reasons for dropping-out or failed to indicate any kind of goal orientation. These seemed to be seeking or simply accepting change for its own sake.

"Constructive" Goals

Many respondents gave no indications of a desire for escape. They seemed to be motivated by an honest desire for a better way of life for themselves in terms of their own attitudes. A 22-year-old female from Riverside, California, states, "I turned-on to acid and began to see the emptiness of my past existence—in addition to the growing hypocrisies which I was perpetuating within myself."

A 24-year-old male from California speaks of dropping-out as simply "a way to achieve human fulfillment." While a 21-year-old male whose family home is in England describes it as "to stop existing and start to live—to stop hating and begin to love."

Some stated their desires for a better life more in terms of behavior than in attitude. A 19-year-old male, who has used drugs heavily since 1959 and has been locked up on three different occasions, wrote this definition of dropping-out: "To do your thing, what your thing really is though, like 'to thine own self be true,' you dig." Asked to state his reason for dropping-out, he responded, "I never really dropped-in, so it seemed natural really that I'd dropped-out. Right? Right?"

Emphasis is placed on function by an 18-year-old male, a moderate user with one lock-up experience. He wrote, "The term 'dropping-in' means learning how to function stably on a psychical, mystic, and intellectual level." Behavior is also stressed by the 19-year-old male from Seattle, Washington, who defined dropping-out as "The unlearning of certain behavior patterns including thought." His stated reason: "To drop-out is to change. To not change is to not exist. Since I exist I must change; therefore, I am always dropping-out. Drugs have tended to excelerate [*sic*] changes in me."

The statement of a 20-year-old female from San Francisco clearly defines what is often spoken of as the core of the hippie philosophy, covering both behavior and internal attitudes: "Becoming totally aware of the inner self and letting it show through—without playing games. Doing your thing but not imposing your thing on anyone else." "Becoming," "doing," "not imposing" are the key words of the movement incorporated in her response.

Religious or Spiritual Goals

At the opposite end of the continuum from those who expressed anarchy as the goal desired are those who spoke in terms of religious zeal or striving for spiritual growth. These ranged from the fanatical to a seemingly calm devotion to becoming fully loving and at peace.

An evangelical response was given by a 27-year-old man who indicated that he had used pot, LSD, Methedrine, speed pills, STP, DMT, and DET all "often enough" since early 1954. He also had been locked-up in jail, in a mental hospital, and in maximum security in a state prison. He defined dropping-out as "turning my back away from the false life of this world," and said he had dropped-out "because the Lord called me and drew me to Him and His Heaven of Love and Truth."

The teachings of Oriental religion were dominant in the responses of a 22-year-old male who indicated a heavy use of more than six different drugs since 1959. This man had no jail record but had been in a mental hospital for 8 months. His definition: "Finding retreat in one's own Karma and enlightenment of one's needs." His reason for dropping-out: "Lao Tsu teaches man to reject desires. To be humble is man's greatest virtue."

Less specific but with a definite religious flavor were the responses of a 19-year-old youth who indicated frequent use of pot, LSD, and STP since October, 1966: "Following some sort of revelations, turning toward yourself and away from 'society' or whatever. This is a very general definition. A dropping-out is extremely personal." His reason: "It was inevitable. I gave myself freedom to see (left home, etc.) and saw a lot of illusions disappear and a lot of truths appear. What remains now is just myself, love, soul, pride." This boy indicated no serious record of being locked-up other than having been in jail for "minor things."

Spiritual orientation is expressed with simplicity by the 19-year-old male who has used various drugs often since

1963 and who had been jailed for "minor offenses, dates insignificant." His reason for dropping-out: "To achieve a fellowship with the universe."

A 23-year-old male who indicated the use of pot often, LSD and other drugs moderately since 1963, wrote that he had dropped-out "in order to slay my 'self'—to destroy the part of me that prevented the possibility of attaining the states of grace and love."

2. *Give Your Opinion of some of the Problems or Hangups on the New Scene.*

A core "hangup" reported by participants on the new scene is the process of making a vast shift in orientation from the straight to the hippie world. A 35-year-old male hippie from New York states, "America's ancient laws and moral values must be discarded and replaced with ones compatible with the new insights one has attained." Many respondents state that they find it difficult to drop a system of norms and values that they have internalized since birth. As the 22-year-old hippie daughter of a $50,000-a-year industrialist from Southern California comments, "The problems or hangups are in people's heads. My own hangups center around learning to forget the lies I have been taught and believed for so long."

This awareness that "the problems are all in my head" is a basic perception of those on the new scene. The philosopher-priests of the movement harbor little or no hostility toward the outside world. They often see the newly dropped-out novice, in the words of one 19-year-old female from New Jersey who has been using drugs for over three years, as being guilty of "too much protest and complaining [and] lots of misdirected criticism." A 24-year-old female college drop-out from South Bend, Indiana, regards the problem as one of "immaturity . . . too much time is wasted on Establishment fighting instead of helping and understanding."

Many comments refer to the central problem of dropping the old scenes and becoming totally involved with the new:

"One can't inhabit two worlds at the same time." Holding onto the dead past can only cause frustration. Failure to let go can lead, in the words of one 32-year-old Los Angeles woman, to the "schizophrenia of trying to hang on to old values which cause pain."

One 33-year-old college graduate, who led a commune in California, feels that "too many people are dropping-out for reactionary reasons rather than for life-affirming reasons." Related to this is the view of a 26-year-old male from Ohio, who has taken over 25 acid trips. He felt that "most of the people have never actually lived with the society they condemn, except as juveniles, with the disadvantages and handicaps imposed by parents. They tend to identify all society with the actions of their parents."

Love, honesty, and trust are the concepts most often used to characterize the quality of the social relationships with the new scene. A set of problems, from this perspective, relates to actual practices in the hippie world, which deviate from this ideal. A 16-year-old youth from Huntington, New York, sees the new scene often inhabited by "too many fakes preaching love and not giving it—people too much in the drug bag and too busy being different and not themselves." A 23-year-old male from New York, who has been arrested twice for narcotics violations, points to the "phonies on the scene who think being a hippie is the 'in' thing to do and sometimes try profiting on it—like the so-called hippie merchants."

The ideal holds that anyone is welcome to "do their thing," whatever it may be, but as admitted by one 27-year-old male from Tennessee, "We have a long way to go toward true toleration for any personal eccentricity whatever, ideational or otherwise."

The "honest, out-front communication" which is part of the ideal is often obscured by what a 17-year-old Culver City, California, girl sees as "people who still play their funny phony games behind drugs and reality."

A "hangup" seen by many respondents is that drugs are taken as an end in themselves, rather than as a means to an end. An 18-year-old male from New Jersey, who has been using drugs for about one year, reports that "there is a hang-up that the new revolution is done mostly with drugs and not so much with attitude. Drugs may be good if used wisely, but they are not the heart of this revolution." A 19-year-old male ex-college student, also from New Jersey, points out that "there is a false idea that drugs are solely an escape from the pressures of modern society—rather it should be seen that they should be used as a method of exploration for one's inner self."

The usage of non-psychedelic drugs, like Methedrine and the amphetamines, is viewed with alarm as a major problem by many. The "speed-freak" is considered to be a negative role-model. Many respondents answering the questions on Methedrine usage report that they had used it in the past but added comments such as "no more," "never again," or the much repeated warning that "speed kills."

There is a sense of persecution felt by many on the scene. One 19-year-old male from Idaho feels that there exists a condition of "ignorance and a lack of understanding between the hippie and the 'straight world.'" A 28-year-old male with a graduate degree, who first used drugs in 1958, feels the biggest problem is the "coercive and usually destructive response we get from 'regular society.'" One 18-year-old "kicked out" of the University of Alabama contends that "a majority of people don't understand, and treat us, the new world, like savages and murderers."

Newcomers to the scene usually exhibit a great deal of fear about the police and consider this a major hangup.

A major problem, according to the 19-year-old son of a Midwest medical doctor, is "the police and their continued hassling of long-hairs and our established group, and the refusal of the government to legalize marijuana." A 17-year-old male from Granada Hills, California, who reports having had 60 acid trips, feels that "one of the main problems is the police attitude toward drop-outs—also the illegality of certain organics and chemicals."

A factor that seems to influence this orientation to the police is the fear of "getting a record." The philosopher-priest claims to have no fear of being arrested. Being "busted" may, in fact, even be viewed as simply another spiritual experience—an experience from which he will attain additional insights into the workings of the universe.

A great number of the "problems" of the new scene must be seen in this light. What may be considered a concrete hangup to the novitiate is a meaningless unreality to the philosopher-priest. The latter, often operating in the role of teacher or guru, tries to help the novitiate see more clearly that "the hangups are all in your head." In brief, the basic hangup or problems on the new scene are those related to the clash of values, laws, and viewpoints between the "straight" and the "hip" world.

3. *Define the Philosophy of the New Scene.*

> Scenes, like dreams, are intensely personal happenings, impossible to organize or abstract. A million people fill a million universes and there are no space ships.
>
> (Response of a 26-year-old male college drop-out)

Honesty, trust, love, freedom are the words most often used to describe the viewpoint or the philosophy of the new scene. It is a philosophy described as mystical in nature, emphasizing the unity of man and the harmony to be found in the universe. The respondents' philosophical viewpoint reflects an almost total rejection of economic individualism, and the "dog eat dog" or "do unto others before they do you" attitude that is seen by them as the driving force behind contemporary American society. The philosophy is defined in an ideal-type fashion by respondents and often delineates goals to be strived for, but which are difficult, perhaps impossible, to achieve.

According to many respondents, the first step one must

take upon entry into the new scene is a form of self-purification; the old systems of thought and behavior must be discarded. As one 24-year-old male from Pontiac, Michigan, put it, "the prevalent verbal viewpoint seems to be an almost total denunciation of all established beliefs." One must be able, says a nineteen-year-old girl from Boston who had "around 20" LSD trips, "to be uninhibited and relaxed from certain established modes society has laid out; to love and be loved and turn others on to loving and grooving on the world."

The concept of "freedom" is considered of prime importance on the new scene. One wrote, "In order to act with freedom, one must not be constrained by the oppressive systems of orientation and the selfish, meaningless goals that were learned while a member of the up-tight, plastic society." The watchword, as expressed by one 20-year-old male college student from Arlington, Virginia, is "Freedom is the message—freedom to pursue my own life style and do what I really want to do."

The old ways of relating to others are clearly seen as hindering self-actualization and meaningful interaction. "To get out of established symbol systems, to find sexual and spiritual liberation, to attain a sense of joy," this, says the 22-year-old daughter of a Beverly Hills M.D., is part of what the new scene is all about. A 20-year-old male from New Jersey who has used many different drugs, including opium and heroin, writes, "Don't love me because of what I am, but just because I am."

The collective respond is that completely dropping-out entails a disaffiliation with the customary processes through which one defines his place in the world. One respondent wrote, "It involves discarding the roles and labels that are bestowed upon us, the composite of which makes up the social dimension of our personality."

A cardinal rule of the new scene is not play "ego games" and to be "out front" and "open" in relating to other people. As one 19-year-old female, who lived at Strawberry

Fields for four months, states, an important objective of the new scene is the development of "total trust and love to the fullest extent." "This condition cannot be realized unless others have a similar orientation," the 21-year-old son of a West Coast industrialist writes: "we are a group of people that have found a way to exist in a community without having to play games with each other."

The most commonly reported philosophical feeling is "a oneness with the world." They write about transcending the bounds of the limited ego and experiencing the flow of existence and a realization that, in the words of the Chinese mystic Lao-tzu, "by doing nothing, everything is done." On this mergence of ego with the cosmos, one 19-year-old male from Ohio, who has been using LSD and marijuana for over a year, writes, "In my own society, my mind is one and one of many, but the mind must become a non-self so one can easily identify himself with his fellow man."

The relationship with Eastern mysticism is apparent. A 22-year-old male who has taken over 50 acid trips sees in the movement, "the establishment of new collective psychic patterns based on ancient systems." An 18-year-old male from San Diego who reports having 113 acid trips remarks, "The new scene is the recognition of people and that universal love and working for all is the thing." A 21-year-old female, who dropped out of college one semester before graduation and is now living in a rural commune in Northern California, responded: "Energies are freed to be used to grow and learn. No more must time be spent in a defensive shell that is almost necessary for survival in straight society. The potential perfection in each person is here to be developed, and we have 24 beautiful hours each day for this to happen."

The experience is characterized, in the words of one girl from Santa Cruz, California, by "attention to the here and now, holding an awareness of all stimuli—communication beyond words." As an 18-year-old male high school drop-out who has been using drugs for three years said, in refusing to define the philosophy of the new scene, "it's not the words but the feelings." A 24-year-old male who has been using drugs for 10 years writes, "I can't possibly put any *real* expression of ideas in these poor words; verbalizing limits, thoughts are ethereal." From this perspective, a 20-year-old male who has been using drugs for six years says, "God is. Love is. I am."

There is a sense of a missionary zeal reflected in the philosophy. One 18-year-old female college student from New Jersey sees the movement's philosophy as "an attempt to build (or rebuild) humanity on top of a graveyard of dead ideas and non-living existing 'people.'" The 17-year-old daughter of a Southern California $30,000-a-year electronics engineer tells us to "get together and make this world a place of love, cooperation, and expansion." A 19-year-old male hippie from the Pacific Northwest says, "We are searching, and trying to succeed where the society at large has failed."

In conclusion, a 31-year-old Army veteran who reported that his drug usage includes "the Army, greed, ambition, and anxiety" presents his "philosophy" of the new movement this way:

> Eat tacos on Thursday morning and watch black angels swim in the sun. Play monopoly and move the pieces lightly. Wear red and go to sleep after you've been made love to. And don't ask too many questions—it's all O.K.

4. *How Do You Feel About American Society?*

The new scene and its evolution of new values is manifested in its biting comments on American society. When questioned on feelings regarding American society, we find a full spectrum ranging from "it's fucked up" or "it sucks" to "needs improvement but better than many." Though comments run the gamut, those repeated most frequently include the expressions "it's fucked up," or "it's fucked." The latter means more specifically that American society is confused and finished. A New York University drop-out says American society is "a rancid armpit threatening to pollute the world." The son of a $20,000-a-year businessman remarks: "It's a freak scene—Uncle Sam is a Meth monster!" And from the son of a Connecticut doctor we get the poetic diatribe:

> American society!
> Claw hawk—rot eagle
> Hung up claw, caught on smelly snatch—
> Can't prevent or change it but don't
> have to be in it.
>   Wormless insides.

The fact of hippies "dropping-out" and joining the new scene carries with it the clear conclusion that American society is something they can no longer accept in its totality. Rather, it is a "thing" to "drop-out" of or rebel against by confronting it directly instead of attempting to work within its framework. This reaction can be found not only in the overt actions of the people on the new scene but in their pleas for more meaningful interpersonal relationships.

The communal, tribal family attempts on the new scene reveal the rejection of the American family. A 19-year-old girl from Miami who dropped out of college in her sophomore year comments: "The family is falling apart; togetherness is unity in the bag you dig, not home and apple pie." A 21-year-old male college drop-out from Reading, Pennsylvania, writes: "American[s] are very frightened and insecure. Most of them are cut off from really honest human relationships." A graduate engineer with 250 acid trips behind him dropped-out because of "the pseudoistic dictates of a robot society" which does not permit him "to be real."

The hippies' primary criticisms of American society appear to fall into three major areas: the lack of human interpersonal relationships, as discussed above; materialism; and hypocrisy. The latter seems to be the fundamental criticism. A 19-year-old daughter of a United Auto Worker executive whose income, as she puts it, is "a lot," a novice drug user (seven LSD trips in as many weeks), commenting on how she perceives the hypocrisy, states: "American justice is a bunch of bull. Organized religion has turned too political; they're not concentrating on love anymore. The war in Vietnam is ridiculous." A 22-year-old male and veteran of 75 acid trips, from a Roman Catholic Los Angeles home, writes: "What America? It's a shuck. As for my fellow patients—we need truth therapy—less pills, fewer ills, [less] exposure of clergy, politicians, and doctors—and all professional do-gooders as 'sick' people using others' gullibility for therapy." He further projects his perceptions with a poem commenting on his brief stay in a mental hospital:

> Possession of a drugged mind
> Lack of any other place to crash—
> For no money—can't
> Rich people come down
> Poor people crash
> people like me are insane,
> and no one's to blame?
> and if you're Black, your
> gun you aim—

The hypocrisy or disparity in American society between value ideals and actual behavior crops up as a re-occurring theme in the responses. "It [America] lacks something—like its original ideals and values," comments a 22-year-old male college graduate. Another college graduate in engineering from Lido Isle, California, affirms: "It is falling apart from the ideas in which it was supposedly conceived and it's becoming dictatorial." Adding to the consensus, a 24-year-old male from a Protestant Council Bluffs, Iowa, family, who has been on 25 acid trips, says, "They [American society] are forgetting the right guaranteed everyone in the Constitution in their attempt to control the individual. They want everyone to be in their bag." Why did he drop out? "Basically, because of the contradictory nature of almost everything taught, believed, and practiced by straight society."

Frequently, government becomes the scapegoat when the hippie attempts to identify the causes of the hypocritical society. "It [the government] is run by power hungry immature mentally ill and not too intelligent lower intellectual class failures," writes a 20-year-old student from upstate New York who feels he is trying to drop-out but also that "society dropped him at birth." A 19-year-old, whose father earns $18,000 a year as a Lockheed employee, is not yet sure of her drop-out status though she has "tripped out" 15 times. Pointing to the hypocrisy in American government, she states: "It's pretty fucked up as far as I'm concerned—it's being run by a bunch of hypocrites out for their own good." An 18-year-old youth from an Ithaca, New York, Catholic home points his criticism at both the lack of honest relationships and government with: "It [American society] is a bunch of selfish people ruled by a stupid and senseless government."

The whole tone of hypocrisy with respect to American society as perceived by members of the new scene can probably best be summed up by a 34-year-old college graduate who "opted out" and a 27-year-old rabbinical student who dropped-out. "It is at a crossroads between its ideals and its realities," writes the former. The ex-rabbinical student comments woefully, "American society sucks. It has stolen from youth the American dream."

Competing strongly with the critical current regarding hypocrisy in American society is a sentiment against materialism. Considering the upper socio-economic background of most hippies, anti-materialism as a value explicitly calls for active rebellion, and as one said, "putting down the parents who produced and protected them in the womb of affluence." A 19-year-old girl, veteran of 105 acid trips, whose father's $23,000-a-year income supports a Catholic home in Mt. Vernon, Washington, comments: "Bullshit! They [American society] only worry about money and judge too much by color, creed, and if people are dressed according to society." She says it is important to "give up willingly material possessions that aren't necessary." American society is "material and not spiritual. What more can be said?" confirms a

24-year-old college drop-out whose father, a Southern California merchant, earns $20,000 a year. A 23-year-old college drop-out, who has been jailed for civil rights demonstrations, used drugs since 1962, and lived in communes from New York to San Francisco, writes: "We have reached a high level of material development, many people have become hypnotized and obsessed with a desire for material good. There is a strong feeling of 'us' and 'them.' . . . This is a negative part of contemporary American life and is blocking people from seeing the essence of one another." The son of a designer from South Bend, Indiana, who desires a tribal way of life and who has "tripped-out 18 times on acid" since he first started using drugs in 1963, comments that American society is "an aggregation of individuals who have unfortunately decided to pursue wealth and let God find them."

Supporting the anti-materialistic position is a 20-year-old university student from London, son of Jewish parents, who during a recent visit to this country observed: "After a few weeks here only, it's obvious how unbearably materialistic the average American is. He is so busy earning dollars that he has no time to think and see the beauty of commonplace things around him." The young English student participated in the new scene in New York and had this to say about it: "The [hippie] idea is fantastic and those living here have shown courage in sticking to their beliefs."

In addition to the three main currents of questionnaire response of the new scene's negativism toward American society, there are many smaller currents which should be woven into the broader concepts already discussed. There are the negative attitudes the hippies hold toward "programming" and "categories." As a 23-year-old daughter from a Jewish home in White Plains, New York, who has an M.A. in English, writes about American society: "It's dead! What is American society? I'm ashamed of you for asking such a silly question and talking of programming people—this surely is a program." The rebellion against the plastic, programmed, or conditioned society can be understood in terms of the hippie's repeated philosophy of "letting each person do his own thing."

Religion is another undercurrent in the new scenes' responses about American society. "In general, it [American society] needs to see more of God," writes a 23-year-old girl from Southern California who has used drugs since 1959. And a 21-year-old college junior, daughter of a Sears department manager, on drugs for three years with 30 acid trips behind her, states that American society "has no soul, being spiritually dead itself, it tries to destroy everyone's soul and make them as false and dead as it is." She adds, "I want every action I make to be at one with my individual self and God."

The responses are essentially an appeal for the resurrection of warm human interpersonal relationships built on honesty, and a demand for the burial of hypocrisy in the same grave with materialism. This general view of American society's failure was summarized by a 19-year-old boy from a $20,000-a-year Congregationalist family in Sacramento, California, who had for several years used LSD, marijuana, Methedrine, belladonna, and "speed" pills. He writes, "American society is materialistic and stupid. It has no respect for philosophy, and it is hypocritical. People, on the other hand, as opposed to society, are confused, but by nature try to love God and man. I think the new scene is about to return to the true meaning of middle-class values which have their origin in the philosophical and religious traditions of the West. . . . I'm writing this in New York, a monument to previous mistakes. I hope American society won't make such bad mistakes again. Good luck on the book. Love."

Glossary

Bag: a personal area of involvement or interest, as in "that's his bag"

Behind-it: sincerely committed to a particular subject of action

Bread: money

Bug: bother, annoy

Bummer: an emotionally unpleasant or upsetting experience; also, a negative drug reaction as an "LSD bummer"

Burned: cheated

Busted: arrested

Clark Kent hippies: part-timers who live mainly in straight society; week-end hippies

Cop-out: to confess, or to compromise one's position or beliefs

Cool: to be tuned-in, into things

Cut out: leave

Dig: enjoy, appreciate, understand

Far out: unusual, extraordinary; bizarre or avant-garde

Flash-on: to think about; become intensely aware of or remember

Freak-out: to lose control, to have bizarre patterns of thought or behavior. Often occurring under the influence of a drug

Grass: marijuana

Groove: to "swing," to enjoy, to be "with it"

Hassle: an annoyance or a conflict situation

Head: a frequent user of psychedelic drugs, as in acid-head or pot-head

Heat: police

Hip: to be "in," "with it," emotionally wise, in the know
Joint: marijuana cigaret
Man (the): police; or drug dealer
Out front: open; honest; or the preface to a statement
Out of sight: so good that words fail to describe it
Rap: to talk; or present one's particular point of view
Roach: butt of a marijuana cigaret
Spade: a Negro. Used in a non-discriminatory way
Split: to leave
Square: a person or thing, not tuned-in or in the know
Stoned: very high on drugs
Teenybopper: a teenage "plastic" hippie
Turn-on: to use a drug; to get into the new scene
Up-tight: overly anxious or nervous

Lewis Yablonsky

ROBOPATHS

The robopaths are the people who pull the triggers at My Lai, Kent State, and Attica, make policy in Washington . . . and live next door. Dehumanized by regimentation, bureaucratization, and indiscriminate violence, they are rapidly increasing in modern post-technological society. The outcome of the struggle between people and their technological servants—whether computers, automobiles, or H-bombs—"may not be the total physical annihilation of people," writes Lewis Yablonsky. "Instead, people may in a subtle fashion become robot-like in their interaction and become human robots, or robopaths." What can be done? Yablonsky doesn't claim to have the final answers, any more than Charles Reich or Alvin Toffler. Like them, however, he believes that we must persist with the questions.

Richard Fairfield

COMMUNES USA
A Personal Tour

An exciting personal report on the American communal movement. Richard Fairfield has had five years' experience with communes and the people in them. Hippies, utopians, self-proclaimed messiahs, anarchists, traditional Christians, and dropouts from suburbia attempting group marriage are all covered in this unique book. To Fairfield, a commune is "an arrangement of three or more persons among whom the primary bond is some form of sharing"—and the sharing can take in anything from work to sex. In most communes, he says, honest and successful efforts are being made to create new ways of life. Alone in contemporary writing, *Communes USA* offers a truly intimate view of this growing, but little-known, sub-culture. Illustrated with photographs.

Lewis Yablonsky

SYNANON
The Tunnel Back

A thorough and absorbing account of the Synanon program for treating and rehabilitating drug addicts. The author examines the origins, philosophy, methods, and life style of this unique community. Drawing on extensive research, case histories, and recorded conversations, he describes the function of the intense group sessions in treating the problems of addicts. He also shows how Synanon's methods differ from those employed by traditional institutions and describes the impact this new program has had on current correctional techniques.

Lewis Yablonsky

THE VIOLENT GANG (Rev. Ed.)

A classic sociological study of youthful urban gangs. Drawing on "live research" and personal interviews, the author provides the "natural history" of two New York gangs, including their patterns of organization, leadership, alliances, warfare, and violence. Yablonsky carefully analyzes the social setting of gang activity, reviews recent sociological theory on the subject, and explores the sociopathic character of gang members. There is a discussion of programs for dealing with such groups as well as Yablonsky's own plan for gang control.

Benjamin DeMott

SURVIVING THE 70'S

A survival manual for the 1970's by one of America's top social critics. In these pages Benjamin DeMott considers the liberated woman, the college dropout, the "ecological summons," the new sexuality, and various other patterns of thought and action that characterize the contemporary scene. He asks: "How can a human being cope with the tilts of assumption and belief now occurring regularly in all corners of the culture? . . . What kinds of order can a mind work out for itself?" In answering such questions, *Surviving the 70's* looks not only at the mixed nature of experience today but also at the opportunities that lie beyond.